THE COMPLETE IDIOT'S GUIDE® TO

Eating Local

by Diane A. Welland, M.S., R.D.

A
ALPHA

A member of Penguin Group (USA) Inc.

ALPHA BOOKS

Published by the Penguin Group

Penguin Group (USA) Inc., 375 Hudson Street, New York, New York 10014, USA

Penguin Group (Canada), 90 Eglinton Avenue East, Suite 700, Toronto, Ontario M4P 2Y3, Canada (a division of Pearson Penguin Canada Inc.)

Penguin Books Ltd., 80 Strand, London WC2R 0RL, England

Penguin Ireland, 25 St. Stephen's Green, Dublin 2, Ireland (a division of Penguin Books Ltd.)

Penguin Group (Australia), 250 Camberwell Road, Camberwell, Victoria 3124, Australia (a division of Pearson Australia Group Pty. Ltd.)

Penguin Books India Pvt. Ltd., 11 Community Centre, Panchsheel Park, New Delhi—110 017, India

Penguin Group (NZ), 67 Apollo Drive, Rosedale, North Shore, Auckland 1311, New Zealand (a division of Pearson New Zealand Ltd.)

Penguin Books (South Africa) (Pty.) Ltd., 24 Sturdee Avenue, Rosebank, Johannesburg 2196, South Africa

Penguin Books Ltd., Registered Offices: 80 Strand, London WC2R 0RL, England

Copyright © 2011 by Diane A. Welland, M.S., R.D.

International Standard Book Number: 978-1-61564-076-8
Library of Congress Catalog Card Number: 2010915380

13 12 11   8 7 6 5 4 3 2 1

Interpretation of the printing code: The rightmost number of the first series of numbers is the year of the book's printing; the rightmost number of the second series of numbers is the number of the book's printing. For example, a printing code of 11-1 shows that the first printing occurred in 2011.

Printed in the United States of America

Note: This publication contains the opinions and ideas of its author. It is intended to provide helpful and informative material on the subject matter covered. It is sold with the understanding that the author and publisher are not engaged in rendering professional services in the book. If the reader requires personal assistance or advice, a competent professional should be consulted.

The author and publisher specifically disclaim any responsibility for any liability, loss, or risk, personal or otherwise, which is incurred as a consequence, directly or indirectly, of the use and application of any of the contents of this book.

Most Alpha books are available at special quantity discounts for bulk purchases for sales promotions, premiums, fund-raising, or educational use. Special books, or book excerpts, can also be created to fit specific needs.

For details, write: Special Markets, Alpha Books, 375 Hudson Street, New York, NY 10014.

Publisher: *Marie Butler-Knight*

Associate Publisher: *Mike Sanders*

Executive Managing Editor: *Billy Fields*

Senior Acquisitions Editor: *Paul Dinas*

Senior Development Editor: *Christy Wagner*

Senior Production Editor: *Janette Lynn*

Copy Editor: *Cate Schwenk*

Cover Designer: *Kurt Owens*

Book Designers: *William Thomas, Rebecca Batchelor*

Indexer: *Tonya Heard*

Layout: *Brian Massey*

Proofreader: *John Etchison*

I would like to dedicate this book to all the community farmers and ranchers who work so hard to provide us with local treasures and the people who come out in droves to buy them.

Contents

Part 3: Local Food in Your Community 101

8 Farm-Fresh Markets 103

9 Food Festivals and Fairs 115

Appendixes

Introduction

Eating local is all about eating close to the land. It's about eating foods grown and raised in the same region where you live. In this book, you learn why so many people are "going local," how to find local foods, and what to do with them once you have them.

Many people choose local foods simply because they taste better than conventional, well-traveled foods. And they do! Picked ripe right off the vine and transported usually only a few short miles, local food is about as fresh as you can get. Animals live happy lives and are treated humanely from start to finish. Local foods are so much healthier for you than processed, shipped-from-afar foods.

Just as important, however, are the social and environmental implications. Knowing where your food comes from and connecting with farmers who produce it gives you a sense of satisfaction and comfort—people who eat local don't worry about food safety issues—not to mention supports your local farmers and your community.

Eating local also means eating "green." It means protecting the earth's resources for future generations to come and being part of the solution rather than the problem. This book covers all the environmental issues surrounding this topic.

For people who are used to shopping at conventional supermarkets, buying and cooking local food may take some getting used to, but the challenge is well worth the effort. Local foods offer incredible diversity, and I've given you many ideas to search out and find these local treasures. Also included is a wealth of ideas and tips for cooking, saving, and storing seasonal foods—ultimately saving you money and time.

As you learn more about the many benefits of eating local, you may decide to become a vocal advocate for this cause. Already the local food movement is making a difference at restaurants, schools, and universities. This book shows you how to live the local food lifestyle outside of your home, too.

Turn the pages to explore the many ways you can incorporate healthy local food into your life. The move will not only have you feeling better about yourself, your community, and your planet but also have you enjoying delicious, nutritious food you and your family will love!

How This Book Is Organized

This book is divided into five parts. Each part focuses on a different part of what it means to eat local:

Part 1, An Introduction to Eating Local, begins our journey into eating local at the first and crucial step: defining exactly what *local* means. Here you get a sense of why eating local means different things to different people and how local eating can be a part of your lifestyle. I also discuss the many benefits local eating offers to your health, your community, and your planet Earth. Finally, I dispel many of the myths surrounding local eating, so you can buy and prepare these foods with a clear conscience.

Part 2, The Local Pantry, provides an in-depth look into your local food supply. In these chapters, you learn about heirloom vegetables; seasonal fruits; the wealth of dairy products available; and best buys for meat, poultry, and seafood. I also offer a great section on locally prepared foods like breads, jams, and sauces, all handcrafted by neighborhood artisans.

Part 3, Local Food in Your Community, introduces you to all the many places you can find local food in your community. Here you'll find tips and tricks for shopping local at farmers' markets, food festivals, community supported agriculture (CSA), U-pick farms, food co-ops, and conventional supermarkets, and even gathering food from the wild. For those who have a green thumb or want to have one, I also include a chapter on vegetable gardening.

Part 4, Cooking Local, offers you realistic suggestions on how to manage your menu with seasonal food. This includes ways to stretch the harvest through a variety of preservation techniques as well as tips on cooking and storing fresh meat and produce.

Part 5, Living a Local Lifestyle, helps you eat local when dining out and gives you advice on navigating the menu and choosing local items. I also discuss the many types of farm-to-table restaurants now popping up across the country. Schools are another avenue where local food is making inroads, and this section presents the many challenges and successes institutional foodservice operators face.

At the back of the book, I've included several appendixes where you'll find helpful information and places to dig deeper into the local food culture. First you'll find a glossary of new terms, followed by recommendations for further reading. Appendix C is all about local eating by region, breaking down the United States into six geographical regions with local foods for each area. Appendix D puts these regional foods into practice by featuring 25 regional recipes from all over the country.

Extras

In every chapter, you'll find sidebars that share important information you should know about eating and living local. Here's what to look for:

A CLOSER LOOK

These sidebars offer insights into local food, community, and culinary arts.

KEEP YOUR DISTANCE

These sidebars alert you to potential problems or pitfalls you want to steer clear of.

LOCAL LINGO

Look to these sidebars for definitions of new words or concepts.

NATIVE KNOWLEDGE

These sidebars contain tips or tricks to help you buy, cook, or eat local food.

Acknowledgments

I would like to express my heartfelt thanks to all the people who have helped make this book possible: especially Marilyn Allen of Allen O'Shea Agency; all the staff at Alpha Books, including Paul Dinas and Christy Wagner, for their invaluable input, advice, and suggestions; and all my friends and family for their enthusiasm, support, and guidance while I was immersed in this project.

Special thanks also go to everyone who answered my many questions, including Renee Brooks Catacalos, former editor of *Edible Chesapeake Magazine* and a vocal advocate for local food; Kristi Bahrenburg Janzen, another pioneer in the local foods movement; Katie Gimes and Alexandra Greeley of the Slow Food DC Chapter; Rich Pirog, associate director of the Leopold Center for Sustainable Agriculture; Bruce Butterfield at the National Gardening Association; Karlene Webster, who manages the food pantry at the Lorton Community Action Center; and California chef Jenny Huston.

Finally, I would like to thank all the real heroes out there: the farmers, packers, home-gardeners, and organizers who work hard to bring real local food to our table every day.

Trademarks

All terms mentioned in this book that are known to be or are suspected of being trademarks or service marks have been appropriately capitalized. Alpha Books and Penguin Group (USA) Inc. cannot attest to the accuracy of this information. Use of a term in this book should not be regarded as affecting the validity of any trademark or service mark.

An Introduction to Eating Local

Eating local is more than just eating foods from your own backyard. It also means understanding how the food you eat was grown and raised, and how it got from the farm to your plate. Part 1 explains exactly what *local* means and why *local* means different things to different people. It also covers both local foods and locally prepared foods and discusses how local fits into the organic scene. (Some local foods are organic, and some are not.) Then it tackles the next step: how far is local?

If you're wondering why you should eat local, this part helps answer that question, too, by explaining the many benefits eating local has to offer. You'll see why eating local is better for your health, your community, and your planet.

Finally, maybe you've heard some things about local food that you're not too sure about. In the last chapter of this part, I set the record straight by dispelling some of the most common myths people have about eating local. Part 1 will set your mind at ease as you discover eating local is not as expensive or hard as you may have expected.

What Is Eating Local?

In This Chapter

- A closer look at the local food movement
- Putting a distance on "local"
- Defining "local food"
- Learning a new, local lifestyle
- Making a commitment to eating local

For thousands of years, man has been eating food grown, raised, or hunted on the land where he lived. Local farms sustained farmers as well as nearby city dwellers and created a network of thriving agricultural and urban communities. Unfortunately, that's not the case anymore. With the advent of superhighways, trains, planes, and ships, we've grown farther and farther away from the land and the food it supplies, both physically and mentally.

Luckily, a growing local food movement is bringing back this lost culture and becoming more and more popular. But in this globalized world, rediscovering local food can be a challenge. In this chapter, I explain the local food movement and look at just how far "local" can be. Then I discuss what "local food" really means and how you can adapt your lifestyle to eating this way.

Once you start thinking local, you'll be surprised at all the incredible culinary opportunities you'll find so close around you. It's a journey that can take you farther than you ever imagined!

The Local Food Movement

Eating local, by definition, means eating close to the land you live on—but if you dig deeper, you'll find it's really much more than that. Eating local also means understanding where food comes from and exactly what it took to get that food from the farm to your plate. Its building locally based, self-reliant food economies that are not only financially sound but also environmentally friendly—which means they don't use up precious natural resources. And most of all, it's connecting with the people and places that produce these goods and services.

To sum it up, the local food movement is a collaborative effort to encourage and support local community food systems. But don't be overwhelmed by such a lofty-sounding goal. The truth is, you can do all these things simply by buying and eating locally grown food; in short, by becoming a *locavore*.

LOCAL LINGO

Coined in 2005 in San Francisco, **locavore**—*New Oxford American Dictionary* 2007 Word of the Year—refers to a person who tries to eat mainly locally grown or produced food, with "locally grown" meaning within a 50-, 100-, or 150-mile radius.

Unfortunately, eating local is not as easy as it sounds. Conventional grocery stores are home to thousands of products, many of them from faraway places. Stroll down the produce aisle, and you're more likely to see fruits and vegetables from Chile, Mexico, or Canada than from the United States. Look closer still, and you'll find pork from Denmark; seafood from Thailand; and dozens of processed and prepared foods from India, China, Spain, and many other countries. Over the last few decades, the volume and variety of foods imported to this country have risen dramatically—nearly 50 percent of the fruit and vegetables Americans eat is imported. That's about twice the amount it was even in 1992.

Even domestic produce isn't likely to be local, particularly if you're living on the East Coast. That's because the majority of the produce grown in this country comes from California, Florida, and Washington State, and is shipped across the country daily.

So where *do* you go to buy local? Farmers' markets, nearby farms, food co-ops, and occasionally supermarkets and specialty stores are prime spots. I explore all these local options and more in later chapters, and share more secrets about buying and shopping close to home. First, however, you need to define your parameters.

How Far Is Local?

Although most people have a sense of what's local and what's not, there's no universally accepted definition of "local." In the Food, Conservation, and Energy Act of 2008, Congress defined a "locally produced agricultural food product" as any food product sold or marketed either 400 miles or fewer from the place where it was originally grown or raised *or* in the state where the product is produced.

That's one definition. But among consumers, "local food" has many different meanings, especially when it comes to the distance considered local—how far you are away from where the food is grown, raised, or produced. That distance can range anywhere from 50 to 250 miles, or more, depending on your own ideas and the land where you live. If distance is your biggest concern, one way to determine your local food zone is to put a pencil or compass on your city or neighborhood map and draw a circle around what you feel would be local to you. The radius of that circle is the number of miles around your home you could gather food. All the food grown and raised within your circle would be local.

This works well if you live in a moderate or small city. For instance, in *Plenty: Eating Locally on the 100-Mile Diet* (Clarkson Potter, 2008), authors Alisa Smith and J.B. Mackinnon use a 100-mile radius as their boundary for eating local in Vancouver, Canada. On the other hand, author Gary Paul Nabhan extended this gap in his book *Coming Home to Eat* (W.W. Norton & Company, 2009), eating only food found within a 250-mile radius of his northern Arizona home. This longer distance might also be a better idea for people living in big cities like New York, where 100 miles away may still be very built up.

Another way to set your local boundaries is to keep track of how far the food travels from the place where it's grown to the place where it's sold. This is called *food miles*. Food miles can be gauged in increments such as 50, 100, 150, or 200 miles or simply by the distance driven by car or truck. For people watching their food miles, this usually means eating foods that can be trucked in to your region on a single day's drive. A reasonable day's distance is one that can be done round trip—no more than four or five hours one way.

LOCAL LINGO

Food miles refers to the distance food travels from where it's grown to where it's ultimately purchased or eaten.

Look at Geographic Boundaries

Rather than look at numbers, sometimes it makes more sense to define local regions based on the physical characteristics of the land. Mountains, valleys, rivers, plains, and deserts form natural boundaries and often divide regions by climate and soil characteristics. Popular areas you may have heard defined by their geography include the Front Range in Colorado, Hill Country in Texas, and the Appalachian Mountains of the South.

Oftentimes, the lay of the land naturally creates a foodshed. A foodshed is local region that supplies food to a specific population base or urban center. Similar to watersheds, foodsheds must be maintained and managed with renewable resources as well as be economically and ecologically viable.

Think Stateside

Some people define "local" by looking to a specific metropolitan area, city, county, or state. This not only fosters a strong sense of community, but it also promotes regional pride and loyalty to the place where you live.

Qualifying local according to political boundaries like states has other advantages, too. If you live in a small state like Rhode Island or Maryland, or if you live in a part of the state that closely borders other states, you may want to include several states in your definition of local. For example, if you live in northern New Jersey, chances are you also consider food grown in New York and Connecticut local. If you live in the southern part of New Jersey, Pennsylvania might fall within your local parameters. Other times, a single moderate-size state such as Colorado or Iowa is local enough.

> **NATIVE KNOWLEDGE**
>
> When it comes to eating local by state, you may want to further narrow it down for large states such as Alaska, Texas, and California. These states are the largest in the union, making up about 30 percent of the United States. Traveling across state in these areas is like travelling across several small European countries. Not exactly the definition of local.

Determining how far your local food comes from is a personal decision and one you should spend some time thinking about. And don't feel like you have to choose just one way. Most people consider components from each aspect—distance, geography, and state or county areas—when deciding on their local food supply. The key is to pick what works best for you.

Local Food Versus Local Product

When you're truly committed to eating close to the land, local food becomes more than just about "where" the food comes from. You'll also think about "how" and "by whom" those foods are produced.

You want to be sure the farming methods are healthy, the land is nourished, and the animals are treated well. You also want to support local farmers and their community. These factors not only determine where you'll find your local food, but also what foods you'll classify as local.

Start with Fresh Food

Think local, and think healthy, whole, natural, unprocessed foods plucked straight from the land where they were grown. Think fresh fruits, vegetables, and meat grown or raised in a socially and environmentally conscious fashion. Think small-scale, diverse farms with a variety of crops and a farmer who knows exactly how each harvest is doing. Think a short, local supply chain with direct interaction between you (the consumer) and the farmer (the producer).

Just as significant is what this *doesn't* mean. This doesn't mean plants are heavily doused with herbicides and pesticides, grown in large centralized single-crop factory farms by big industrialized companies, and sold via a mega-distribution system.

Local values are the core of the local food movement and essential for defining local food. In fact, for many people, they're even more important than the actual location of the food. Consequently, how much worth you assign each of these factors ultimately influences what kinds of local food you purchase.

Prepared from Scratch

Local products are made from local foods and sold at local food markets. They can be homemade or prepared by more commercial methods, but either way, they follow the same tenets as whole, fresh foods. Locally prepared food is …

- Made by artisan chefs or bakers.
- Made with local ingredients.
- As close to their natural state as possible.
- Prepared on a small scale.

- Produced with socially and environmentally sound methods.
- Sold at local marketplaces.

Although not every product will meet each one of the criteria, it should meet most of them.

KEEP YOUR DISTANCE

Many people also expect local foods to be inherently healthy. Although many are, some are not.

A good example of a responsibly produced local product is a Mexican salsa, made from an old family recipe with locally grown tomatoes and cilantro, with no additives, preservatives, or artificial ingredients. Oftentimes, the producer can even tell you which farm the vegetables came from for each batch. Sold in recyclable glass or plastic bottles with a simple label (not overly packaged), this is the ideal locally prepared food.

You also have to take into account the spirit of the operation or product making the food. A bakery in Portland, Oregon, for example, makes its artisan loaves only for city dwellers and their surrounding neighbors. The store uses locally sourced grain, all-natural ingredients, and environmentally and socially sound practices. Although it's a large-scale operation, using modern equipment, the spirit and the care it takes when making its bread qualify it as a true local product.

Some products, however, are not so transparent. Their producers may claim to be local or imply that they are, but they lack local values. These products include highly processed junk food loaded with refined fats and sugars as well as calories or foods produced by big food companies with large-scale farming operations.

Also beware of products that may be grown and sold locally but shipped miles away for processing, sometimes even out of the country. For example, crab fished out of the nearby Pacific Ocean then sent halfway across the world to southeast Asia to be "picked"—is this picked crab local? Closer to home, think about cattle, born and raised in Iowa or Kansas, but processed hundreds of miles away in Chicago. After its long trip, this meat returns to its native state as "local" beef. Don't assume that because a product calls itself local, it really is. Ask questions before you buy.

Keep in mind, too, that as the local food movement gains momentum among consumers, more and more major food companies will seek creative ways to get a piece of the local pie. How they can do this without compromising local values is yet to be seen.

Minimally Processed

Local food is food in its whole, natural state. Most can be eaten raw, while some need to be cooked, but in general, it has changed little from when it was picked off the plant or fished from the ocean. Local products, on the other hand, are processed, meaning they've been changed in some way.

This isn't always a bad thing. Local prepared foods like apple butter, sauerkraut, and tomato sauce are processed. Local meat and poultry also must be processed before it's sold. This means it's slaughtered, butchered, and cut into retail pieces. Chicken is killed, cleaned, and plucked. Few of us can process our own meats … or would want to.

The difference between these products and most of the processed and ultraprocessed products we see in the supermarket is the fact that local products are *minimally* processed. Producers and chefs strive to preserve the original fruit, vegetable, or whole grain, which is their main ingredient and the nutritional integrity of the food. The main goal is to *enhance* flavor rather than cover it up. So although sugar or salt may be an added ingredient, it's often used sparingly.

A CLOSER LOOK

According to a 2010 study in the *Journal of World Public Health Nutrition Association,* all food falls into one of these three categories: (1) Unprocessed or minimally processed foods—foods that don't change the nutritional value of the food. (2) Processed foods—foods altered in such a way that they've been depleted of nutrients and provide only calories (flours, starches, sugars, sweeteners). (3) Ultraprocessed foods—foods made up of a combination of processed foods containing little if any unprocessed or minimally processed foods.

Furthermore, processing methods are often more in line with environmental and ecological practices. The best example I can give for this is olive oil. In places where olives grow, olive oil is a natural result. For thousands of years, in fact, olives have been pressed between large stones to yield this liquid gold. Thus, locally produced olive oil is a popular, albeit ancient, product—minimally processed.

Compare this to another common oil: corn oil. Although Mexicans and Native Americans have grown corn just as long and maybe even longer than those in the Mediterranean have cultivated the olive, corn oil did not exist until the late 1890s, when scientists discovered a way to mechanically and chemically extract the oil, a complicated and involved procedure. Therefore, corn oil is a highly processed refined product and not something you'd find at a farmers' market, even in corn-producing states.

What About Organic?

Many people equate *local* with *organic*, and although many local values are certainly in line with organic ideals, not all local food is organic and vice versa. This is partly because of strict U.S. regulations defining what's organic; partly because of the places where organic produce and other foods are produced; and partly because some organic companies are now owned by large, multinational companies.

LOCAL LINGO

Certified organic is a label applied to food produced without synthetic fertilizers, herbicides and pesticides (natural ones are allowed), sewage sludge, genetic engineering, or irradiation. For animals, organic means raised without growth hormones or antibiotics, fed only organic feed without animal by-products, and given access to the outdoors.

Why Not Organic?

Most farmers' markets have at least one vendor certified organic. In order to become certified organic from the U.S. Department of Agriculture (USDA), farmers must adhere to specific rules regarding pesticide, herbicide, and fertilizer use; use farming practices that are gentle to the environment; and keep detailed documents every step of the way. It is this burdensome and expensive last step that prohibits some local farmers from becoming certified organic, even though they may be following organic principles and cultivating the land in an environmentally natural and healthy way.

Other local farmers may want the flexibility of using low-strength pesticides on certain plants if they need to. For instance, a farmer once told me he only uses pesticides on peaches, apples, and cherries, and only when he has to, because otherwise, "We wouldn't have a crop." All the rest of his vegetables and fruits are pesticide-free.

The best way to find out what your farmer does is talk to him directly. Ask him about the pesticides and fertilizers he uses, including when, how, and on what foods he uses them. You may even want to ask why he uses them. Remember, the farmer and his family eat this food, too, so if you're concerned about something specific, he probably wants to know about it.

When it comes to raising local beef, poultry, pork, or other meat, becoming organically certified is an expense few can afford. Remember, these small farms are not subsidized by the government the way large mega-farms are. Other farmers don't see organic certification as meaningful or necessary because they're already following humane and ecologically favorable practices—which they are usually happy to talk about.

When Local Is Better

While buying local and organic produce and meat is the ideal for people who can afford it, it's not always possible, nor is it always necessary. In fact, in some cases, buying local is better than buying organic.

This is true when organic foods are imported and must be shipped thousands of miles to get to your door. To meet growing demand, more and more organic fruits and vegetables sold in the United States are coming from countries like China and Chile.

If organic foods don't support local economies, such as those products produced by large industrial farms run by international food companies, opt for local instead.

If you find that organic food manufacturers use questionable organic methods, don't support that brand, choose local instead of organic if you can. Like all big industries, some companies stretch the rules. In the organic industry, one of the biggest loopholes concerns the meat and dairy industry and the interpretation of the phrase, "access to the outdoors." While most people assume this means cows grazing lazily on lush green pastures, for unscrupulous companies, this could be nothing more than a small barren dirt lot or cement patio.

KEEP YOUR DISTANCE

Beware of organic foods that are highly processed junk foods filled with sugar, fat, salt, and excess calories. Skip them and opt for fresher, local foods.

What Local Eating Means to You

Determining what local means to you depends on a variety of factors, including your time, family, budget, and location. But once you make the commitment to supporting local agriculture, you'll be surprised at how easily you'll adjust.

Also keep in mind that eating local is not an all-or-nothing proposition. Some people only eat local during harvest season (summer and fall) or commit to only eating local produce. This is usually the case for those people living in warm climates with lush, long growing seasons. Others may choose to take a different route, depending on their climate and locale, choosing only one or two local items. For instance, in Minnesota, where quality meat and milk are readily available, you might want to start buying local eggs, milk, and chicken.

Choosing only a few foods is also a great way to get your feet wet and introduce yourself to the world of local. Then you can expand your local repertoire gradually, in small steps, as you become more comfortable with the lifestyle by exploring local meats, cheeses, and other proteins. You may even begin buying local during the off season or winter months. When thinking about local, consider your lifestyle, location, and budget.

Keep in mind, however, that even those people totally committed to eating local rarely eat local 100 percent year-round. Often they pick a few favorite items as exceptions such as bananas, coffee, chocolate, or certain spices. The key is to choose as much food produced locally as possible—meat, fish, poultry, fruits, and vegetables, for example. I encourage you to strive for a 75 to 80 percent local diet. This strategy not only makes a difference to your environment and the local farmers you support, but it can also improve your health, your diet, and your quality of life.

Making an Attitude Adjustment

Even if you do decide to start slow, eating local still requires you to think about food in an entirely new way. For one thing, it means you have to eat with the seasons. During the in season, food is abundant, but when the season is over, so is the fruit or veggie. If you eat with the local seasons, you probably can't get fresh strawberries in November, tomatoes in January, or peppers in March.

Because most produce available in supermarkets is now sold year-round, many people aren't even aware of the seasonal nature of food (I talk more about this in later chapters) nor are they willing to give it up. Doing without, however, does have its benefits.

The anticipation of seasonal specialties like asparagus in spring or zucchini during the summer months provides for a wealth of culinary opportunities. When they do appear, you'll value and appreciate these foods on a new level. You'll also find they even taste better than their year-round counterparts.

Eating with the seasons means you also have to rethink the way you plan meals. In this globalized food world, meal planning often involves finding a recipe and buying the ingredients—oftentimes not even realizing that the food can come from all over the world. Processed products are also customary components in typical American meals, with no connection to time, place, or season.

 A CLOSER LOOK

A typical American meal contains ingredients from five foreign countries.

Buying local, on the other hand, is just the opposite. Meal planning revolves around what's in season, and you adjust your menu accordingly. Thus, meals reflect not only what's growing during the time, but also what's available in your region.

Living a Local Lifestyle

Eating local food has many benefits, including better health for you and your family, your community, and your planet. But it is a commitment and a lifestyle far different from the typical convenient, grab-and-go food most of us are used to eating.

As you embark on a locavore lifestyle, keep in mind that eating local takes time. In the beginning, most of your time is spent researching and tracking down local sources for the different foods in your region. However, once you discover these places, most of the work is done.

You also need to allow more time to plan, prepare, and cook meals. Luckily, this time commitment also drops as you become better and more efficient in the kitchen.

And don't count on one-stop shopping. Although large farmers' markets do have a wide variety of products, including meat, produce, and dairy, chances are you may still need to frequent several local markets to get everything you need. And because freshness is the key to eating local, you'll probably need to shop more than once a week for your food.

Eating local also means consuming mostly whole, natural, unprocessed food you prepare at home. If you're used to relying on frozen dinners and convenience products, this can be quite a shock. But the benefits are many. Aside from being a better cook, you'll be eating healthier, better-tasting food that you'll appreciate and enjoy all the more knowing where and how you got it.

The Least You Need to Know

- Locavores are people who eat food close to the place where they live. Local food can be determined by miles, geography, or state.
- The local food movement cares about how the food is grown or raised and processed as well as where it comes from.
- A big part of eating local is supporting local, small-scale farmers.
- Although some farmers do offer organic food, not all local food is organic, nor does it have to be.
- People who eat local spend more time getting, preparing, and cooking their food. In return, they have a healthy, quality, fresh-tasting diet they believe in.

The Benefits of Eating Local

In This Chapter

- It's all about fresh and healthy food
- A look at nutrition on the local level
- Creating healthy communities
- Getting to know your farmer
- Protecting the earth's natural resources

People who eat local do so for all sorts of reasons, but top on the list are always taste, quality, and freshness. These three factors are the driving force behind the local food movement and the biggest motivators for most locavores. But eating local food gives you more than just great flavor. Whole, natural, farm-fresh foods are often better for you than many conventionally bought groceries, and considering the recent outbreaks of food-borne illness, they may be safer, too.

Beyond good, nutritious food, however, is how local food helps your community and your planet. Supporting small farmers builds healthy, local economies; preserves our food culture; and creates more jobs. These farmers also have a vested interest in nurturing and protecting our natural resources, making them particularly environmentally conscious.

In this chapter, I explore all the many benefits eating local has to offer and discuss why happy people lead to happy farmers, happy communities, and a happy planet.

Building a Better You

When you start eating local, you automatically begin eating more fresh fruits and vegetables. I doubt you'll be able to resist the overflowing baskets of leafy greens, colorful tomatoes, and unusual squashes as you frequent farmers' markets. Also, because produce is the main cash crop for the majority of small local American farmers, this is what you'll see the most of at the market.

That's a good thing, because a diet rich in fruits and vegetables offers a multitude of health advantages. Fresh produce is loaded with fiber, essential vitamins and minerals, and a wealth of beneficial plant compounds (called *phytochemicals*) that boost overall nutrition. Fruits and vegetables are our main source of beta-carotene (the plant form of vitamin A), vitamin C, vitamin K, folic acid, and potassium. And because they're naturally low in calories and fill you up, they can help you maintain your weight, too.

Other staples you'll find at local markets, like nuts, seeds, whole grains, and beans or dried peas, also pack a nutritional punch, providing a variety of brain-boosting B vitamins, vitamin E, magnesium, zinc, selenium, and copper.

LOCAL LINGO

Phytochemicals are the plant compounds that give fruits, vegetables, and grains their distinctive colors, textures, and flavors. In the body they provide no calories but are biologically active and believed to protect you from disease and promote overall good health.

Although some of these foods, like almonds, avocado, walnuts, pumpkin seeds, and peanuts, are high in fat, luckily it's the good kind of fat. Good fats are unsaturated, meaning they're liquid at room temperature and include both monounsaturated and polyunsaturated fats. When used in place of saturated fats as part of a low-fat diet, unsaturated fats help reduce blood cholesterol levels and lower your risk of heart disease and stroke. Recent research suggests monounsaturated fats in the form of olives, olive oil, peanuts, and most other nuts may even protect you from other chronic illnesses.

Then there's omega-3 fats, another good fat found primarily in seafood, both shellfish and finfish, and particularly fatty fish like salmon, sardines, and trout. Omega-3 fats not only guard against heart disease, but may also defend against high blood pressure and inflammation and keep your brain sharp.

Saturated fats, on the other hand, are the fats you want to stay away from. They're solid at room temperature and are mostly found in animal products like milk, cheese, meat, and poultry (with a few exceptions like coconut, palm and palm kernel oil, and cocoa butter). Fortunately, not all saturated fats are created equal, and neither are the foods that contain them.

Local foods in particular may have an edge. That's because meats raised in open pastures tend to be leaner and less fatty than traditional supermarket beef, chicken, or pork. Experts say the composition of the fat, especially in game animals, is also better, and has a higher ratio of polyunsaturated to saturated fats.

Getting More of the Good Stuff

According to the U.S. Department of Agriculture (USDA) Dietary Guidelines, we should be eating about 5 cups of fruits and vegetables a day (2 cups fruit, 3 cups vegetables) or 10 (½-cup) servings total. As you may have already guessed, most Americans fall far short in this category.

A 2010 report by the Centers for Disease Control and Prevention (CDC) showed only 32.5 percent of Americans eat the recommended amount of fruit daily (about 2 cups) and just over a quarter (26 percent) eat three or more servings of vegetables a day. Put them together, and the numbers drop even lower. According to the CDC, only 14 percent of adult Americans eat the suggested amount of *both* fruits and vegetables daily.

What's more, the produce we do choose tends to be pretty limited. Thus the majority of our intake comes from just a handful of fruits and vegetables.

A CLOSER LOOK

More than half of U.S. adults' vegetable intake comes from these four veggies: potatoes, lettuce, onions, and tomatoes. Top fruits are oranges, grapes, apples, and bananas.

Shopping at farmers' markets makes it easier for you to increase your fruit and veggie intake, mostly because of the fresh, high-quality produce readily available there. Rows of colorful produce and more choices within each of these categories (instead of four lettuces to buy from you have ten, instead of two types of melons there are eight) encourage you to expand your culinary offerings and explore new foods.

To ensure you're getting all the right nutrients you need, think about choosing foods based on the colors of the rainbow. As you shop, pick up the following:

- All shades of green, especially dark leafy greens like lettuces and cooking greens, asparagus, broccoli, green beans, and cabbage

- Orange and yellow foods like squashes, melons, peaches, apricots, carrots, pumpkin, and sweet potato

- Reds like red peppers, radishes, strawberries, red apples, tomatoes, and grapes

- Purples and blues like eggplant, purple peppers, blueberries, blackberries, and plums

- Whites like cauliflower, potatoes, onions, turnips, and parsnips

In addition to adding more excitement to your plate via bright colors, flavors, and interesting textures, these foods are good for your health, too. They fight off obesity, diabetes, heart disease, high blood pressure, and some cancers.

Stealth Health

Scientists continue to debate whether local produce is more nutritious than conventional produce, but many locavores believe local fruits and vegetables are superior to their conventional counterparts. Because these foods are allowed to ripen on the plant longer, there's more time for the fruit or vegetable to mature, producing optimum nutrient content. And local produce doesn't have to travel in storage for days or even weeks. It's during that storage and transit time when fragile vitamins and minerals are apt to be lost.

In fact, if all things were equal—variety, production method, handling, storage, processing, and packaging—local produce would definitely have the advantage over conventional produce. Unfortunately, it's not always easy to compare.

Even with nutrient content aside, a local diet is still a healthy one, emphasizing fresh meat, fish, or poultry and wholesome fruits, vegetables, beans, and grains. More than just the type of food that's eaten is the *way* it is eaten. Locavores generally eat more in line with U.S. Department of Agriculture (USDA) dietary guidelines, consuming a wide variety of foods; small amounts of meat, fish, and poultry; moderate amounts of fat; and hefty quantities of leafy greens, fruits, and vegetables.

> **NATIVE KNOWLEDGE**
>
> The USDA Dietary Guidelines are a list of recommendations designed to help healthy Americans make good food choices. They are updated every five years, and the latest was released in 2010. For more information go to health.gov/dietaryguidelines.

Plus, all this fresh food leaves little room for the many processed, prepared, and convenience foods so prevalent in the typical American diet. So without even really realizing it, you'll be eating less salt, sugar, fat, and calories.

Dining out, particularly on fast food, is also something most locavores don't make a habit of. Although restaurants that serve locally grown food are growing in number, they're still hard to come by—and may be expensive. Furthermore, the basic principles behind buying local food—eating whole, natural foods, and supporting local agriculture and the environment—encourage preparing, cooking, and serving your meals at home.

Food prepared at home tends to be more nutritious than food served in restaurants, so people who eat local generally have a healthier diet than those following a typical American meal pattern. The result is a style of eating that not only boosts energy, improves health, and reduces your risk of chronic illness, but also makes you feel good eating it, especially when you know exactly where your food has come from.

Fresh Food Tastes Better

Your tongue is covered with thousands of taste buds. Those buds detect five basic sensations:

- Sweet
- Salty
- Sour
- Bitter
- *Umami*

> **LOCAL LINGO**
>
> Long recognized in Japanese cuisine, **umami** comes from the Japanese word meaning "delicious." It's considered the fifth taste and refers to a food's savory richness or meatiness. It's caused by the naturally occurring amino acid glutamate.

Beyond that, however, you can decipher little else, taste-wise. So how do you identify the earthiness of a tender beet or the fruity tartness of an apricot? It's your sense of *smell*. Odor molecules travel up your nose and through your mouth and signal your brain, so you can tell the difference between an orange and a grapefruit or a piece of broccoli and a piece of cauliflower. That's right: it's your powerful sense of *smell* that allows you to determine the *flavor* of the food. In fact, experts say 70 to 75 percent of what we perceive as taste is actually smell.

Local foods, because they're ripened on the plant rather than in storage, develop high levels of aromatic compounds that help give the food its characteristic taste and heightened flavor. This is most noticeable in fruits, where the intoxicating scent of fresh-picked strawberries or peaches can signal the start of the season even before you pop one in your mouth.

Another reason why local food tastes better has to do with timing. The longer a food travels, the more flavor and aroma compounds it loses during transit. Because produce is often brought to market within 24 hours of being picked and is at the peak of freshness and ripeness, this isn't an issue for local farmers. It may, however, be a big concern for food traveling from California to New York.

Finally, local produce tastes better because it *is* better, inherently. Over the years, supermarket produce varieties have been chosen for their ability to be shipped long distances and withstand harvesting equipment, bulk handling, and processing. They're bred for sturdiness, stability, and looks, not taste. As a result, we've gained the ability to have peaches in the dead of winter and apples in April, but at what cost? Bite into any of these off-season fruits, and you're likely to find a dry, mealy texture with only a hint of its natural flavor.

On the other hand, local foods are just the opposite. Small farmers care most about taste, quality, and diversity of crops. Raised according to the natural seasons, local produce is picked at the peak of flavor and ripeness and quickly transported for a quick sale.

Safer Food

Concerns about food-borne illness have escalated lately due to the fact that recent outbreaks have moved beyond traditional foods like meat, poultry, dairy, and eggs to seemingly healthy produce like spinach and processed foods like peanut butter. Because most of these outbreaks occurred on large industrial farms or from imported products, many people are turning to local foods over store-bought conventional ones for safety alone.

Although any food can become contaminated from improper handling or tainted water, local foods offer something supermarket foods can't: direct access to the farmer who grew or raised the food. Local farms are generally small operations, so if the farmer doesn't sell her food to you herself, it's usually someone else in her family who does. If a distributor or processor is involved, this is usually someone the farmer has personally chosen because he shares her values and the farmer trusts him. Direct communication with the farmer helps you understand the process and handling of food once it's picked or, when referring to meat, butchered. It also allows you to ask questions about the farms' food safety practices so you can decide whether or not to buy.

This is quite unlike conventional produce and meat operations, where the farmer has little control over how the food is handled after it leaves his operation. Furthermore, to get from farm to supermarket requires going through many stops, including processors, packagers, transporters, and distributors. The longer this supply chain, the more likely it is that something can happen to the food along the way. Short supply chains, on the other hand, can be more tightly controlled, reducing the risk of food-borne illness, not to mention improving quality and freshness.

You also may find comfort in knowing that the lettuce you're purchasing comes from only one farm. In some large-scale processing plants or slaughterhouses, foods are pooled together from many different places. As a result, if one product is contaminated, it can contaminate all the products, causing a more serious and widespread outbreak of food-borne illness. In the past, this has happened with both bagged spinach and ground beef products.

Often simply establishing a relationship with your farmer can alleviate food safety concerns. Most farmers care deeply about the food they sell and encourage customers to come and visit the farm and see how the crops are grown or the animals raised. Some even proudly post pictures of their animals or farmland on their website and at farmers' markets so customers can see.

Building a Better Community

When you buy local, remember that you're helping more than just your small local farmer; you're also helping your community. Healthy local food systems boost local economies in many ways, and over the last few years, have saved many struggling rural communities from ruin. How do they make such an impact?

Farms growing fruits and vegetables generate local jobs. Those jobs include picking, packing, processing, and selling produce.

In addition, farmers need seeds, supplies, farm equipment, fertilizer, and financial services to run their business. Thus, they support and promote other local businesses involved in the industry.

Local food markets stimulate other business activity by improving business skills and opportunities. This is apparent at farmers' markets, where start-up companies have the ability to test out their product at a relatively low-risk and nurturing venue.

Finally, local food systems keep consumer spending and money in the community. Although this sounds simple enough, much of the money you spend on food leaves your local area via imported products and faraway processors, retailers, wholesalers, truckers, and others. In all, only 7 percent of every food dollar spent at a grocery store today stays locally in the community.

A CLOSER LOOK

When the Leopold Center for Sustainable Agriculture at Iowa State University conducted an economic analysis of fruit and vegetable production in southwest Iowa (where corn and soybeans currently dominate the agriculture), it found upping fruit and vegetable production in a 10-county region increased labor income by $2.67 million and created 45 more farm-level jobs.

Making an Investment

By buying local, you not only support local small farmers, you also invest in future generations of farmers. Many small farms are family run on land that's been owned by their family for several generations. Since the mid-twentieth century, however, the number of these small farms has been dwindling rapidly in favor of large-scale industrial operations.

Economics has been the main reason for this demise. Despite the fact that productivity has more than doubled over the last four decades, income for small farmers has stayed the same—and in some cases even dropped, with farmers earning less than they did in 1969. To make ends meet, more than 60 percent of farmers work another job off the farm.

Now thanks to the burgeoning interest in local food, this trend is finally changing. For the first time since World War II, the USDA 2007 Census reported a 4 percent increase in the number of farms nationwide, crediting most of this rise to a greater number of small operations.

And while farmers receive on average only 20 cents on every food dollar spent at traditional supermarkets, when sold at local outlets like farmers' markets, they make 90 to 100 percent of every food dollar spent.

More money in the farmers' pockets means more money spent supporting the economy on local services like haircuts and movies. It also means small farmers can now produce a viable income they can actually live on. That's something most couldn't do before.

Putting a Face on Your Food

Although farmers have been the backbone of this country from the beginning, until recently, few people in urban and suburban communities actually knew a farmer, nor did they know where their food came from. Sure, local markets connect consumers with farmers, but what they're really all about is building relationships. Those relationships raise awareness of what it takes to put food on the table, foster appreciation and value for the hard work farming requires, and breathe new life into a struggling industry.

The result is a vibrant, enthusiastic culture that has helped farmers make a profitable living and attracted new, younger people committed to the land and what it can produce to enter the field.

For consumers, this means not only access to wonderful, fresh, quality food, but it also brings a certain sense of responsibility and respect for the farmer. You'll think twice about throwing away a tomato or letting fruit sit in your produce bin until it goes bad if you know the care and hard work that went into picking, packing, and selling that produce.

Taking advantage of this growing interest in local farming, the USDA recently launched the "Know Your Farmer, Know Your Food" initiative. Designed to strengthen the link between consumer and farmer, it encourages healthy eating, eco-friendly farming, and local food systems in rural communities. Log on to www.usda.gov/knowyourfarmer to learn more.

Preserving Food Traditions

Every country has its own food traditions based on regional foods, and America is no exception. What makes this country so unique is the fact that it is so large. Vast geographic diversity coupled with a melting pot of cultures has resulted in a wide range of regional options. (See Appendix C for more information on regional foods.) Unfortunately, many of these foods never make it to most conventional supermarkets, which value uniformity and market share over food culture.

Local food markets, on the other hand, have no such stipulations and actually seek out regional foods. Why? Mostly because these native foods grow best in the climate and soil where they naturally thrive. They also offer variety and excitement, which many consumers find attractive.

In addition to regional foods, you'll also find many local prepared products such as sauces, jams, or jellies. For instance, if you're in Oregon, a state known for its abundant hazelnuts, you might find hazelnut butter, hazelnut candies, or hazelnut-coated cheeses. Across the United States in Amish Country, Pennsylvania, chances are you'll see something quite different, like bread-and-butter pickles, pickled beets, churned fresh butter, and a variety of sweet fruit pies.

The local markets enable these food artisans to prepare their traditional wares, find a market for them, and keep their customs alive.

Building a Better Planet

Protecting Earth's natural resources is something we all need to be concerned about. Large-scale monocrop farms damage soil, deplete water systems, and burn through lots of energy. Small local farm operations rarely do this.

As committed stewards to the land, local producers are dedicated to treating the land, soil, and water they use with respect and integrity. Many are well versed in environmentally friendly farming practices, use organic methods, employ gentle pesticides or herbicides (only if necessary), and avoid chemical fertilizers.

In return, they get not only an abundant bounty of crops, but also an economically viable land that will produce for many years to come. In this way, local farmers preserve large tracts of this nation's natural green farmlands and pastures as well as surrounding wooded areas that would otherwise be developed or end up in disrepair.

Simply Sustainable

The best local farmers use *sustainable agricultural* practices. Sustainable farms produce food using healthy food production systems in harmony with the land and the community that surrounds them.

LOCAL LINGO

Sustainable agriculture protects and replenishes the earth's natural resources. It integrates profitable farming with environmental and social consciousness by promoting continuous yet environmentally protective farming techniques.

To do this, sustainable farmers …

- Take care of the earth's natural resources such as land and water by carefully monitoring quality as well as quantity.
- Do not harm the environment.
- Treat animals humanely and feed them a vegetarian diet.
- Do not use any unnecessary antibiotics or hormones.
- Pay farm workers a fair wage and treat them with respect.

Sustainable agriculture, however, is more than just doing the right thing. It also makes good business sense. By taking care of their land, their animals, and their workers, farmers are investing in their most valuable and profitable assets.

How do you know the farmer you're buying from uses sustainable practices? First, look around. Does the produce look fresh and lush? Do the workers look happy and friendly? When you talk to the farmer, ask him how he grows his vegetables, what type of irrigation he uses, if he uses any pesticides or herbicides, and how he takes care of his land during the off season.

Many small farms are family operations so often brothers, uncles, cousins, sons, and daughters are involved in the business. Talk to them about who takes care of the farm.

Like anything else, some people are better at it than others. Consequently, some farmers use more sustainable practices than others, depending how committed they are to following sustainable principles. Talk to several different farmers about their methods, and choose the one you feel most comfortable with. For more information on sustainable agriculture, visit www.sustainabletable.org.

Biodynamic Farming

Another popular local farming method gaining ground, particularly among environmentalists, is called biodynamic farming. Developed in the 1920s, well before the organic movement, biodynamic farming is chemical-free agriculture that works closely with nature.

This holistic approach to farming emphasizes balance and views the soil and the farm as living organisms. Planting, harvesting, and/or raising livestock is based on the interrelationships between the soil, plants, animals, and nature.

Biodynamic farms strive to be self-sufficient and self-contained entities that raise diverse plants and animals. Emphasis is on crop and livestock rotation and recycling of nutrients to maintain a healthy, fertile soil. The goal of the farmer is to set up a system in which all the processes of nature—earth, sun, animals, and plants—work together in the most harmonious and efficient way possible.

A good example of a biodynamic farm is Polyface farm in the Shenandoah Mountains of Virginia. Owned by farmer Joel Salatin and his family, Polyface raises cows, chickens, pigs, turkeys, and rabbits using natural ecological practices that keep the soil healthy and vibrant. For more information on Polyface and biodynamic farming, visit polyfacefarms.com and biodynamics.com.

Reducing Your Carbon Footprint

Global food systems use large amounts of fossil fuels and energy to plant, tend, harvest, and transport their foods. When burned, these fuels emit tons of carbon dioxide, a greenhouse gas known to contribute to global warming.

Nowadays people talk about global warming by looking at *carbon footprints*. Conventional food systems have a large carbon footprint, but eating local reduces your carbon footprint significantly. Here's how:

LOCAL LINGO

A **carbon footprint** is a measure of the impact of an individual's activities on the environment, and in particular climate change. It's how much greenhouse gases you produce in your everyday life through burning fossil fuels for electricity, heating, driving, and other activities.

Fewer food miles. There's no doubt conventionally grown foods travel farther than local ones. How far depends on where you live. Fresh produce delivered to one Midwestern market logged about 1,500 miles on average, while the same produce grown locally traveled only 56 miles. And some local food travels less than that. Either way, staying close to home is the best way to reduce your carbon footprint.

Avoid processed foods. Processed foods automatically drive up the carbon rating due to the fact they have to be prepared, packaged, transported, and stored. This doesn't even count gathering up the many ingredients they contain. In contrast, local foods, sold in their natural state, take little energy to ship and sell.

Eat less meat; eat better meat. Some of our biggest problems from greenhouse gases are a result of concentrated animal feeding operations (CAFOs). These overcrowded feedlots produce large lagoons of liquefied manure loaded with methane (another greenhouse gas), thanks mostly to poor-quality feed. Local livestock raised in pastures and fed on grass don't have this problem and produce little methane.

A CLOSER LOOK

According to the National Resources Defense Council, if all Americans eliminated just one 4-ounce serving of beef per week, the reduction in global warming would be equivalent to taking 4 to 6 million cars off the road.

Eat with the seasons. Local foods are seasonal foods, so they require less energy to grow and flourish. Plant foods also naturally reduce your carbon footprint.

Minimize waste. Forty percent of the food produced in the United States is thrown out. On the consumer level, we throw away more than a quarter of the food we buy. Not only is this a waste of the precious water and fuel used to raise and harvest produce, but decomposing food produces carbon dioxide. Be smart. Buy local and buy only what you know you can use.

The Least You Need to Know

- Fresh, local food promotes a healthy diet by emphasizing wholesome fruits and vegetables and fresh meat.
- Many consumers feel local food is safer because they know where and how the food was produced.
- Local farms support rural communities by boosting the economy.
- Environmentally conscious local farmers use sustainable or biodynamic practices to run their farm.
- Eating locally can significantly reduce your carbon footprint.

Myths About Eating Local

In This Chapter

- How much do local foods really cost?
- Taking a look at transportation
- Discover a world of choices
- Finding local markets

Even if you believe in eating local, making a commitment can be scary, especially when you've heard negative rumors or myths about it. Will you get bored? Where will you get the food? Is it expensive? Does it really matter?

Through the years, we've gotten so accustomed to buying our food at slick super-stores loaded with year-round produce cut, washed, and ready-to-eat, and aisles of boxes, bags, and cans of nearly everything else, the notion of living on locally grown food seems overwhelming, stressful, and at times even silly.

Don't let your fears get the best of you. Eating local is easy, accessible, and affordable—and it's one of the best ways to support your environment and your community. Plus, once you start doing it, you'll get better and better at sourcing, buying, and cooking these kinds of foods.

This chapter is dedicated to putting your mind at ease by dispelling some of the popular misconceptions and fallacies surrounding local food. So relax and read on to find out the real scoop on eating food close to home.

Myth: Local Food Is More Expensive

As far as reasons why not to go local, this is the one I've heard most often. It's also a very easy excuse to use. In reality, however, it's really not true.

Before they do much research, most people think local foods are more expensive than nonlocal foods. Part of this has to do with marketing, and part of it has to do with the fact that some foods *are* more expensive than their conventional counterparts and always will be, like meat. Other local foods, however, balance out the higher-priced items. Plus, local food can save you money in more places than just your food bill. Add up all these factors, and a local diet almost always comes out on top—not only cheaper, but healthier, too. Each of these areas is discussed in detail later on in this chapter and in other parts of the book, so read on to find out why you don't have to spend more buying local foods and how you can even save money.

A CLOSER LOOK

America has the cheapest food in the world. In 2009, only 9.5 percent of our total disposal income was spent on food—this includes both food eaten out (3.93 percent) *and* prepared at home (5.55 percent). For food eaten at home, that's about half the amount of income spent by Germans and nearly one quarter of the income spent by Italians.

Why do local fruits and vegetables seem priced higher than industrial produce? For one thing, most fruits and vegetables available at a farmers' market or other local market are usually sold by the *piece* versus the *pound*, as is more common at regular supermarkets. For example, a bunch of Swiss chard at a local market may sell for $1.50, but at the grocery store, it's 69¢ a pound. The grocery store version sounds cheaper, right? Sure … until you weigh it at the checkout and realize the same Swiss chard costs $2.

A recent Iowa study comparing seven local vegetables to supermarket varieties found that buying 1 pound of each vegetable cost $8.84 local and $10.45 nonlocal.

Most of the cost advantage of local produce stems from competition during peak season, when farmers often have more produce than they can handle so they drop their prices. While driving through the countryside, I once stopped at a stand for fresh-picked raspberries. At early summer, the height of raspberry season, they cost $4.50 for 1 quart. What a deal!

Sometimes weather can make a difference, too. After a heavy rain storm, my local farmers' market sold cherries, which were cracked from water damage but otherwise perfectly fine, for $2 a quart—less than half the price of the regular cherries at $6 a quart. Other times, bruised apples or fruits that may have fallen off the tree before they could be picked are deeply discounted and sometimes even offered for free. For these items, the trick is to use them quickly before they become over-ripe or go bad.

Even if local produce prices aren't lower, they're usually close enough that it doesn't make much of a difference. The one exception to this is proteins like meat, poultry, and fish. This is because it costs significantly more to humanely raise livestock than the way it's conventionally raised on large feedlots. The result, however, is a better-tasting and better-for-you product. Plus, you'll appreciate it more, knowing the animal was taken care of.

Despite the fact that conventional food may be cheaper to buy than locally grown products, the costs to your environment, your land, and your health are higher.

Costs and Balances

Despite the recent hikes, U.S. food prices have stayed relatively low over the last few decades, particularly when compared to average income levels. High-tech agriculture along with large-volume operations that drive down cost-per-unit as production increases have kept food costs low, but at a price.

By focusing on efficiency and streamlining operations to cater to only one crop, usually a grain like corn or soybeans, these massive factory farms have become very good at producing cheap food. Today, the average large conventional farmer can feed 129 Americans compared with 19 people in 1940. While this may sound impressive, cheap food is not, particularly for the small farmer (as well as everyone else, as you'll see later). Without the high volume of industrialized farms, small and even medium-size farmers get less money for the food they grow, making it harder and harder for farmers to feed themselves and their families and forcing many to give up farming. This has led to even more consolidation, resulting in even bigger (and more efficient) factory farms.

Planting single crops is another common practice at factory farms. Even if these plants are rotated annually, it's not good for the soil and fosters soil erosion. More single-crop farms also mean we need to get more of our dietary needs elsewhere. Many times this means turning to imported products for foods we used to produce ourselves when crop variety was still valued. With fewer farmers and a more limited food supply to feed a larger nation, food security has now become an issue and has led many people to question our domestic agriculture.

> **NATIVE KNOWLEDGE**
>
> When it comes to meat, choose medium-size companies over small. Very low-volume operations, particularly for livestock, need to charge higher prices just to cover their expenses. In this case, bigger operations may be a better bet for cost because they sell more. So be sure to shop around.

Government subsidies given to these huge single-crop or single-animal farms are another way conventional farmers offset costs, artificially keeping prices low and food cheap. Many of the crops they do grow—mainly soybeans, corn, and wheat—are mostly used in processed foods.

Fruit and vegetable farmers get no such subsidies. On top of that, they have extra costs such as higher insurance rates or extra paperwork due to the fact that the system is designed for more industrial-type farms. Small farmers cannot spread these costs over a large volume of product, so they must pass them directly to consumers.

Perhaps your biggest cost, as a consumer, is to the environment. In order to keep yield high and soil healthy, conventional farmers use powerful chemical fertilizers and herbicides. Over the last few decades, the use of these fertilizers has risen dramatically. Runoff from the fields of heavily fertilized farms has polluted a great number of our rivers and streams. The most contaminated are called dead zones because they have such low oxygen levels they can support little aquatic life. Each year a dead zone about the size of New Jersey appears where the mouth of the Mississippi and the Gulf of Mexico meet, and lately this has been growing.

So while conventional food may be cheaper, more of our tax dollars now go to cleaning up the environmental damage this type of factory farming produces, indirectly upping costs.

Quality, Not Quantity

It doesn't take much to see that most of the so-called "cheap" food in our current food supply is of poor quality. Cheap food like bread, pasta, cookies, cakes, and fast food are loaded with refined carbohydrates, sugar or fat, and plenty of calories. Many processed foods are included in these ranks.

So it comes as no surprise to find that grains and fats, which supply the lowest cost per calorie, are also the foods subsidized by the government. Unfortunately, these foods are also the least nutritious, supplying us with more empty calories than healthy vitamins, minerals, and protein. Fruits and vegetables, on the other hand, cost more per calorie—primarily because they're low-calorie foods—but have the lowest cost per nutrient.

What does this mean in practical terms? For a few dollars, you can get a hamburger, french fries, and a soft drink amounting to 1,100 calories or more and little nutrition. Or for the same amount of money, you can buy a variety of locally grown fruits and vegetables (about 2 pounds' worth) giving you about a quarter of the calories or less but containing much more fiber, vitamins, and minerals—good nutrition! Furthermore, while the processed food can only feed one person one time, the fruits and vegetables can be stretched into three or four servings. Unfortunately, most people choose the former over the latter.

Not surprisingly, poor diet is responsible for many of the health problems that plague this country—obesity, diabetes, heart disease, and cancer—and ultimately the high health costs many people pay down the road, not to mention how it affects quality of life. Local foods, because they're healthier, are typically not associated with these hidden costs. Rather, their costs are right up front.

Focusing on quality over quantity means you'll be paying more to the farmer, but spending less (on health care) in the long run. Looks like cheap food isn't so cheap after all.

KEEP YOUR DISTANCE

It pays to eat your fruits and vegetables! A 2010 report from the National Fruit and Vegetable Alliance attributed inadequate fruit and vegetable consumption to $56.2 billion as the economic cost to society (including health care). This is an increase of more than 90 percent compared to 10 years ago.

Buying Local Foods on a Budget

So what can you do to save money and buy local on the cheap right now? Aside from shopping at local markets regularly, there's plenty you can do. Here are some ideas:

- Buy only in season.

- Join a CSA.

- Go to the farmers' market early to get the best deals.

- Visit a pick-your-own farm.

- Buy in bulk and "put up" your harvest so you'll have enough for winter months.

Stocking up on healthy, locally grown produce, proteins, and prepared foods is the best way to ensure you get the most nutritional bang for your buck, not to mention wonderful food every night. In upcoming chapters, I cover each of these money-saving tips in more detail. As a result, you can make delicious, nutritious meals you can be proud of—and best of all, won't break the bank!

Myth: Local Foods Burn More Fuel

Some people argue that local foods actually burn more fuel than conventional farming because farmers transport small amounts of food by inefficient commercial vehicles that use more gas. But this isn't always the case. Obviously, the closer you are to the source of your food, the less fossil fuel you will burn no matter what, but mode of transportation makes a big difference.

Planes are notorious gas guzzlers, emitting tons of greenhouse gases annually; consequently, they have the highest carbon footprint. Next in line come trucks like large semi-tractor trailers. Surprisingly, trains and ships are better and more efficient than either of these two other transportation systems, especially considering how much food they can haul. This often throws a twist into the local mix.

Take the case of the Maine potato and its well-traveled cousin from Idaho. For consumers on the East Coast, you'd think the Maine potato arriving by long-haul truck would be the clear winner, eco-wise. But in reality, the Idaho potato traveling by energy-efficient train has a smaller carbon footprint despite larger food miles. Food miles are a good way to determine how local a food is, but they don't always tell the whole story when it comes to environmental impact. (For more information on food miles, check out "How Far Is Local?" in Chapter 1.)

Learn the Life Cycle

According to Rich Pirog, associate director of the Leopold Center for Sustainable Agriculture at Iowa State University, it's the entire life cycle of the food supply chain that counts. This includes when, how, and where the food was grown or raised as well as what happens to it after it's picked or processed. For example, foods grown in cool climates in heated greenhouses use more fuel than those grown in warmer climates. Do they need extra water or irrigation? What has to be done to them after they're picked? For example, do nuts need to be de-hulled or cracked? Are dried peas shelled? All these factors play a role in determining how much energy your food uses.

Processed foods especially require more energy to produce. Consider that these foods need to be shipped to a processing plant (with ingredients coming from all over) and then peeled, cut, mixed, and formed or shaped into some type of dinner, lunch, or snack food. Then they have to be packaged, labeled, and shipped out again, usually to a storage area and then to their markets.

Organic foods, on the other hand, conserve energy. They use sustainable agricultural practices that don't damage the soil or the environment. They're grown under natural conditions and mostly sold in their whole, natural state. They need no packaging or labeling or storage, and when they're sold locally, no storage is needed and only minimal transportation is required.

Because they're grown in season; use environmentally friendly methods; and are in their whole, natural form, local foods often win out over conventional food practices. Try to choose foods you know are native to your soil, climate, and region because others may require more energy to produce. Even with a larger carbon footprint for local foods than some conventional foods, local foods are still the better bet when it comes to saving energy. Why? Because conventional foods have to be cleaned, cut, and packaged, not to mention stored usually in a central facility miles away for several weeks and then trucked to the store—extra fossil-fuel-burning steps local foods just don't have.

A CLOSER LOOK

A 2001 Iowa-based study evaluated fuel and gas emissions of trucks based on three different systems: local, regional, and conventional. The study found that conventional large tractor trailers used anywhere from 4 to 17 times more fuel and emitted 5 to 17 times more carbon dioxide gas than both the local small, light trucks and regional midsize trucks.

Taking Control

Buying fresh, whole, natural local foods is the best way to support your community, your farmer, and your environment, as well as reduce your carbon footprint. But you can help keep your planet green in other ways, too. Check out these easy ways you can make your local foods even greener than they already are:

Eat less meat and more plants. The meat and dairy industry is responsible for a huge amount of air and water pollution. Chicken and fish are eco-friendlier, but still have issues. Replacing just one of your meat meals a week with a vegan/plant-based dish (no cheese) would make a big difference. Here's where more (plant foods) is definitely better.

Plan no-cook days. Being green means conserving energy, and what better way than have one day a week a "raw day"? Skip the oven or stovetop, and instead make a main dish salad, veggie burrito, or cool cucumber-yogurt soup.

Use your microwave. Compared to a conventional oven, microwaves can reduce energy by about two thirds or more. This is mainly due to faster cooking times. Some microwaves can even automatically shut off when food is cooked. Most people don't think about *cooking* with a microwave, only heating things up. Shake things up a bit and try planning dinner with your microwave in mind.

Make multiple dinners with one meal. The next time you're sautéing vegetables, cooking a pot of beans, or roasting chicken or fish, plan for another meal and double up the recipe. Reheating a meal uses much less energy than cooking from scratch, and it takes less time, too.

Don't waste food. Be a green-conscious cook, and aim for less waste whenever you're in the kitchen. Leave the skin on your fruits or vegetables whenever possible, and use extra scraps in soups or stews. Prepare your meals with leftovers in mind. If the recipe is too big, try cutting it in half to make exactly what you think you need. Less trash means less landfill waste and less pollution.

For more ideas about being green in the kitchen, take a look at Jackie Newgent's *Big Green Cookbook* (John Wiley and Sons, 2009) or Kate Geagan's *Go Green Get Lean* (Rodale Press, 2009).

Myth: Local Foods Mean Limited Options

People who haven't eaten local before may complain of the food being boring, limited, and lacking in variety. Talk to a locavore, however, and you'll discover that nothing can be further from the truth. In fact, in no time at all, you'll begin to realize that local foods offer a world of diversity that conventional products simply can't match.

Mother Nature has provided us with tens of thousands of flavorful varieties of fruits, vegetables, greens, grains, nuts, and seeds; oceans teeming with fish; and all types of game, fowl, and four-legged creatures. More than 7,000 species of plants have been consumed by humans throughout history. Even among familiar foods, there's incredible diversity evident in the 4,000 known varieties of tomatoes, more than 100 varieties of apples, 650 varieties of potatoes, and at least 40 different types of lettuces—just to name a few.

Yet the typical supermarket rarely highlights these homegrown specialties, stocking only a small amount of local produce (most are imported or from more than a thousand miles away), only five or six types of meat and poultry, and one or two dozen kinds of seafood.

Look closely, and you'll see the majority of our conventional food is actually based on only three foods: corn, soybean, and wheat, processed in all kinds of ways. If in doubt, try to find foods without high-fructose corn syrup or cornstarch (corn), wheat flour or modified food starch (wheat), or soybean oil. According to author Michael Pollan in his book *Ominvore's Dilemna*, only four crops—corn, soy, wheat, and rice—account for two thirds of the calories we eat. Who's limited now?

Discover New Foods

Eating local is a great way to discover new foods. Such foods can appear as unusual or rare varieties of a familiar food, like purple tomatoes or golden beets. They can be a part of a plant we don't typically eat, like garlic scapes or cactus pads. Or they can be an entirely different vegetable, like scorzonera, a long, black, root vegetable with a creamy white interior that tastes something like artichoke or kohlrabi, a round bulbous vegetable that is part of the broccoli family and has a mild sweet taste. Either way, these foods are worth seeking out, not only for their nutritional value, color, and crunch, but also for their unique taste.

Look for these and other unusual foods anywhere local foods are sold. If in doubt, ask your merchant or farmer what's new or interesting. Chances are, he or she is eager to point it out. Your local farmer can also give you tips on how to prepare and cook the food as well as what it goes best with.

Fostering new foods is one of the ways neighboring farmers promote the biological diversity or *biodiversity* of a region.

LOCAL LINGO

Biodiversity refers to all the variety of life in a certain region. This includes species diversity, such as plant and animal variety; genetic diversity, the variety of genes in individual organisms; and ecological diversity, the kinds of habitats, biological communities, and ecosystems that exist there.

Local farmers celebrate biodiversity for a number of reasons. Planting a wide variety of plants keeps the soil healthy and protects plants from insects and viruses. From an economic perspective, it ensures success because if one crop fails, you always have another to fall back on.

Ecologically, biodiversity preserves plants that would otherwise be lost or become extinct. Where do farmers find such seeds? Sometimes it's from customers, like me and you, or friends who had a certain plant in their family for generations. Sometimes it's from farms that have closed down. Sometimes they buy them at special seed banks or "seed" festivals like the Southern Exposure Seed Exchange Heritage Festival at the home of Thomas Jefferson in Monticello, Virginia. Here farmers can buy or exchange heirloom seeds as well as learn about sustainable gardening practices and local foods. For more information, log on to heritageharvestfestival.com.

A Multicultural Melting Pot

In the strict sense of the words, *local food* refers to foods that are native to the sur-rounding land. But what about immigrants who came to this country, years or even generations ago, bringing along the plants and seeds of their homeland as well as their own farming traditions? Are these foods, grown and raised on local soil, still consid-ered our own? Most people would say yes.

Born of European or Asian ancestry, these foods have now become part of the agri-cultural fabric of the region. Furthermore, many of these immigrant cultures place a high value on farming, thus they have strong roots in the local farming community.

The Amish, for example, have been a major force in revitalizing the local food move-ment in Pennsylvania and Ohio. The Hmongs from Laos have done much to foster the growth of farmers' markets in the Midwest and northern states, where their pop-ulations are greatest. And the Chinese, Korean, Vietnamese, and southeast Asians have a strong influence in California's farmers' markets.

A CLOSER LOOK

Minnesota is home to an estimated 60,000 to 70,000 Hmong, making it the second state with the largest Hmong population, close behind California. Many of these Hmong were farmers in their home country.

Unfortunately, locally grown ethnic vegetables like the Laos bitter melon or one of the dozens of Asian greens (with names so hard to pronounce some farmers don't even label them) may not be so easy to find outside big-city local markets. This is mostly because some farmers hesitate to sell them, thinking there's not a market for them.

If you do get the chance to buy a locally grown ethnic vegetable, definitely take advantage of this opportunity. Then tell the farmer how much you enjoyed the vegetable. Maybe you could start a trend!

While you're at it, talk to the farmer about what else he or she grows. Certain vegetables may look similar but may taste slightly different because they're native to a faraway country. This can be the case with squash or leafy greens. Other times, they are a part of the plant we don't typically see, like "top squash"—the leafy green top part of a type of Laos squash grown in the United States.

Either way, exploring ethnic foods can offer many new and unusual foods for you to try.

Myth: Local Foods Are Hard to Find

Over the last two decades, the local food scene has taken off at a phenomenal rate, both in size and scope, making homegrown specialties more and more accessible to the average consumer. Most of this growth has mushroomed in urban and suburban neighborhoods, particularly on the coasts, where demand is greatest, but rural communities have also benefited. What will you find in your community?

Farmers' markets. Once only welcome in country neighborhoods, local farmers' markets can now be found in nearly every major metropolitan city across the United States, with big cities boasting several different ones. They're typically located in parks, parking lots, and out-of-the-way places, and most locavores have a list of hot spots they regularly frequent.

Community supported agriculture organizations (CSAs). At CSAs, consumers buy directly from the farmer. In cities, most CSAs drop off their products at strategic, easy-to-get-to places. They are also involved in buying groups. LocalHarvest, for example, has the largest database of CSAs, connecting consumers to 2,500 farms across the country. Log on to localharvest.org to learn more.

Specialty and regular food stores. Thanks to pressure from consumers, many specialty and regular grocery stores now carry local items. Keep an eye out during peak summer season. If you want to know for sure, ask a manager. If he or she doesn't currently stock any local items, if you keep asking for them, you might someday find them in stock.

Food co-ops. Owned by consumer "members," co-op stores are great places to find local goods. They're also becoming more and more popular as the local food market grows.

Thriving online local food communities. Most local foods are only a click away, now that many farmers have websites. You can also go online and hook up with local buyers' clubs and delivery services. To find a buyers' club, first try going to the site of the specific farm you'd like to buy from, and search there. You may even want to put in a query to the farmer and ask him if he has any buyers' clubs in your area. Another option is to visit www.greenpeople.org, click CSAs Buying Clubs, and search there. Otherwise, you can do a Google search.

Right now, most local foods are sold directly by farmers at small outlets, but as the market matures, it will develop a more solid infrastructure. This, in turn, will create a larger and more efficient distribution network, expanding the local market.

A CLOSER LOOK

Today, the direct-to-consumer market represents about $1.2 billion in sales. Advocates expect this is only the tip of the iceberg.

The Least You Need to Know

- Whole, natural local foods are generally less expensive than their globe-trotting counterparts.
- Quality, taste, and freshness are the main reasons why consumers choose local food over conventional produce.
- Local markets boast a wide variety of homegrown foods, including new types of produce and ethnic brands.
- A food's environmental impact is determined by how it's grown, shipped, and processed as well as its food miles.
- More and more local food is popping up all across the country in a variety of outlets. Look for farmers' markets, CSAs, food co-ops, and farms in local newspapers, online, and in nearby neighborhoods.

The Local Pantry

When many people think "local food," fruits and vegetables come to mind. That's a good thing. It's true the local pantry is filled with a wealth of produce, and in the following chapters, we're going to look at all the different kinds out there.

But local food is more than just green fruits and veggies. It includes a wide range of nuts, legumes, dried beans and peas, herbs, and whole grains. Beyond these plant foods, Part 2 explores meat, fish, poultry, cheese, milk, dairy products, and eggs. These basic foods are the backbone of local cuisine, and we'll look at each one in turn.

Plus, don't forget prepared foods like preserves, salsas, and baked goods. The final chapter in Part 2 uncovers the wealth of local beverages, both alcoholic and nonalcoholic, now being made in different regions. You'll be surprised at the many kinds of local food available in your region. Not only will you discover the unique advantages of choosing local foods over conventional ones—taste, quality, and variety—you'll also explore new foods you may not have tried—or even known existed!

Local Produce

In This Chapter

- Exploring veggies close to home
- Fantastic fruits
- Getting your daily bread
- Learning to shop local
- What to do after the fall harvest

Produce plays a major role in the locavore's diet year-round. Some of this comes by way of sheer abundance as harvest time delivers a cornucopia of offerings impossible to ignore. Other times, variety is the driving force, as fruits and vegetables along with whole grains and nuts supply myriad colors, tastes, and textures, adding excitement and adventure to meals. Last but not least, there's the health aspect. All these foods are super nutritious, providing a wealth of vitamins, minerals, and fiber. And as a bonus: fruits and vegetables are virtually fat-free and naturally low in calories.

With all these benefits, it's easy to see why produce holds a place of esteem in the locavore lineup. In fact, once you start eating local, you'll find more and more things to love about them. In the meantime, let's go over what you need to know about each of these local foods.

All About Veggies

Unlike conventional produce, locally grown vegetables are always sold in their whole, natural state, uncut and unprocessed. Often this means root vegetables like beets, turnips, and carrots still have their greens attached; corn is still in the husk; and while you may find shelled peas, it's more likely you'll see them still in their pod. Certain vegetables like Swiss chard, kale, and lettuces tend to be sold in a bunch, plastic bag, or basket. Most other vegetables are marketed individually by the pound or the piece.

Because these foods are generally brought from farm to market in a short period of time, they don't need any special treatment, like waxes. To protect it during storage and transit, most supermarket produce is typically cleaned and coated with wax. According to the U.S. Food and Drug Administration (FDA), food-grade wax or resin is made from a base of either vegetable, petroleum, beeswax, or shellac—sounds appetizing, right?

KEEP YOUR DISTANCE

Many farmers try to clean their produce before they sell it to you, but dirt is a fact of life and hard to avoid. It's particularly stubborn on leafy greens and root vegetables. Be sure to wash all local produce thoroughly before eating or cooking with it.

The first time you go shopping for local vegetables, you might be surprised at what you find—and what you don't find. Keeping in mind what veggies grow in what season gives you an idea of what you'll find at the market. In addition to the season, climate, weather, and region have an influence on what grows when. Remember, too, that some vegetables like onions grow year-round (although flavor changes along the way), while many others extend only into the next season. Here's a quick guide to help you sort out local food by growing season:

Spring:

artichokes	lettuces
arugula	morels
asparagus	onions
beets	parsley
carrots	potatoes
cauliflower	radishes
English peas	rhubarb
fava beans	shallots
fiddleheads	snow peas

spinach   turnips

Swiss chard

Summer:

arugula	garlic
avocado	kohlrabi
basil	okra
beans—snap or green	onions
collards	peppers (all types)
corn	Swiss chard
cucumbers	tomatoes
dried beans	yellow squash
eggplant	zucchini

Fall:

arugula	hot peppers
beans	kale
beets	mushrooms
broccoli	onions
broccoli rabe	parsnips
Brussels sprouts	potatoes
carrots	pumpkin
cauliflower	radishes
celery root	squash (all types)
collards	sweet potatoes
cranberries	sweet red peppers
fennel	tomatoes
garlic	turnips

Beans, Dried Peas, and Lentils

Beans, dried peas, and lentils are part of the *legume* family. (Legumes are edible seeds grown in pods.) They're high in protein; have plenty of folate; contain some B vitamins; and have a variety of important minerals like iron, potassium, magnesium, calcium, and copper. But their biggest claim to fame is in the fiber department.

One cup of beans can provide as much as 15 grams fiber—more than half your required daily intake of 25 grams. Aside from lowering your cholesterol and reducing your risk of heart disease, high-fiber foods keep you feeling full and satisfied longer than low-fiber ones, making them an ideal food if you're watching your weight.

For people concerned about blood sugar levels (like diabetics) beans offer even more of an advantage. Because they're absorbed and digested slowly, they help control glucose levels better than other carbohydrate foods.

Lucky for us, the ubiquitous bean is a staple in regional cuisines throughout the United States, and each region has its favorite. Midwesterners love their limas; Northeasterners have their Italian fava beans, broad beans, chickpeas, or cannellis; New Englanders their navy beans; and in the Southwest, pinto beans and black beans are the stars. But none can compare to the passionate pea-eaters of the South! Here you'll find all types of beans usually in late summer, fall, and winter.

Most legumes fall into three camps:

- Fresh shell beans or peas

- Dried beans or peas

- Lentils

Fresh shell beans are basically young beans, newly picked, sold in their pod or shelled. They're less starchy than dried beans and taste creamy and sweet. They also take about half the time or less to cook. If left in their pods to dry out, shelled beans will eventually become dried beans.

The same holds true for peas. In the South, shell field peas come in a rainbow of colors and flavors. Cowpeas, known as black-eyed peas, are probably the most well known, but other varieties include crowders, Purple Hull, Lady Peas, and many more.

NATIVE KNOWLEDGE

If you live in Arizona or New Mexico, try buying tepary beans. Native to the desert regions of the American Southwest and parts of Mexico, tepary beans are drought-resistant and adapt well to arid conditions. They come in a number of colors—reddish-brown, white, black, speckled—and have a unique nutty flavor.

Not all dried beans can be bought in their fresh form. In fact, some dried beans or peas are never sold fresh, only dried. These dried legumes are called *pulses* and are a staple farm crop in the prairies.

Lentils, dried peas (better known as split peas), and chickpeas are the three most common pulses grown in the United States. All pulses are legumes, but not all legumes are pulses—for example, peanuts are not a pulse. Lentils, which are cousins to the bean, come in a range of colors from bright orange (red) to grayish-brown to black.

Fresh Herbs

Fresh herbs are indispensable in the locavore kitchen. All it takes is a small amount of this herb or that herb to liven up vegetables, meat, poultry, or fish and turn a ho-hum meal into an extraordinary one. And by varying the herb you use, you can create completely different dishes with the same foods.

Multiply this variety tenfold for people who grow their own herbs or buy them at farmers' markets. Imagine the number of cultivars they have available at their fingertips! Lemon verbena, English thyme, pineapple sage—there are 60 varieties of basil alone! Next time you're shopping, buy a bunch and don't be afraid to experiment with different herbs.

If you have the inclination, try planting an herb garden. Most herbs are a hardy lot and don't take much effort to grow. Many can thrive year-round, indoors in windowsill planters or container gardens. They don't need much space. You can plant a half-dozen or more varieties in one pot. Best of all, growing herbs saves you lots of money!

From farmers, you can buy local herbs fresh-cut or potted in soil and ready to plant. The latter ensures you have a steady supply of fresh herbs throughout the season and maybe even the year if you dry and store the leaves. The former are great when you need a bunch to cook with right away.

Taste-wise, nothing compares to fresh herbs just plucked from their branches. Not only are they stronger in flavor but (unlike supermarket varieties), when chopped, their scent fills the air, giving your food a fresh, aromatic quality.

Fruit Finds

Fruit isn't called "nature's candy" for nothing. Sweet, juicy, and delicious, it's a favorite among adults as well as children. Local fruit is particularly succulent because it's allowed to ripen right on the vine, meaning all the starches have naturally turned to sugar. This makes it perfect for pies, pastries, or desserts—or for eating right out of your hand!—but not for long storage. Eat it within a week or so.

A CLOSER LOOK

Supermarket fruit is typically picked under-ripe in its starchy state and artificially ripened either in storage or transit.

Because most local fruit doesn't last more than a few days, if you stock up on strawberries, cherries, blackberries, peaches, or anything else, be sure you have time for baking, freezing, canning, or preserving the fruits before they go bad.

Also be prepared to pay a higher price for local fruit than for vegetables at local markets. A lot of this has to do with how much work is involved in growing the fruit. Unlike supermarket fruit, which is mechanically picked when its under-ripe and hard, local fruit is picked ripe, so it's more fragile and requires more labor to pick, pack, and bring to market. If you'd like to do some of the work yourself, on a U-pick farm (see Chapter 10), you can get your fruit for much cheaper.

Keeping the fruit on the vine longer also increases the risk of pests—birds and bugs like fruit as much as we do. For this reason, some local farmers are more apt to use pesticides. If that's a concern for you, you can opt for organic fruit.

Weather can be an issue and can easily wipe out a crop. Fruits are much more finicky about their environment than vegetables. Some need warm days and cool nights to thrive; others need long, hot summers. Citrus, for example, grows best in hot, humid weather. Northern climates, which may have a good selection of pears, apples, and berries, simply won't be able to sustain peaches, nectarines, or plums because the season is just too short.

Most typical American consumers take the fruit we buy at grocery stores for granted, but locavores quickly develop an appreciation for these sweet treats. They've learned that fruit is not only a precious and valuable commodity, but with its relatively short season and delicate nature, it's a luxury to be savored and enjoyed during peak season … and anxiously anticipated when it's not.

Nuts to You, Too!

Most people can think of only a handful of nut varieties. Almonds, walnuts, pecans, pistachios, hazelnuts, and cashews most often come to mind, but when you explore local food, you'll discover many more varieties.

Many of these native nuts have seen their numbers dwindle drastically over the years, and some have even been close to extinction. Luckily, the local food movement, along with dedicated conservationists, are bringing them back.

Here are a few nuts you're likely to see at your local markets:

Hickory nuts, butter nuts, and black walnuts. Native to the Midwest and East, these nuts are similar to the common English walnut, but each has a unique flavor. Black walnuts have a strong, musky flavor, while hickory nuts are more mild, and butter nuts are smooth-tasting and milder still.

American chestnut. Almost wiped out by a blight in 1904, scattered trees of this nut can be found from Maine to Ohio and Georgia to Alabama. Small and sweet, they're most often roasted, baked, ground, or used in stuffings.

Acorns. Not just squirrel food, acorns have been an important food staple in the diet of Native American peoples for hundreds of years. More than 60 types of oak trees grow in North America, and all produce edible acorns. Some are better tasting than others, however. That's because acorns naturally contain a bitter compound called tannic acid. These levels can vary from very high to very low (sweet-acorn varieties). In the United States, the sweet edible varieties grow wild in Arizona, southern California, and other southwestern states. They're eaten raw, ground into meal, or sometimes roasted. You can still eat the bitter ones, but they must be soaked or boiled first to remove the bitter tannins.

Beechnuts. The beechnut comes from the beech tree, which thrives in temperate climates. American beech trees (there are 10 varieties) can be found from Kentucky to Central Michigan, and from New Jersey to parts of Florida and Texas. The nut grows in small, prickly burs that split open and drop on the ground, usually by the first frost, revealing two or three triangular kernels surrounded by a thin, smooth shell that can be difficult to remove. Beechnuts have a mild nutty taste, similar to hazelnuts, and have a high fat content, so they must be used quickly before they spoil.

Pinyons. Pinyon nuts are the American version of pine nuts (almost all the pine nuts you see in stores are grown in China). Native to northern Arizona, New Mexico, and Nevada, pinyons have a slightly sweet, rich taste.

Even more common nuts have a better, brighter flavor when freshly picked off the tree and eaten.

If you're wondering what type of nuts to expect in your climate, here they are in a nutshell:

- Almonds grow best in the warm Mediterranean-like climate of California.

- Walnuts thrive in the Midwest and the West Coast.

- Hazelnuts like the moist, mild climate of the Northwest.

- Pecans enjoy the sandy soil of the Southwest but are also famously grown in the Southeast, especially Louisiana, Georgia, and North and South Carolina, giving rise to the famous praline (made with native pecans).

Most locally grown nuts are relatively small operations, so farmers must do most of the work of picking, sorting, and cracking the nuts by hand themselves. For this reason, nuts are often sold at a premium price.

A CLOSER LOOK

Although classified as a nut, peanuts are technically a legume. They're a cash crop in Southern states like Alabama, Georgia, North Carolina, and Virginia, where it's not hard to find locally grown "green" peanuts. Similar to fresh shell beans, fresh peanuts are typically boiled in salted water and eaten out of hand.

What About Wheat?

Wheat is so ingrained in our food culture, few Americans can imagine their diet without it. Who can live without bread, pasta, pies, or muffins?

Throughout most of the nineteenth century, communities grew their own local wheat, and grain mills dotted the countryside. To give you an idea of how important this industry was, just 150 years ago 10,000 mills were producing flour in northern New England.

With the advent of the railroad and the opening of the West in the late 1800s, grain-growing moved to the prairies, where it stayed. Today, North Dakota, South Dakota, Nebraska, Kansas, and Minnesota supply most of our commercial wheat. Mass-produced in large factories, this is standardized wheat bred for uniformity.

Interest in local food, however, has sparked a resurrection of some of these old wheat fields and uncommon wheat varieties. As a result, boutique local flours have been popping up everywhere from Oregon to New Mexico to New York State.

Unlike commercial flour, small-batch, high-quality flours have a musky fragrance, with a distinct taste and texture that brings complexity to baked goods. Many are whole-grain or stone-ground, which means they can go rancid in weeks if not frozen or refrigerated. They can also vary greatly from season to season, farm to farm, and even field to field. So the wheat you bought one year might not taste the same or even perform the same way in baking as the same wheat, produced by the same farm, you bought the next year. For this reason, consider each season like a new culinary adventure.

Finding a Miller

The toughest part of buying local wheat usually isn't finding the wheat itself, but turning it into flour. Most mills were abandoned long ago, but luckily, some are being renovated and brought back to life, so check around your area. If not, here are some other options:

- Check with the farmer who grew the wheat. He may know someone.

- Take a class on threshing, cleaning, and milling wheat. For instance, the Northeast Organic Wheat consortium in New York regularly holds workshops like this. Log on to growseed.org/now.html to learn more, or search the Internet for a group like this near you.

- Buy a second-hand milling machine, and grind it yourself.

- Strike up a relationship with a local baker.

- Find other people who buy whole wheat, and form a buyers group. Remember, there's strength in numbers!

Go Wheat-Free

Beyond wheat, many other types of grains can be milled into flour. In the South, for instance, corn dominated the agriculture and was once much more popular than wheat. Locally grown, stone-ground cornmeal is still the favorite. Artisan mills are also now experimenting with a wide range of options including spelt, buckwheat, rye, and oats. Look around at your local markets to see what you can find.

And don't forget about rice. This familiar grain was first introduced to colonists in Charleston, South Carolina, in 1685 by sailors coming from Madagascar. The low-lying marshes bordered by fresh tidal water of the Carolinas and Georgia proved to be ideal for production. A long-grain rice with a golden color, it soon became known as "Carolina Gold." The crop quickly spread throughout the South, giving rise to a wealthy plantation culture. But after the Civil War and with the loss of slave labor, the labor-intensive rice industry of the South suffered.

With the mechanization of agriculture, rice moved westward and new rice varieties were developed. By the end of the Great Depression, Carolina gold was nearly extinct. Luckily, a Savannah farmer collected some seeds and began growing the crop in the 1980s. Today, the revived heirloom rice can be found in North Carolina, South Carolina, Louisiana, Georgia, and Texas. Look for it at local farmers' markets in those areas.

Best Bets for Bakeries

If buying local flour and making your own bread isn't really your thing, consider frequenting local bakeries. This supports your community as well as your local food system. Some bakeries will even source locally produced wheat, within a reasonable distance.

What makes a good bakery? It should be independently owned and operated—in short, the owner should be there to greet you at least sometimes. He or she should make artisan bread, pastries, etc. fresh daily with no artificially additives or preservatives—handmade, if possible. And generally, the business would be a small operation (although not necessary) that sells to the local neighborhood.

If you don't know where to look, start at your local farmers' market. Most host at least one and sometimes two bakeries. This also gives you the chance to sample the products and talk to the employees before buying.

Let's Hear It for Heirlooms!

Some of the foods you come across at local markets hail from *heirloom* seeds. According to Seed Savers Exchange (seedsavers.org), a nonprofit organization dedicated to preserving and sharing rare seeds, heirloom plants are from seeds that have been passed down through generations. For locavores, produce from heirloom plants is the ultimate local cuisine.

LOCAL LINGO

Heirloom plants include any garden plant (fruit, vegetable, grain, or bean) that has a history of being passed down within a family. These heritage plants are unique in that they're genetically distinct from mass-produced commercial plants.

Heirlooms protect the genetic diversity of the world's food crops by promoting agricultural variety. Over the last few decades, crop genetic diversity and, consequently, variety has eroded at an unprecedented rate. As a result, we have lost precious ecological systems along with thousands of fruit and vegetable plant varieties.

Genetic diversity allows plants to change and adapt to their environment. Without it, we rely on single varieties or just a handful of food crops, which increases the risk of devastation by emerging diseases and pests. It also makes it harder to develop new crops.

But more important than plant characteristics is how this diversity affects appearance, flavor, and maybe even nutrition. Whereas industrial produce strives for conformity, often sacrificing taste along the way, heirlooms celebrate uniqueness, reveling in interesting and what most people consider "superior" flavor. They also have to fight off insects and other pests, meaning they have more protective phytochemicals than codified conventional plants.

By purchasing heirlooms, you ensure these plants have a future in our ecosystem for years to come. Luckily, shopping for these extraordinary fruits and vegetables, even in local markets, is easy to do—just look for the unusual-looking produce. Some dead giveaways include yellow tomatoes with red stripes, mauve-colored eggplant, or black radishes. Colorful names like Mortgage Lifter Tomatoes, Green Nutmeg Cantaloupe, and Purple Glow in the Dark Peppers are other tip-offs.

Off-Season Options

Although year-round farmers' markets are still not as popular as seasonal ones, they are becoming a common sight as consumer demand grows for the products they offer. Consumer demand is also behind the growing trend for winter community supported agriculture (CSA) membership (I talk more about CSAs in Chapter 11), which often fill up fast.

Places with mild winters like in the South, parts of the West, California, and the Northwest naturally favor a 12-month growing season simply because of their climate and long growing season. As a result, the kinds of foods you'll find off season vary tremendously depending on where you live.

Nevertheless, here are a few foods you're likely to see:

broccoli	kale
broccoli rabe	kumquats
Brussels sprouts	leeks
carrots	lemons
cauliflower	limes
celery root	onions
chicory	oranges
collards	persimmons
grapefruit	pomelos
jicama	pumpkins

Winter Climates

Despite frigid temperatures, you can still find local food grown in many states, including Nebraska, Illinois, Minnesota, and Maine. In these cold climates, root vegetables like parsnips, sweet and white potatoes, carrots, onions, beets, rutabagas, turnips, and winter squash rule the roost. These are followed by a multitude of hardy greens like lacinato (a type of kale), escarole, and collards, and winter fruits such as apples, pears, and dates.

A CLOSER LOOK

Green City Market is Chicago's only all-year-long farmers' market. Learn more at chicagogreencitymarket.org.

This time of year can also be heavy on meat, cheese, and eggs. Traditionally fall was harvest season for animals, which means a bounty of meat is available for the winter. Because these foods generally store well (meats are frozen) and cold weather tends to perk up appetites, many people tend to eat more meat in the winter.

Prepared items are another common site, particularly because many farmers "put up" their own green beans, tomatoes, beets, and more, selling these items during the winter months. There may also be a fair number of jams, jellies, preserves, and sauces. And don't be surprised to find a number of bright winter salad greens.

Surprising Advances

Farmers are always looking for ways to get better at what they do, and often this means extending the growing season. Greenhouses are one of the ways they do that. A houselike structure with glass panels to let the sun in, greenhouses allow farmers to nurture hardy plants in the winter and plant spring plants early. Although solar-style greenhouses do exist, many greenhouses need to be heated, particularly in the cold winter months.

Recently, however, farmers have begun to experiment with hoop houses or high tunnels. Used at the White House garden in the winter of 2009, hoop houses are simply clear plastic stretched over large hoops. High tunnels are similar but are high enough for a person to stand up in them. Both are less expensive than a greenhouse to build. Depending on the location, some hoop houses are heated, and some are not.

Other innovations in cold storage technology allow apples to be sold in spring and summer. In "controlled atmosphere" cold storage, apples are stored in low temperatures in an airtight room with most of the oxygen removed. The process basically puts apples into hibernation for the winter, and can be a boon for small farmers. I've tasted several apples from local farmers in May and June because of this storage method, and they are wonderful. You'd never know they were picked off the tree months earlier.

Mastering the Local Mind-Set

Living like a locavore means enjoying the bounty of nature when you have it and stocking up for the leaner winter and early spring months. Local food picked ripe must be eaten or prepared for storage pretty much immediately. As a locavore, you always have to think ahead about how you can preserve fragrant peaches or sweet berries or cook up mounds of zucchini.

This is quite different from the way we approach conventional supermarket produce. More than just how much we buy and how we use produce, the way we select fruits and vegetables also changes. Most of us have grown accustomed to choosing produce based on looks alone. Thus supermarket produce was grown to look model perfect, which as you know, doesn't always translate into a good-tasting food.

For local food however, looks are not a deciding factor. Quite often, quirky-looking tomatoes, bumpy squash, or odd-shaped peppers are surprisingly more flavorful and delicious than beautiful-looking, store-bought ones.

Look around at your local market, and you'll be surprised at all the different kinds of produce you see. Even if you're a newcomer to the local scene, you'll quickly notice how the seasons and produce change from week to week and month to month. Ask your farmer what's in season, and take advantage of these options. Consider it an opportunity to explore and experiment in a new culinary world. You won't be disappointed.

The Least You Need to Know

- Produce plays an important role in the locavore diet.
- Locally grown vegetables, fruits, nuts, beans, and peas boast a wide variety of tastes, textures, and colors.
- Many locally grown foods come from heirloom seeds.
- Off-season markets even in the cold winter climates offer an abundant amount of locally grown food and make it easy to eat local year-round.
- Because local foods are picked ripe, they need to be eaten or used immediately.
- Looks don't always determine quality, as you'll quickly learn after a trip to your local market.

Meat, Poultry, and Fish

In This Chapter

- The benefits of grass-fed beef
- When chickens *should* fly the coop
- Getting more game on the dinner table
- Tips for buying local meats
- Fishing for local seafood—what you should know

Switching from buying typical supermarket meat, poultry, and fish to buying local is, for most new locavores, one of the toughest steps to take. For one thing, cost can be an issue. The price differential between local and conventional proteins is greater than almost any other local food. This is mostly due to the expense of humanely caring for a living animal, usually on a small scale, which costs much more than the meat cranked out at high-volume, overpopulated factory farms. Fishing or hunting responsibly also takes more work.

Local meats, fish, and poultry—although they're getting more and more popular—may still be harder to find than other local food. This is mostly because fewer farmers raise meat than grow produce. But explosive growth in the last few years is quickly changing that, as more and more farmers are getting into the act.

And even when they *can* find it, some consumers don't feel comfortable buying local meats because they don't know what to look for. Well, get ready to learn the ropes!

In this chapter, I explain why local proteins do more than provide great-tasting, flavorful main entrées—they also protect the earth's natural resources, help ensure the animals are treated with respect and dignity, and are better for you. I introduce you to some interesting and unusual meats and fish you just might find in your neighborhood and also give you some tips for buying locally produced meat, poultry, or fish.

Naturally Fed

Feeding cattle is big business in more ways than one. Cows eat a lot, which means they're not only expensive to take care of but they also put a strain on our natural resources. What they eat affects the environment, the community, and their meat. Typical conventionally raised livestock eats mainly corn, which can also be mixed with soybeans, cottonseed meal, hay, and other vegetable and animal by-products. The problem with this is that cows (as well as chickens and pigs) are not meant to be grain-eaters. Cows, along with buffalo, sheep, and goats are, by nature, grass-eaters (or worm- and bug-eaters, in the case of poultry; pigs eat a variety of plant and animal foods). Feeding cows and pigs a steady diet of grain makes them gain weight quickly, but it also increases their likelihood of getting sick, which is why farmers then give them antibiotics.

Furthermore, the vast stretches of corn fields needed to feed our growing demand for meat do more harm to the earth than good. They require large amounts of fossil fuel–burning fertilizers and pesticides, erode topsoil, and increase pollution-laden water runoff.

What About Grass?

Locally raised beef is more likely to be grass-fed than corn-fed. By U.S. Department of Agriculture (USDA) definition, *grass-fed* means the animal consumes only mother's milk, grass, and forage its entire life. Simply looking for a label isn't enough, however, because grass-fed animals can still be held in confined lots or CAFOs. Ideally, you should look for grass-fed beef or meat, pasture-raised year-round.

Grass-fed beef is not only healthier for the cow, it's healthier for the land and for you. Cattle graze on a given pasture only about four or five days. Then they are rotated to another pasture. During that time their manure fertilizes the ground and protects precious topsoil, making room for new grass to grow once the animals move on. Chewing down this grass also exposes more bugs, worms, and seeds for other animals (specifically birds and chickens) to enjoy. This starts the cycle all over again.

Nutritionally, grass-fed beef is leaner than traditionally raised beef. Compared to conventional beef, grass-fed meat is lower in saturated fat and higher in omega-3 fatty acids (the same "good" fat found in fish), beta-carotene (vitamin A), and conjugated linoleic acid (CLA; a nutrient associated with lower heart disease and cancer risk). And because grass-fed cows tend to be healthier than conventional cows, they're less likely to have been given antibiotics or growth hormones.

KEEP YOUR DISTANCE

Conventionally processed feedlot cows have a higher risk of E. coli contamination than grass-fed cows, mostly because corn-fed diets increase acidity in the gut, which increases E. coli susceptibility.

But nutrition isn't the only difference between corn-fed and grass-fed red meat. Taste is different, too. Grass-fed beef has a more distinct flavor, often characterized as more earthy, robust, and meaty-tasting than regular corn-fed beef. For people who are accustomed to a bland, somewhat buttery-tasting meat (thanks to a high level of marbling, or the amount of fat found throughout the meat—it looks like little white veins), grass-fed beef can be an acquired taste. I like to think of it as the difference between a multigrain whole-wheat bread and white bread. Once you get used to the chewy, nuttiness of whole-wheat bread, all white bread just tastes bland.

In the kitchen, cooking techniques also need to be adjusted. Because grass-fed beef is so lean, it cooks quickly—so quickly, in fact, it can easily turn tough and stringy. For this reason, tender cuts should be served on the rare side, while less-tender ones do best slowly braised over a low temperature.

Organic Options

Organic beef is free of antibiotics and growth hormones. Organically raised cows also must be fed only certified organic vegetarian feed, but unless your organic beef is labeled "grass-fed," don't assume it is. Most organic beef is from corn-fed cows. Unfortunately, local organic grass-fed beef can be hard to find. It's also pretty expensive. Given the choice between a local organic or a local grass-fed cow, I'd choose the local grass-fed, for a few reasons.

First, many local farmers pasture-raise grass-fed beef using organic methods, even though they may not be certified organic. Also, grass-fed cows get their food directly from the land they live on, rather than having their food trucked in from faraway cornfields, making grass-fed beef more in-line with local ideals. Finally, grass-fed beef has a better nutritional profile, as discussed earlier, making it better for you even than organic corn-fed cows.

Sometimes farmers will give their livestock both grass and grain. Other times you'll see the term "grass-fed grain-finished" or just "grain-finished." This means the animals are given grain only for a few months before slaughter to fatten them up. Unfortunately, grain-finishing changes the composition of the meat, and many of the healthy aspects of grass-fed beef are reduced or negated when this is done. This also changes the flavor of the meat, making it taste more like corn-fed meat and less like grass-fed.

Meaty Issues

According to 2008 USDA data, Americans eat more than 61 pounds of beef a year and 46 pounds of pork. Factor in lamb and veal, and you're looking at a total consumption of more than 108 pounds of red meat annually. (Yes, pork is a red meat, despite what the pork industry advertises.) That's a lot of red meat!

Goat, although very popular in the rest of the world, is not a big seller here in the United States. But it is available at local markets, and consumer demand is slowly growing.

Government subsidies, along with large factory farms (CAFOs), whose main goal is efficiency, keep prices low for our major commodity meats beef and pork, but at what cost? To satisfy our voracious appetite for red meat, we've sacrificed much in the way of food quality and animal welfare, not to mention the effects it has had on our environment and our health. Ranchers raising local meats seek to change this system by treating animals humanely, improving the quality of the meat, and introducing new breeds. At the same time, they also care about the earth and our natural resources, working toward a sustainable and healthy industry. Creating such an industry is vital for the future of our communities, our country, and our planet, but it's not cheap.

Quality Comes at a Cost

The biggest issue facing locally raised meat, poultry, or fish is price. While some Americans rarely blink an eye at paying more for a better car, bigger house, or luxury vacation, they do balk at paying more for food, even when it's a higher-quality product. For some reason, the "you get what you pay for" attitude doesn't always transfer to the grocery store.

It's not that locally raised meat is so expensive; it's that much of what we see in the grocery store is extraordinarily *in*expensive. Conventionally raised meat is so cheap partly because the government sinks large subsidies into industrial beef operations and partly because of the rise of large factory farms that take advantage of *economies of scale*.

Economies of scale relates to the size of the operation. The bigger the output, or the number of cows, the less it cost to raise, process, and sell each one. Thus, profit margins are driven by volume rather than quality. These large factory farms, known as concentrated animal feeding operations (CAFOs), contain a minimum of 1,000 cattle, 2,500 hogs, or 125,000 chickens, all in one space usually the size of a few football fields, where the animals have little or no access to the outdoors.

Living in such close quarters, animals are regularly given drugs to prevent illness and keep them healthy. (Antibiotic-free meat can still come from a factory farm—usually given antimicrobial drugs.) They also produce a huge amount of land and water pollution in the form of liquefied manure. In addition to these health and environmental issues, the animals are not treated well. Many people oppose factory farming simply for that reason.

Locally raised livestock, on the other hand, is raised in small numbers, on open pastures, and with humane treatment. While the price of locally raised meat will never be as low as factory farm-raised proteins, you can rest assured that if responsibly raised, this meat is of higher quality and value.

To find out how your local meat is raised, ask questions—and don't stop at one!—and check online. Many local farmers now have websites to explain how they run their operations.

Heritage Breeds

Like heirloom plants, heritage breeds are farm-raised traditional animals—some breeds date as far back as three centuries ago. Although not necessarily rare, heritage animals—raised through natural, sustainable, nonindustrial methods—are unique in that their genetic traits have adapted to withstand disease and survive in harsh environmental conditions. They also are well suited to live outside on pasture land.

Why are these animals important? For one thing, heritage breeds' resilient genetic diversity is critical to a food supply that currently relies on only a handful of breeds for the majority of its needs. What's more, many of these breeds are in danger of disappearing altogether. According to the United Nations' Food and Agricultural Organization (FAO), in the last 15 years, more than one third of the world's farm animals have become extinct, and many more are threatened. And because they forage in open pastures, do not receive any antibiotics or growth hormones, and reproduce naturally, heritage breeds are less damaging to the environment than other animals. Their meat is also healthier and of higher quality than conventional breeds.

From a culinary standpoint, the meat from heritage animals offers a unique dining experience. More flavorful and intense than conventional meats, the meat is greatly influenced by the quality and age of the animal, how it was raised, and what it was fed.

The best thing consumers can do to preserve heritage meats is to eat them. That increases demand and increases supply. Most heritage meats appear in restaurants, bought by locavore chefs. But as interest continues to grow, more of these breeds are moving into the retail sector. Now you can buy them at stores like Whole Foods (wholefoodsmarket.com), directly from farmers, or via specialty food brokers you can find online. Heritage Foods USA is one such broker. Check them out at heritagefoodsusa.com.

Be prepared to pay a premium price because heritage breeds are much more costly to raise. This is partly due to the fact that these breeds grow more slowly than commercial varieties.

Best Buys for Meats

Shopping for local meats isn't as easy as going to your corner supermarket, but retail venues are growing in leaps and bounds. And as competition and demand heat up, prices cool down, making local meats more and more affordable to average consumers.

So where do you go to find local meats? Here are a few places:

- Farmers' markets.
- Direct from the farm at farm stores (retail cuts).
- CSAs, which bring different meat products right to your door every week.

- Buy a part or "share" of the animal—pig, cow, lamb, or goat. The farm usually takes care of the processing, inspection, and packaging, and because you buy in bulk, the price per pound is generally much lower.

- *Buyers' clubs.*

- Local butcher shops.

LOCAL LINGO

A **buyers' club** is a group of individuals usually based in a metropolitan area that strikes up a deal with a producer to regularly buy local meat, which is delivered directly from the farm to a central location (usually a buyers' club host's house). Because they buy large quantities, pricing is usually better.

The Rise of the Local Butcher

For farmers, the hardest part of selling responsible meat is not raising the animals, but getting them processed. With the rise of industrial agriculture, local slaughterhouses are few and far between, forcing some farmers to travel long distances and even cross state lines to have their meat processed by someone they can trust. This ultimately ends up costing you, the consumer, more money as it ups the price of the meat.

Luckily, times are changing, as small-scale slaughterhouses and local butcher shops are working to fill this local niche. While most butcher shops just cut the meat and don't slaughter it, some small country slaughterhouse operations do it all, offering a small retail outlet for customers.

Fresh Frozen

The majority of local meat sold at farmers' markets, on farms, and through buyers' clubs is fresh frozen and vacuum-packed right after processing. This guarantees the meat is safe and of high quality, prevents freezer burn, and greatly prolongs storage life. The same holds true for poultry.

Fresh local meat, which is most often sold in foodservice, can be found at some local butcher shops and is only around for a day or two due to its perishable nature. Then it's usually frozen. Be sure to ask about the origin of the meat because most butcher shops sell both local and nonlocal products.

Local farms are usually small operations, only slaughtering meat during certain times of the year (usually late summer or fall), so finding fresh local meat available all year long can be a challenge. If this is a concern for you, be sure to talk to your butcher. He can let you know when he expects fresh meat to be coming in.

Buying in Bulk

Most people are used to buying meat by the part or piece. In fact, some stores don't even sell whole chickens or larger cuts of meat anymore. But in the locavore world, exactly the opposite is true.

Bulk meat (like an entire side of a steer, lamb, or pig) and whole chickens are the best deals, economically. Plus, buying in bulk means you have local meat throughout the year.

If you plan on buying a slab of local meat, here's what you need to know:

Shop around. Buying half or part of an animal is a huge investment—several hundred dollars. Be sure you visit the farm, trust the farmer and butcher, and most of all, like the meat. Here's where tasting the meat before you buy it is crucial.

Split it with some friends. A side of beef yields roughly 200 pounds of meat. Some farmers have custom-cut options, selling bulk meat in 100-pound increments especially for pork or lamb, but that's still a lot of meat. Be sure to have your friends lined up to divvy up your bounty as soon as you get it.

Get to know your cuts. Buying a side of beef means getting a wide variety of cuts—not all of them premium. A Delmonico, standing rib roast, and rib-eye steak are all from the same piece of meat, just cut differently, so don't count on getting all three. Also, if you want special cuts like hangar steak and short ribs, be sure to tell your butcher this before he processes your meat. Be specific.

Be creative in the kitchen. When you buy an animal share, you buy the entire animal—including some things you might not be accustomed to using, like organ meats, fatback, and soup bones. With a little ingenuity, you'll be surprised at how tasty some of these parts can be.

A CLOSER LOOK

The Amish are experts at utilizing all parts of their livestock. Consider their famous dish *pon hoss,* otherwise known as scrapple, made from pork scraps, organ meats, broth, and flour or cornmeal. The mixture is arranged in a loaf pan and thinly sliced and fried. It's particularly popular in the South.

Make room in your freezer. Stocking up on beef, pork, goat, or lamb means you need to have freezer space to store it. Usually two empty shelves are sufficient. Be sure you have the space.

Birds of a Feather

Almost all chickens produced in the United States spend their life in enormous, overcrowded confinement buildings that look like long, white windowless sheds. Most of these birds are bred to get so big, so fast, if they lived to maturity, their legs would collapse. They also are unable to survive outdoors.

Instead of contributing to this inhumane treatment, look for local poultry that's pasture-raised outdoors. Even better is a heritage breed because most of the poultry raised in this country come from a very narrow gene pool. Depending on where you live and what farmer you use, locally raised chickens may not be available year-round. So if you can, stock up when they're in.

Remember, too, that whole birds are a better purchase than chicken parts because they're the least processed, the most affordable, and cheaper in the long-run.

Free-Range Free-for-All

Free-range or *free-roaming* is a term that's been bandied around for years. Although it can be used with any animal, it most commonly refers to chickens or turkeys. The USDA defines free range as having some access to the outdoors, but what that outdoors is isn't specified. It can be anything from a cement patio to a green pasture. Consequently, a chicken labeled "free range" doesn't really mean much unless you know exactly how "free" that chicken really is and how it was really raised.

Free-range eggs is another term you're likely to see, and it can be even more problematic. It implies that egg-laying chickens are lounging around on green pastures in the outdoors before going inside to lay their eggs. But in reality, free-range egg-laying chickens, like free-range meat chickens, need only have access to the outdoors. Thus, free-range eggs can come from caged chickens.

Like everything else, your best bet is to buy from a credible, trustworthy vendor and ask questions. Usually this means going straight to the source and talking directly to the farmer.

Raising Your Own

Recent media attention to the plight of poultry, along with the surge in eating local, has resulted in a new trend: urban chicken farmers. These city or suburban dwellers usually raise a handful of chickens in their backyard and have the advantage of fresh eggs whenever they want them. If they do want a chicken dinner from their flock, USDA-approved mobile slaughterhouses will do the trick.

If you're interested in raising your own brood, be sure to check with local officials first to see if it's legal in your neighborhood. If you live in an urban or suburban area, there may be rules or regulations relating to not only if you can have chickens but how many you can have per a certain amount of space and where you can have them. Roosters are usually not permitted in most cities.

Chickens are relatively easy to take care, don't need a lot of space (a chicken requires anywhere from 5 to 10 square feet of space depending on the breed), and eat mainly bugs, worms, green leaves, and grass, supplemented with a high-protein or organic feed, so they're relatively low maintenance compared to raising other livestock. It's not likely you'll see a cow or a goat in someone's backyard in the city. But chickens still take time, energy, and a certain amount of know-how.

Start small with only a few birds—three is a good start and will still give you a good egg yield. When you're used to those three, you can work your way up to adding more to your flock. If you want chickens for meat, you'll probably need more. You'll also need a different breed. There are egg-laying breeds, meat breeds, and dual-purpose breeds, which are kept for both meat and eggs.

If you're still intent on trying your hand at raising chickens pick up a copy of *The Complete Idiot's Guide to Raising Chickens* (Alpha Books, 2010), which covers everything from choosing the right chickens (discussing heritage breeds) and what to feed them to handling eggs, including how to sell them. You can also find information on how to take care of chickens as well as a wealth of other ways to provide for you and your family in *The Complete Idiot's Guide to Urban Homesteading* (Alpha Books, 2011).

Starting a Turkey Tradition

Even though turkey consumption has more than doubled in the last 25 years, most people only think of serving this big bird during the holidays. Granted, Thanksgiving would be just another holiday without the turkey. This holiday season, try starting a new tradition and buy a local farm-raised heritage bird.

Like other livestock, commercial turkey is typically raised in confinement on large, industrial-size factory farms. During processing, their white meat is often injected with a salt or sugar solution to make it more juicy and flavorful. Furthermore, 99 percent of all the turkey Americans consume comes from one single breed, the Broad-Breasted White turkey.

It was this last fact that prompted the American Livestock Breed Conservancy and Slow Food USA to launch the Heritage Turkey Project in 2001, a program designed to re-introduce Americans to the unique flavor of heritage birds and save eight heritage breeds—Black, Bronze, Narragansett, White Holland, Slate, Bourbon Red, Beltsville Small White, and Royal Palm—from extinction. At the time, only 1,200 breeding birds existed. Thanks to their efforts, the number of heritage turkey breeds more than tripled by 2004. Today, the project, which has since added a few other breeds, estimates a breeding stock of 15,000 and counts the growing demand for heritage turkeys as part of their success.

A CLOSER LOOK

American Livestock Breeds Conservancy (albc-usa.org) is a nonprofit organization working to protect more than 180 breeds of livestock and poultry from extinction. Slow Food USA (slowfoodusa.org) is a grassroots organization dedicated to preserving old-world foods and food traditions and reconnecting Americans with the plants, animals, and people that produce our food. There are more than 200 chapters nationwide.

While gracing your table with a locally raised heritage turkey is ideal, they still may not be easy to find or easy to get. You may need to order weeks in advance or talk to your farmer about getting on a customer list that lets you know when the turkeys are available to order. Plus, these birds can be pretty pricey.

If buying a heritage bird isn't possible, another option is to buy a local certified organic turkey that's been raised with no antibiotics or growth hormones. But because many small, local turkey farmers often use sustainable, organic practices without being certified, you may even be able to forgo the organic part in lieu of a well-cared-for, less-expensive local bird. Talk to your farmer, find out his practices, and don't wait until late fall to start thinking about your holiday turkey. Most farmers will be able to tell you exactly when is the best time to buy or order your turkey. Heed their advice, or you might miss out on a bird.

Game Time

Over the last few years, game meats and birds have gained lots of attention, particularly among people who eat local. Some of the most common animals are deer, elk, moose, rabbit, wild boar, grouse, pheasant, and quail. Buffalo or bison, although considered a game meat, has seen a boom in demand recently. As a result, much of it is conventionally raised (i.e., corn-fed), making it more similar to traditional beef. To get the real deal, look for grass-fed local bison sold directly by ranchers.

The Eastern cousin of the bovine breed, yaks are another big game animal you might come upon when searching out local proteins. Growing demand for the lean, tender red meat, especially among chefs, is raising its profile, particularly in local circles. Currently Colorado, New Mexico, Wyoming, and Montana are home to ranches raising yak for meat.

If you like to hunt or know someone who does, getting good game meat is easy. It's also about as local as it gets (if you hunt in a nearby forest, that is), not to mention inexpensive. Depending on the size and type of the animal, one successful hunt can often feed a family of four or larger all year long.

Game meat is healthy for you, too. Because these animals eat plants, seeds, nuts, and foliage Mother Nature provides, you don't have to worry about antibiotics, growth hormones, or any other additives. This natural diet, combined with the fact that wild animals are more active than conventionally raised domestic livestock, results in meat that's darker, leaner, and lower in artery-clogging fat than its conventional counterpart. Even the type of fat is better, because game meat is high in heart-healthy omega-3 fatty acids and provides a wealth of vitamins and minerals.

Once you've gotten your game, the next step is getting it processed. Many hunters either butcher their own meat or have a local butcher do the honor. Either way, be sure to utilize as many parts of the animal as you can. For example, if you've shot a deer, you can make venison roasts, burgers (ground meat), sausage, steaks, stew meat, and more. Remember, like grass-fed beef, game has to be cooked gently and slowly or it will be too tough to eat. It also pairs well with robust flavors and hardy herbs and spices like rosemary, wine, juniper berries, sage, and chile peppers.

And don't forget about organ meats like tongue, liver, and kidneys (see Chapter 14 for more about offal). If you have more than you can give away or eat, think about donating it to the local food bank. This is a great way to promote local foods to your community.

If you're not a hunter and you don't know any, getting good game meat is still possible, especially if you live in the open spaces of western states like Montana, Wyoming, South Dakota, North Dakota, and Colorado. In these places, you may be able to find game at food co-ops and some farmers' markets. Even grocery stores like Whole Foods may carry some local game meat.

An Ocean of Seafood

If you're lucky enough to live near the Atlantic or Pacific Ocean, you have a wealth of local seafood to explore—shrimp, oysters, scallops, mahi-mahi, halibut, fluke, porgy, hake, herring, salmon, … the list goes on and on. Get up early and visit a local fish market. Become familiar with what your region has to offer. Many times, these local species are unique and distinct.

> **NATIVE KNOWLEDGE**
>
> For more information about how to identify, buy, and prepare seafood, check out these two gems: *Field Guide to Seafood: How to Identify, Select, and Prepare Virtually Every Fish and Shellfish at the Market* by Aliza Green (Quirk Books, 2007) and *Fish: The Complete Guide to Buying and Cooking* by Mark Bittman (Wiley, 1999).

Consider the simple crab. Stone crabs are a favorite in Florida, blue crabs are famous in the Chesapeake Bay area, Dungeness crabs are popular in the Northwest, and King crab abounds in Alaska. And that's not the only fish in the sea. Ocean fishermen often sell a wide range of both finfish and shellfish. You may also want to experiment with underutilized fish like sardines, mackerel, dogfish, and shad. These are often less expensive but still tasty. Talk to your fishmonger about different types of fish, and explore new and unusual seafood. You might be surprised!

At the same time, you want to be sure you choose sustainable finfish and shellfish, from healthy, reliable stock and environmentally sound resources. You also want to be sure the fish is caught in a responsible manner, without harming other creatures of the sea. This preserves our local bounty for future generations and protects our oceans and waterways.

Keep in mind that like produce, seafood is seasonal. Many fish migrate up and down the coast based on the water temperature of the ocean. Spawning cycles also naturally contract and expand fish populations regulating catches. Thus, the type of seafood you see throughout the year is likely to change depending on the climate and time of year. Talk to your fishmonger to learn what kind of fish is available in each season so you can make the best choices.

Where else would you buy local seafood? Many farmers' markets located near the coast often host several fish vendors. Usually these markets require the fishermen to personally catch the majority of what they sell. Searching out seafood festivals is another good way to try some local seafood. Seafood states like Louisiana (especially New Orleans) and Maryland host a dozen or more each year (see Chapter 9).

Why not go fishing yourself? Check the Internet for fishing clubs, day trips, and newsletters in your area. Be sure the water is safe and unpolluted. (The Environmental Protection Agency regularly puts out fishing advisories.)

For an extra fee, some places will even clean, cut, and wrap what you catch if you're not up to it. This is a great way to experience local dining at its best.

> **NATIVE KNOWLEDGE**
>
> If you're concerned about overfishing and sustainability, the Monterey Bay Aquarium offers Seafood Watch Pocket Guides. The guides, available at montereybayaquarium.org, categorizes fish into best choices, good alternatives, and those to avoid.

Lakes and Rivers

If you don't live near the ocean, you probably do live by a lake or river that can feed your seafood cravings. Freshwater lakes, especially in the north, are home to hundreds of fish, including bass, trout, perch, and walleye.

Also, keep in mind that the mighty Mississippi is only one of dozens of rivers that crisscross this country. Fish caught from local rivers supply an abundance of local seafood. To find out what's available in your area, talk with your local fishmonger.

Freshwater lakes especially often have problems with contamination, so be particularly vigilant about checking the U.S. Environmental Protection Agency's site (www.epa.gov) for your state before going out. Keep in mind that certain high-risk individuals like pregnant women, infants, children, nursing mothers, and women of child-bearing years may have limits on how much of a certain seafood is recommended to eat.

Wild-Caught Versus Farm-Raised

When it comes to which fish to buy, wild-caught is generally the preferred choice. This is certainly the case with salmon, where wild-caught is superior not only in taste, but from an environmental standpoint as well.

Nevertheless, don't assume that simply because a species of fish is local, eating that species is best for the environment. For example, wild salmon is abundant in the West and a great local choice if you live on the coast of Oregon or Washington. Go to the East Coast, however, and wild salmon is not recommended. After years of overfishing and exploitation, the local Atlantic wild salmon is now in danger of becoming extinct. Be choosy about which local fish you purchase.

As with everything, there are always exceptions to the rule, and while wild-caught is the norm, don't discount local farm-raised seafood. Some farm-raised fish such as salmon are harvested in large factory farms with environmentally questionable practices, but small local operations use sustainable methods. Your best bet here is to talk directly to the farmer handling the fish, if possible. Find out exactly how the fish is treated, fed, and processed. Then decide if you'd like to include this in your seafood diet. Catfish, for example, is a local delicacy in the Mississippi Delta region, but local farm-raised operations operate in that area as well.

To build a healthy, sustainable food system, some fishermen are also trying their hand at farm-raised shellfish like shrimp and oysters. These small-scale, experimental operations usually sell seafood only on the local level. Look around; you might find one near you!

The Least You Need to Know

- Buying local meat and poultry that's grass-fed and pasture-raised is better for your health, the environment, and the community than conventional.
- Local proteins are expensive because farmers are small-scale operations, take good care of their animals, and produce a high-quality product.
- More and more local meats are now available frozen from local butchers, farmers' markets, or the farm itself. If you buy in bulk, prices are a lot cheaper.
- Be sure to explore heritage game and birds in your area.
- You don't have to live near the ocean to eat local seafood; lakes and rivers are also abundant sources.

Dairy Products and Eggs

In This Chapter

- Making milk, pure and simple
- Going organic—does it make a difference?
- Understanding the culture of local cheese
- Choosing local eggs

Every time I go to a farmers' market, I often see several vendors selling cheese, eggs, and other dairy products. Most have a steady stream of customers, and before the day's over, many are sold out.

That's not surprising. Like local produce farmers, small-scale dairy operations are lately enjoying a renaissance among consumers. Much of this reflects the rise of artisan cheeses, but it also points to the fact that more people are eating locally produced yogurt, butter, buttermilk, and ice cream.

Drinkable milk, which has dropped off considerably in the last four decades, is also getting a well-deserved boost by the local food movement, led by mothers looking for a healthier product for their children and milk-loving adults searching for a fresher, tastier product.

Greater demand has led to greater choices. And while this builds healthy competition and better diversity, it can also be somewhat intimidating for newbie shoppers. In this chapter, I tell you what all the fuss is about surrounding local and organic foods. I also arm you with all the knowledge you need to make your own purchasing decisions—healthy, happy, and confident.

Premium Pasteurized Milk

So what's the difference between local and conventional milk? Lots! Conventional milk comes from thousands of cows raised on concentrated animal feeding operation (CAFO) lots, eating corn, soy, and other grains. The milk is pooled together and then pasteurized using a "high temperature/short time" system wherein the milk travels through continuous feed pipes, is quickly cooled, packaged, and shipped several thousand miles to your store. Generally, such milk takes about a week to get from the cow to your door.

Now much of our conventional milk is taken a step further, undergoing ultrapasteurization (UHT). UHT is when milk is heated at or above 280°F for about 2 seconds. This process allows for a longer storage period and easier transportation (UHT milk doesn't have to be refrigerated, but many stores do simply for marketing reasons), making it better for traveling long distances. But it also changes the taste of the milk very drastically.

Local milk, on the other hand, is treated differently. It's usually from a small farm with only a few hundred cows. The best operations humanely raise only grass-fed animals, and some may not even milk them all year long. One farmer I spoke to gives his cows a rest between January and March every year. (Conventional cows are typically milked two or three times a day, every day.)

In these type of operations the milk is heated slowly in big vats until it reaches 145°F, and is held at that temperature for 30 minutes. This is a gentler method of pasteurization that's less likely to affect flavor. It also can only be done in small batches. Some medium-size operations use the high-temperature/short time method heating the milk 17 seconds at 165°F. Although not as gentle as the first type, it still preserves flavor. Plus the milk is from pasture-raised and usually grass-fed cows, from a single, local farm, meaning it usually gets to your market within 24 to 48 hours from milking.

While local milk may or may not be homogenized, I find the best-tasting milk is also the least processed, which means low-pasteurized, unhomogenized milk, producing a "creamline."

Shake It Up

Unhomogenized milk contains large fat globules that naturally separate as it sits. The fat rises, forming a thick layer of cream on top while the bottom is the more watery portion, similar to skim milk. Shaking the milk mixes the two together and was a common practice before drinking. Before World War II, most milk was judged by the thickness of its "creamline" or cream layer. The thicker the creamline, the richer the milk, which was clearly visible in the glass bottles milk was delivered in.

After the war, milk processors switched to packing milk in opaque paper or cardboard containers and shifted toward selling milk in supermarkets rather than home delivery. The move did several things. It prevented homogenized milk from oxidizing and developing an unpleasant flavor—a problem that kept homogenized milk from gaining consumer acceptance—by blocking ultraviolet light from hitting the milk, hence the new containers. It effectively got rid of the creamline so consumers couldn't see the quality of the milk. And the throwaway packaging made milk a modern, convenient product.

Homogenization also allows milk processors to have more control over fat content, as the fat globules can be removed or added back in, in any proportion. Today the typical dairy-cow breed produces milk with milkfat levels ranging from 3.9 to as much as 5.5 percent, with averages around 4 percent, depending on breed, feed, and other factors. Yet most milk doesn't vary from the 3.25 percent milkfat level set for whole milk by the Food and Drug Administration, mostly because processors keep it that way. Extra fat is sold to other food processors for use in products like butter or ice cream.

If you drink local creamline milk, you'll notice a difference. Unhomogenized milk, even with a similar fat content, has a different taste and mouthfeel compared to homogenized milk. In my opinion, unhomogenized milk tastes creamier and richer (even skim milk). Most likely this is due to the fact that homogenization disrupts the fat globules by forcing them through tiny holes that break them into such small sizes they can't reform. The smaller globules don't coat the tongue the same way the larger ones do.

Other things that affect the taste of local milk are the breed of cow. Holstein-Friesians are probably the most common kind of dairy cow used in commercial operations, but at small local dairies, you can find a wider array of choices, including Jerseys, Guernseys, the American Brown Swiss, and others.

What the cows are fed makes a difference, too. Volume is a priority for large farming operations, which is why cows are fed corn. Grass-fed cows may produce less milk, but what they do produce is better tasting and more nutritious.

A CLOSER LOOK

A recent study showed grass-fed cows produce milk with five times more of the unsaturated fat, conjugated linoleic acid (CLA), than cows fed processed grain. People with high levels of CLA concentrations have a lower risk for heart attack than those who don't.

To Be or Not to Be Organic?

After years of being the fastest-growing segment in the organic market and enjoying double-digit growth, organic milk saw a drop in sales in 2008 and 2009, probably because of overproduction and reduced consumer spending. But experts say this trend is already rebounding as sales are slowly climbing and the $520 million industry begins to move more and more major brands into mainstream markets. Prices closer in line to regular milk are most likely the main reason for the turnaround, but interest in healthier "local" products has also given this milk a push.

Still, just because a milk is labeled organic doesn't mean it's local. In fact, if you're buying in a supermarket, it's probably not. Over the years, the success of the organic dairy business has given rise to industrial-size operations, eerily resembling factory farms.

Indeed, the top three or four largest producers of organic milk are now owned by multinational agribusiness firms. Housed in huge facilities in the Rocky Mountains and on the West Coast, organic milk must travel thousands of miles to get to thirsty consumers. Consequently, much of this milk is sold ultrapasteurized.

On the plus side, organic milk, by law, comes from cows not treated with artificial growth hormones like recombinant bovine somatotropin (rBST) or recombinant bovine growth hormone (rBGH), which boosts milk production 10 to 20 percent. They also eat only organic feed free of harmful pesticides, they aren't given antibiotics, and they must have access to pasture.

What's wrong with rBST? Milk from cows given rBST have higher levels of an insulin-like growth factor 1 (IGF-1), and although there's no definitive evidence showing this milk is any different from milk not treated with hormones, concerns still exist on how these synthetic hormones affect humans. (We already know it's not good for cows because these hormones increase rates of infection, which lead to greater antibiotic use.) When it comes to humans, several studies have linked higher levels of IGF-1 to higher rates of breast and prostate cancer. There are also questions about the impact of synthetic hormones on children.

The FDA doesn't require milk containing synthetic hormones like rBST to be labeled, so it's almost impossible to know if your milk contains added hormones or not unless you call the dairy directly or unless you buy organic. Luckily, more and more small local dairies are selling local organic or local noncertified organic milk. Even some of the big companies are beginning to look at local suppliers.

That said, your best bet is to choose locally raised organic milk from grass-fed cows, particularly if you have a family with young children. Such small operations also ensure the animals are raised as humanely as possible (organic alone is no guarantee of this) and usually pasture-raised. Grass-fed cows produce milk that not only tastes different, it also has a higher nutritional composition.

Getting a Raw Deal

For people who like to drink raw milk, buying local (usually directly from the farm) is the only way to get it. Raw milk comes straight from the cow. It's not pasteurized, homogenized, or processed in any way. Raw milk proponents say the fresh stuff is healthier, tastier, and more nutritious than pasteurized. It's also easier to digest, making it good for those with lactose intolerance.

Despite these claims, there's no real nutritional difference between pasteurized and unpasteurized milk of any kind. (The only significant difference is taste, which is influenced by individual preferences.) There is, however, a real concern about safety. Raw milk has a higher risk of foodborne illness from E. coli, Campylobacter jejuni, and other bacteria.

Consider that a 2008 outbreak of E. coli tied to raw milk consumption in Connecticut found that contamination occurred even though the farm had "acceptable milking and sanitation practices." One possible explanation for this is due to the proximity of the cow's anus to the cow's udder, making it difficult for bacteria not to get in the milk. So even for clean, sanitary operations, it's still possible for milk to be tainted, from dirt or fecal matter.

A CLOSER LOOK

Currently, 39 out of the 50 states allow you to legally purchase raw milk (either from a retail outlet or directly from the farm) or get it by owning a "share" of an animal. Raw milk cannot be sold out of state because of the potential for foodborne pathogens.

If you still want to drink raw milk, be sure to weigh the risks and benefits carefully. Visit realrawmilkfacts.com, a website developed by university and government scientists, before making your decision. Especially check out the Q&A section.

To find farms that sell raw milk, search realmilk.com, the Weston A. Price Foundation's website (a group that advocates whole, natural unprocessed foods). It lists sites of farms that sell raw milk.

Making a Good Choice

No matter what type of milk you buy—unhomogenized or homogenized, premium or regular, skim or whole—quality is still your top priority. Quality can vary greatly for any type of farm-fresh milk, depending on the care taken with the product. To be sure you get the best, safest, and highest-quality product you can find, keep these tips in mind when buying any milk, raw or otherwise.

If possible, visit the farm. This is crucial if you're buying raw milk and not so important if you're not. If you do visit the farm, it should be a small operation with grass-fed, pastured animals. Be sure everything is meticulously clean, the cows are scrupulously inspected, and the milk is promptly refrigerated and frequently checked for microbial contamination. If you don't visit the farm, you can still inspect the product (and its surroundings) for cleanliness. Ask lots of questions about how the milk is processed, managed, and stored. Be sure you feel comfortable before you buy.

Buy whole milk. Whole milk has the fat content fully intact and is less processed. It also tastes smooth and creamy. If you just can't stand whole, try unhomogenized skim or reduced fat. These have a creamier mouthfeel than conventional milk and don't taste watery.

Buy in the spring if you can. Bet you didn't know milk is a seasonal product. Quality is at its peak during the spring, when grasses are green and lush and animals are in high-production mode.

Do your homework. Decide what kind of milk you like, and search locally for a farm that produces it. Remember the same milk can taste different from farm to farm, so try to taste as many brands of milk as you can before settling on one.

Also think about experimenting with unique types of milk, say from goat or sheep (sometimes known as ewe's milk). You may also want to think about flavored milks such as chocolate milk. Many local producers offer this as an option as well.

Beyond Bessie

When it comes to drinking milk, locavores have many more options than your typical supermarket shopper. Not only are there many kinds of milks to choose from within a category, such as cow's milk, but there's also the opportunity to buy goat milk and sheep milk. These last two are a welcome change for some, an acquired taste for others, and a staple dairy item for still others. If you're lucky you may even be able to find water buffalo or yak milk!

Get Your Goat

Although it's not true in the United States, worldwide more people drink goat milk than cow's milk. In fact, more than 70 percent of the milk the world drinks comes from goat. It's particularly popular in India and the Middle East.

When you think about it, it's not surprising. Goats are hardy creatures. They adapt well to almost any climate, hot or cold, and can live all over the world. Compared to cows, they're much smaller—the average goat weights 120 to 135 pounds, and dwarf breeds are even smaller at 35 to 85 pounds, whereas an average cow can easily be more than 1,000 pounds. They also require less space, less food (they eat a wide variety of forage), and are overall less expensive to keep. This is also why historically women have raised goats while men typically take care of cattle.

Goats are also highly intelligent, remarkably friendly, and good milk producers. Although there are more than 200 kinds of goats worldwide, only six breeds are the dominant dairy goat breeds: Alpines, Oberhaslis, Saanes, Toggenburgs, LaManchas, and Nubians.

When it comes to goat milk, don't be put off by what you may have heard from our cow's-milk-drinking culture. Goat milk tastes remarkably mild and slightly sweet, and if handled properly, similar to cow's milk. Off flavors are attributed to two things: poor feed (meaning lots of weeds rather than berries and green leaves) and the presence of a buck. Bucks are odoriferous creatures, and their strong, musky odor can permeate a doe's milk, leaving a strong aftertaste. So be sure to ask your dairy farmer how their goats are raised.

Goat milk differs from cow's milk in other ways, too. The milk is noticeably whiter due to the fact that goats convert all their carotene to vitamin A. Carotene gives cow's milk a yellowish tinge. Goat milk tastes richer because the fat globules are smaller and more evenly dispersed. For this reason, it does not separate—no cream-line here—and does not need to be homogenized. This also may be why many people claim goat milk is easier to digest than cow's milk.

KEEP YOUR DISTANCE

Drinking raw goat milk, like drinking raw cow's milk or raw sheep milk, is still risky business. To lower your chances of getting sick, buy pasteurized goat milk.

Nutritionally, goat milk is closer to human milk than cow's milk. It has almost twice as much vitamin A and higher levels of protein, calcium, vitamin B_6, and niacin. Because it contains about 10 percent less lactose than cow's milk, people who are lactose intolerant and can't drink cow's milk may be able to drink goat milk.

Getting Sheepish

Unlike goats, which have been utilized for their milk (mainly for cheese) since early pioneer times, the tradition of milking sheep in this country is relatively new, dating only a few decades. (In the past, sheep were primarily used for meat and wool.) This is despite the fact that sheep have been raised for milk in European countries for thousands of years, even before cows.

Now, thanks to our growing interest in sheep milk cheese, sheep milk as well as other sheep-milk dairy products like yogurt is on the rise and growing in popularity. Compared to cow's milk, sheep milk is denser and richer and contains almost twice as much fat and milk solids. The type of fat is also different because sheep milk fat contains high amounts of protective CLA (conjugated linoleic acid) and a large proportion of short- and medium-chain fatty acids, which don't affect cholesterol levels. More milk solids makes this milk ideal for cheese-making—it takes about half the amount of milk needed from a cow to make the same amount of sheep cheese—and provides a rich, creamy mouthfeel.

On the nutrition front, sheep milk even surpasses goat milk. It's higher in protein, calcium, vitamin C, thiamin, phosphorous, and nearly a dozen other vitamins and minerals.

Taste-wise, sheep milk is richer and creamier than cow's milk, without the tang often associated with goat milk. Plus, like goat milk, sheep milk is easier for some to digest, particularly those with lactose intolerance.

Most sheep's milk is usually used for making cheese or yogurt, so finding milk to drink can be difficult. Your best bet is to ask someone who's making sheep milk cheese. If you do get some milk, be sure to check to see if it's raw or pasteurized.

Made with Milk

In addition to milk and cheese (which I talk about later in this chapter), you can get many other milk products from your local creamery, including half-and-half, whipping cream, butter, crème fraiche, sour cream, buttermilk, eggnog, and ice cream. Within each of these categories, however, even more choices exist, depending on the type of milk used (skim, whole, or reduced fat), how the cow was raised (grass-fed versus corn-fed), and how the food was processed.

Plus, what the creamery makes varies widely as well. Some just do milk, or milk and ice cream, while others make butter and buttermilk, and still others make cheese and drinkable milk only. So you may frequent more than one local creamery depending on what you're looking for.

Following are some of the local specialties you might find.

Better Butter

When it comes to milk products, butter is often the first thing that comes to mind, and rightly so. It's a major by-product of milk, and Americans eat quite a bit of it—more than 5 pounds per capita annually. According to the FDA, to be called "butter," a product must contain no less than 80 percent butterfat, but local butters may have more—even 1 or 2 percent above 80 percent can make a big difference in baking. Other ingredients like salt and coloring can be added, but that's about it.

Virtually all the butter sold in U.S. supermarkets is called "sweet cream" butter because it's made from churning the cream from fresh milk. If you're interested in making your own homemade butter, plenty of instructional videos are available on YouTube (youtube.com), and a variety of food blogs (search on Google) show you how. Local "sweet cream" butter has a distinctive bland, sweet taste based on the type of cow, what it ate (grass-fed versus corn-fed), and how it was processed (low temperature pasteurization compared to higher temps).

If you buy local, you're also more likely to find "cultured" butter. Cultured butter, which is common in Europe, typically has starter cultures (bacteria) added to the milk before processing (similar to those added to yogurt). The milk is then left to age or ripen. Cultured milk has a richer, fuller, more complex flavor than sweet cream butter. To some people, it may taste tangy as the bacteria used in culturing produces lactic acid.

Yo, Yo, Yogurt

Over the years, we've become something of a yogurt culture. Part of this is due to the large influx of yogurt-eating immigrants from Eastern Europe, the Middle East, and India who now call this country home. More likely, however, it's a result of the broadening of our culinary palate (again thanks to many of these immigrants) and our openness to explore new cuisines.

Whatever the reason, yogurt, a fermented milk product with a slightly astringent, tangy taste, is extremely popular and often made at local dairies. Farm-fresh yogurt can be made from cow's milk, goat milk, sheep milk, or even water buffalo milk, depending on the dairy. And like other milk products, a yogurt's taste is influenced by type and quality of milk, what the cows were fed, and how they were raised.

We All Scream for Ice Cream

Ice cream produced by local dairies has plenty of advantages over commercial products. First, these sweet treats are usually made with only a few all-natural ingredients. Therefore, they lack the fillers and additives like guar gum and carrageen typically added to supermarket ice cream. They also start with premium milk or cream, which improves the quality and taste of the finished product.

And because the dairies are usually small-batch operations attuned to local ingredients, their ice cream flavors reflect this. Consequently, you might find fresh strawberry ice cream in spring, blueberry ice cream in summer, or pumpkin ice cream in autumn. Many of these ice cream makers have a creative bent, so don't be surprised to find off-beat combinations as well, such as kobocha squash, honey goat cheese, or sweet potato and pecan flavors.

Cheese to Please

As discussed, milk can make a number of wonderful dairy products—yogurt, buttermilk, butter, crème fraîche, sour cream, and so many others. But none compare to cheese.

Cheese is the perfect way to preserve a highly perishable product—milk. It also has a long-standing farmhouse tradition of being made close to home. So it's only natural that many local small-scale dairies are making fabulous *farmstead* and *artisanal cheeses* right on the farm and offering it up at local cheese shops, farmers' markets, CSAs, and farm stores.

Count on finding a broad variety of tastes, textures, and styles of cheeses, too, as cheesemakers experiment with both fresh and aged products. Here's a sampling of what you can expect to find:

- Traditional European-style cheeses, deliciously and meticulously reproduced

- American originals, produced with ingenuity and creativity

- Combinations of the two, for example, European-style cheese using sheep's milk instead of cow's milk, or a chevre with lavender blossoms

Like all great dairy products, cheese is only as good as the milk it started with. Keep that in mind when purchasing. Look for cheeses from a dairy that produces high-quality milk from grass-fed animals, and you're likely to find some great cheeses!

Types of Cheeses You'll Find Locally

While it's impossible to mention all the kinds of cheeses you may run into when buying local, there are some specific categories of cheese you're likely to see. Here is a brief rundown:

Fresh curd cheeses, like cream cheese, ricotta, mascarpone, quark, or mozzarella, are generally lower in fat than other cheeses. They also have a shorter shelf life. *Chevre* is a French term that, in this country, has become synonymous with "fresh goat cheese." In fact, often the terms are used interchangeably. Feta is another fresh curd cheese you're likely to find. A milky white cheese that's brined and salted, locally produced feta can be made from cow's milk, sheep milk, goat milk, or a combination of two or three. If not labeled, assume it's cow's milk feta.

Aged cheeses tend to be hard and dry. These are the kinds of cheeses that do well grated. Pecorino Romano and Parmesan come to mind, but there are hundreds of aged cheeses. A little goes a long way. Aged cheeses can also be made from a variety of milks.

Blue cheeses are injected with a greenish or blue vein mold. Like aged cheeses, blue cheeses can be made from any type of milk. They can be fresh or aged and crumbly, sweet or tart and tangy.

Semi-soft cheeses have a soft texture and a taste with earthy undertones. These cheeses melt easily and are good in pizza, quesadillas, and pasta dishes. You'll often see semi-soft cheeses in a variety of flavors such as jalapeño, black peppercorn, horseradish, or herb.

Firm cheeses, harder than semi-soft cheeses but softer than hard cheeses, can easily be thinly sliced. They're good for slicing on sandwiches or using in baked dishes. Cheddar, Gouda, and Swiss are prime examples.

Bloomy rind cheeses are rich, luxurious, full-fat cheeses enveloped by a soft-edible mold. Brie and Camembert are king here, but you can also find a range of other cheeses, including goat cheeses, with bloomy rinds.

Washed rind cheeses—the most pungent cheeses—are usually semi-soft with a rind that's periodically washed with salt, wine, beer, spirits, or other things, which toughens them up.

American Artisans

In only a few short decades, American artisanal cheeses have taken this country and the cheese world by storm. Driven by dedicated and passionate cheesemakers, these cheeses can rival many of the European greats. Their claim to fame is ingenuity and creativity often combined with meticulous old-world techniques. The result is nothing short of spectacular.

With this in mind, don't be surprised to find local cheeses produced by small dairies to be diamonds in the rough. These cheeses are made from almost any kind of milk—goat, sheep, cow, or water buffalo by itself or mixed in any combination.

Typical dairy states have the edge because their land is good for raising milk-producing livestock. So if you live in Wisconsin, California, upstate New York, or Vermont, for example, be prepared to find really good locally produced cheese.

If you don't live in these areas, however, never fear! Artisan-made, locally produced cheeses are turning up everywhere from Maine to Hawaii. Some local hotspots include the Pacific Northwest, Oregon and Washington, the Rocky Mountains, especially Boulder, Colorado, and the northern lakes and woods of Minnesota.

Most of these cheeses are clearly labeled "local" in cheese shops or at marketplaces. Keep in mind, though, just because a cheese is local doesn't guarantee you'll love it. Be sure to sample before you buy.

Raw and Uncut, but Is It Aged?

Raw milk cheese is cheese made from unpasteurized milk. In the United States, these cheeses are allowed to be sold as long as they're aged for at least 60 days. This is why you'll never find a fresh raw milk Brie or chevre in this country but you can find it in France or other European countries. You can also buy raw milk feta; however, it's aged for 60 days.

Nevertheless, you're likely to find plenty of wonderful pasteurized or aged raw milk cheeses to explore in your region. Searching Local Harvest (localharvest.org) is probably the quickest and easiest way to find local cheesemakers in your area, but you can also browse the Internet and visit cheese shops and marketplaces where you live.

Farm-Fresh Eggs

When it comes to eggs, the fresher the better, which is why many people are willing to buy local eggs, despite the sometimes higher price tag. The best local eggs have been laid only a day or two earlier, as opposed to the week or more conventional eggs spend in transit. Nor do fresh eggs have to be shipped cross country, decreasing their carbon footprint significantly.

Freshness, however, isn't the only thing that makes local eggs taste better. Here are a few more things to consider:

Their diet. Locally raised chickens generally get their food from the land they graze, eating bugs, worms, seeds, and natural vegetation. (Chickens are not vegetarian by nature.) Sometimes this is supplemented by a grain feed, particularly during the winter. If your farmer does use grain, be sure it does not contain any antibiotics, growth hormones, or animal by-products. For this reason, organic feed is best.

The type of feed the chicken eats affects the color of the egg yolk. Grass-fed chickens usually have a deeper-colored yolk.

A CLOSER LOOK

Local eggs can come in a rainbow of colors, including green, brown, and red. Egg color is determined by the breed of the chicken. Egg size, on the other hand, depends on the age of the chicken.

Their lifestyle. How the chickens are treated means a lot. Pasture-raised hens produce more nutritious eggs than conventionally raised caged birds. They're also allowed to stretch, nest, perch, and scratch—things caged birds can't do. Some farmers move their hen houses around in mobile coops to different parts of the pasture for hens to graze.

Time of the year. Spring is naturally the most prolific egg laying time for hens, while fall and winter are typically the leanest, when hens molt and the weather is coldest. In fact, many chickens stop laying eggs completely in the winter months (this is directly related to the number of daylight hours). So if you can, try to stock up on eggs in spring and summer.

Another advantage of buying local eggs is having the option of more than one type of egg, such as duck eggs or quail eggs. If you have the opportunity to buy these kinds of eggs, don't pass them by. They're quite a delicacy.

If you want to buy eggs from hens treated humanely and responsibly, looking at labels doesn't help much. Terms like *cage-free*, *free-range*, and *certified organic* are vague and don't guarantee the hens are treated any better than caged hens. Your best bet is to discuss these issues with your local farmer. Top priority would be pasture-time, living conditions, feed, supplements, antibiotics, and molting practices. (Hens on large egg-producing farms are sometimes forced to molt by starvation—this process speeds up egg production.)

KEEP YOUR DISTANCE

Local eggs may be fresher than conventional, but they can still carry salmonella if not handled properly. Always buy eggs from a reputable dealer you trust, that are free of contamination, aren't cracked or broken, and are kept refrigerated.

The Least You Need to Know

- Locally produced organic milk from pasture-raised, grass-fed cows is a premium product that's better for you and for the environment than conventional milk.
- Local dairies make a variety of different types of milk and milk products, including raw, pasteurized, and premium products using milk from cows, goats, or sheep.
- Local milk can be sold homogenized or unhomogenized.
- An array of high-quality, locally produced cheeses are widely available throughout the country.
- Many people prefer buying fresh local eggs because they taste better, and the hens are treated humanely.

Local Specialties You Won't Want to Miss

In This Chapter

- Amazing local breads, preserves, salsas, and more
- Olive oil homegrown in America
- Simple local sweets
- Favorite fermented and pickled foods
- Brewing up local liquors and ciders

Eating local means more than just buying fresh produce, meats, and dairy. It's about connecting with the food, the people who make it, and the culture of the region. It's about using what you have responsibly, respectfully, and joyously. And that brings us to the next level of the locavore diet: locally prepared foods.

Locally prepared items take the bounty of the land and transform it into something delicious, while still valuing the place where it came from. Most of these foods grew out of abundance and our desire to preserve the harvest for leaner times. Others are simply a celebration of the foods and flavors of the land and the people who live there. Either way, buying locally prepared food supports the community where you live and builds thriving, healthy businesses, not to mention provides you with some great-tasting dishes!

Because locally prepared products are so region-specific and so varied, it's impossible to cover everything you're likely to find wherever you are in just one chapter. But I can give you a good overview of the types of products to expect and some great tips on sniffing out high-quality, locally prepared products right in your own backyard. You just might be pleasantly surprised at what you'll find!

What to Expect

When it comes to buying locally prepared foods, it's the spirit of the food along with the quality and taste that counts. Keep this in mind, and you'll understand why not all local food is prepared with 100 percent locally grown ingredients. (For some items, it's just not feasibly possible.) Certainly some are, but most are not, although they should all contain at least one local ingredient to qualify as "local." Always ask the producer where he or she gets their main ingredients, and use your own judgment to decide if that's local enough for you.

For instance, you'd expect a tomato sauce supplier to use locally grown tomatoes, at least when they're in season and plentiful, but you shouldn't be too concerned if a local baker doesn't use local wheat—it may not be available, or the supply may be inconsistent. You should, however, find out if they use local fruit, nuts, or vegetables in their breads or cakes.

Remember, too, that just because it's locally prepared doesn't mean it's low in fat and calories or particularly nutritious. Rich fruit pies may be delicious and all-natural, but their high sugar content makes them more like an occasional splurge rather than an everyday food.

Look for simplicity—simple labels, simple packaging, and simple ingredients. The majority of local artisan producers are more concerned with the quality of their product than fancy labels or packaging. Plus, using less plastic is better for the environment.

> **NATIVE KNOWLEDGE**
>
> Most locally prepared foods have unpretentious packaging and simple, easy-to-read labels stating ingredients and location. Look for products that look "homemade."

Be prepared to experiment and explore foods you may not be familiar with. Many locally prepared foods use unique recipes that tap into creativity and meet consumer demand. Sometimes these recipes are old-world style, handed down through generations, and sometimes they're newly developed, embracing the tastes and trends of the times.

Baked Goods and Snacks

Baked goods and snacks fall into two categories: savory and sweet. Savory items include the following:

- Artisan breads
- Flavored loaves like olive, ham, cheese, or tomato
- Quiche
- Empanadas or other stuffed pastries filled with greens, seafood, meat, or chicken
- Homemade tortillas
- Pretzels
- Tacos
- Indian fry bread
- Crackers

The list goes on and on, and so does the variety. On the sweet side the products are more indulgent but no less exhausting:

- Pies
- Sweet pastries
- Doughnuts
- Sweet breads like banana, sweet potato, pumpkin, or zucchini
- Scones
- Muffins
- Cookies
- Croissants
- Tarts

What makes these items special is the care and attention they receive from their bakers, the fact that they are handmade artisan products, their use of seasonal produce (selling rhubarb pie in spring and blueberry muffins in summer), and last but not least, their reflection of the ethnic heritage of the area. Examples of some of these specialties with roots in their region: shoo-fly pie in Pennsylvania Dutch country, key lime pie in southern Florida, Bavarian rye bread in Wisconsin, and French beignets in New Orleans.

If you're lucky, you may even hit it big. Take the small local bakery I recently discovered, for example. The owners of the bakery own an orchard. All their rhubarb, apple, and berry pies use fruit picked right on the orchard. Eggs and butter for the crust are bought locally as well, and every pie is handmade. No wonder their items sell out regularly!

Finding these hidden gems takes some digging, but it's well worth the extra effort. The best advice: ask around, browse the Internet, visit locally owned stores (not chains), and farmers' markets. Some chain stores like Whole Foods do source locally grown products, so check there, too.

Preserves, Jams, and Jellies

Of all the prepared foods, *preserves*, *jams*, and *jellies* are probably the ones you see most often and the ones most associated with local foods. (Nut and fruit butters also fall into this category.) They're also the ones with the widest range in flavor and quality, which is why sampling is so important.

While you're shopping (and sampling), find out where the fruit, vegetable, or nut comes from. The best local products come from farms or orchards located nearby. In fact, sometimes the farms are owned directly by the company that makes the products. For example, a cherry orchard in Portland not only grows cherries and sells them fresh in season, they also make cherry jam, dried cherries, and chocolate-covered cherries.

Highlighting a unique or local ingredient is another advantage when buying local and one you shouldn't pass by. Search out tart cherries in Michigan, wild blueberries in Maine, or hazelnuts in Oregon.

Most of these sweets are made in small batches, so you can often find unusual, albeit appetizing, flavor combinations like apricot-rosemary, plum-vanilla, and elderberry wine. Hot and savory ingredients are also popular, such as pepper jellies (habanero jelly is a hot one!) or spicy vegetable-type jams; think tomato jam. *Membrillo*, the Spanish name for quince paste, is another local sweet you may find. Quince might not be native to your area, but some creative cooks are preparing membrillo using cranberries and pecans, figs, and other fruits and nuts.

Look for products you know you won't find in conventional markets, such as lavender jam. If you're lucky, you might even find the perfumey herb highlighted in fruits such as lavender-peach preserves or lavender-raspberry-chipotle preserves.

> **LOCAL LINGO**
>
> **Jelly** is a sweet fruit gel made with strained fruit juice. **Jam** is similar to jelly, but fruit pulp is used in addition to juice. **Preserves** add whole fruit or fruit pieces to the fruit gel. Although technically the Spanish term refers only to quince paste, *membrillo* is sometimes used to signify any fruit and nut paste, such as cranberry membrillo.

Sauces, Salsas, and Spreads

Like jams and jellies, sauces, salsas, and spreads encompass a large group of products. Chutneys fall into this category as well. Of those, the ones that rule the roost include any type of tomato sauce, tomato or tomatillo salsas, and all kinds of basil pesto or pepper spreads or dips. These can be sweet or hot peppers and include a wide range of products, featuring everything from red or green sweet peppers to chipotle or jalapeño varieties and many more.

Cold cheese spreads are another item you may find, particularly in the South, where pimento cheese spread is considered a Southern delicacy. Often these products use locally made cheeses, but if you're not sure, ask.

If you live in a coastal region, seafood spreads will also be part of your local lineup. Here you'll get a taste of shrimp, crab, or oysters, to name a few, depending on which coast you live on.

Mustards are another local find. Although it does like cool conditions, the hardy mustard plant can be grown almost anywhere in the United States, but it has been particularly successful in New Mexico. Here, as well as in other places, you can buy unique artisan mustards like "real" honey mustard, dill mustard, green and red chile mustard, pinon nut mustard, and dozens more. There's even a monastery in Oregon (monasterymustard.com) that makes mustard.

Again, look for handcrafted, small-batch brands with an eye toward local ingredients and unique or interesting flavors. Ask questions, and be sure to sample before buying.

Sweets and Sundries

I can't cover every prepared item you'll find in your local market, but a few miscellaneous categories are worth noting. I call them miscellaneous because they can encompass a wide range of products, which your local market may or may carry. You can often find them at larger city markets.

Some, like chocolate, are not truly local, but if you frequent local farmers' markets, sooner or later you'll come upon "locally" produced artisan, hand-crafted chocolate products.

Chocolates and Confections

Chocolate is not native to North America. It comes from the cacao bean, which is found in the football-shaped fruit or pod of the cacao tree. These trees thrive in tropical climates, primarily Central and South America and Africa. In the United States, the only place it grows is Hawaii, and lucky for us, a few enterprising farmers have recently started growing single-origin Hawaiian chocolate. While this is great for people living in Hawaii, what about the rest of the country? How can chocolates be sold at local mainland U.S. markets?

It depends on the market. While the chocolate itself may not be local, the ingredients used to flavor these chocolates generally are, which is how they can qualify as local. They are also likely to be handcrafted, artisan products using high-quality ingredients, which in some places may be enough to be sold by a vendor at your farmers' market. Use your own judgment as to whether you will include chocolate in your local diet.

If you do decide to try local chocolate, look for responsibly produced fair-trade chocolate that uses only local ingredients—for instance, chocolate flavored with home-grown spearmint or peppermint and berries bought from a nearby farm. Nuts, too, can be garnered locally.

The best kinds of companies offer seasonal chocolates, highlighting fresh pumpkin in autumn, strawberries in spring, and raspberries or cherries in summer. Some are sweetened simply with honey or maple syrup rather than using more processed and nonlocal white sugar.

Be sure to ask questions before you buy, and don't assume that because a chocolate contains apricots, which are available locally, that local apricots are being used.

Charcuterie and Smoked Fish

Charcuterie is the art of salting, smoking, and curing meat, usually pork, but you can also find lamb, beef, seafood, goat, and game treated this way. Some local ranchers produce their own charcuterie from their own livestock, managing every step of the process on the same farm. Others specialize in just the actual practice of making these products, using meat they purchased from nearby farms. For the rancher, charcuterie offers a way to preserve his meat, use less-desirable cuts like liver and kidney, and add extra value to his meats.

For the locavore, buying homemade charcuterie has just as many benefits if not more. First off, by buying local, you're less likely to be getting unnatural additives, fillers, and artificial ingredients, which are typically added to conventional products. You know exactly what you're getting and where it came from. (Remember to read the label!) If you choose grass-fed, pasture-raised meat, you can also rest assured you won't be getting any growth hormones or antibiotics in your meat.

Well-made charcuterie can also introduce you to foods you never thought you'd like. I don't like liver, for example, but I do enjoy a good pate. The robust spices and seasonings usually added to these foods, like pistachios, carrots, or wine, often mask the meat's strong taste, producing a more mellow flavor.

And because charcuterie is a way of keeping fresh meat longer—by curing, salting, etc.—it helps you extend the season and eat meat when fresh isn't available.

> **NATIVE KNOWLEDGE**
>
> Charcuterie originates from the French term *chair cuit*, which means "cooked meat." Dating to nearly 6,000 years ago, these foods became popular during the Roman Empire. It wasn't until the Middle Ages, however, that the French brought this skill to an art.

What kind of charcuterie you can find depends on the processor and the region of the country. Sausage is the most well known of these types of meats and can be found fresh or dried. After that, there's bacon, prosciutto, pancetta, ham, guanciale (Italian unsmoked bacon made from the pig jowls or cheek), pate, terrines, and galatines. The last three are made with seasoned, finely ground meat, which usually has nuts or vegetables added to it. If you don't know what type of meat it is, ask! Many times vendors have these products available to taste.

Wherever fresh seafood is sold, you're probably likely to find local smoked versions. Smoked salmon, of course, is particularly common at markets in the Northwest. You may also find naturally smoked oysters and mussels. In other parts of the country, look for smoked trout, white fish, cod, and shrimp, to name a few.

Extra Virgin, Please

When most people think of olive oil, they think of Italy, Greece, and Spain. But America? Yes, it's true! America has a burgeoning olive oil industry that's been around since the mid-nineteenth century.

The southern part of California grows some wonderful olives and produces some spectacular olive oil. Fertile soil and rolling hills (some say the landscape mimics Tuscany) are only part of the story; the rest is thanks to a Mediterranean climate, which explains why grapes as well as olives thrive there.

Local olive oils range in price and flavor, from mild and buttery to peppery and sweet, but with more than 200 California olive oil producers growing over 100 olive cultivars, finding local olive oil you like shouldn't be hard to do.

Other states are following suit now, too. In Texas, the olive oil business is spreading fast, with companies boasting brands with a cowboy twist like lime, chipotle chili pepper, and roasted garlic–flavored olive oil. Recently, Arizona started growing and marketing olives for their own liquid gold. And since 2002, Victory Estates in the Willamette Valley of Oregon has been perfecting their olive cultivar, producing not only extra-virgin olive oil, but a variety of stuffed and flavored olives as well.

A CLOSER LOOK

Queen's Creek Olive Oil Mill, located in Queen's Creek, Arizona, is the state's one and only working olive farm and mill. It produces boutique, handcrafted extra-virgin olive oil using nine varieties of olives. Exotic-flavored oils include blood orange, Meyer lemon, and chocolate.

Simple Sweets Close to Home

Locavores mainly rely on two natural sources of concentrated sweets. These are ones Native Americans used long before Europeans arrived and are a natural part of this land's ecosystem—namely, honey and maple syrup. Long known as local delicacies, honey and maple syrup are two sweet treats you won't want to miss. Many people consider them staples in the diet with a depth of flavor and range of tastes unparalleled in the food world. But even above and beyond their culinary prowess, couldn't we all do with a little more sweet stuff in our life? Plus, they're local!

A Honey of a Time

If you have a sweet tooth, buying local honey is the best way to satisfy it. More importantly, though, buying local honey means you're supporting and helping save a valuable industry that's been slowly dying of colony collapse disorder—the bees just disappear or die. No one really knows for sure the cause for this, but experts suspect pesticides or pollen from genetically modified plants may play a role. Even shipping commercial bees hundreds of miles from home to pollinate fields and then driving them back to their original destination can have an impact, disrupting the bees' natural homing system.

Buying local honey not only helps your beekeeper and your local bees stay in business—and stay healthy—it also provides you with a superior product. Local honey is far less processed than commercial honey. Many local brands are labeled "raw," and although there's no legal definition of "raw" for honey in this country, it usually means the product is unheated (hive temperature ranges around 100°F), it's unpasteurized, and nothing is removed or added. Because of this, local honey often looks cloudy and may have tiny bits of pollen or wax from the hive floating in it.

Commercial honey, on the other hand, is often heated to 160°F during processing so it will remain liquid for several months. Processing the honey this way also allows it to be highly filtered (removing many of its healthy nutrients) to give you a crystal-clear liquid.

Then there's the taste factor. Local honey is a direct reflection of the flora of the region. So don't expect wildflower honey to taste the same in Vermont as it does in Virginia. Even single-flower honeys vary depending on season, climate, and region. It's this unique quality that makes honey so precious to the locavore diet.

Color, flavor, and texture of local honey run the gamut from dark and rich to light and thin, from sweet and flowery to pungent and tart. Each one is different, and each one is inherently complex in its own way, so if you're used to the bland clover honey most supermarkets carry, you're in for a pleasant surprise when you go local.

> **NATIVE KNOWLEDGE**
>
> When it comes to honey, generally the darker the color the stronger the taste. Dark honeys like buckwheat and chestnut are the most full-bodied, while golden-rod and lavender are some of the lightest.

To give people an idea of all the possibilities out there, and because honey preferences are so personal, many beekeepers will line up 10 or 11 honeys for people to sample. If you can taste every one of them before making your decision, the better off you are. Even if you're not a die-hard honey fan, it's hard not to walk away with a jar in hand.

Meet Me by the Maple Tree

How can you talk about local without mentioning maple syrup? Popular in cold climates, it comes from boiling down the sap from the maple tree. And although there are several varieties of maple trees, the best producers are sugar maple and black maple. Both are native to the northeastern part of the United States.

To get the best maple syrup quality and quantity, you need cool nights and warm (but not too warm) days, so the best maple syrup comes from New England and particularly Vermont. In fact, Vermont is the leading producer of commercial maple syrup in the country, followed by Maine and New York. When in season (sap is collected in late winter and early spring), local maple syrup products are easy to find in these states.

If you don't live in New England, don't worry. You can find locally produced maple syrup as far west as Minnesota and as far south as North Carolina. Maple Creek Farm in Yancey County, North Carolina, is the southernmost maple syrup producer in the country (maplecreekfarm.net). All in all, 17 states produce maple syrup, including Wisconsin, Ohio, Illinois, New Hampshire, Michigan, Connecticut, and Massachusetts, most of which are sold locally in their region. To celebrate "sugaring" season, many states host maple syrup weekends or maple syrup festivals, usually in March. Google "maple syrup festivals" to find out when and where the closest maple celebration is.

Keep in mind, though, that maple syrup, like any regional product, can vary—sometimes greatly—from state to state and region to region, depending on the climate, soil, weather, age of tree, and processing technique. So don't expect maple syrup from Wisconsin to taste the same as that from Vermont or Virginia.

All maple syrup is broken down into grades; Vermont has its own system compared to the rest of the country. Grade A or AA is considered the lightest in color (light amber) and most delicate in flavor—it's also usually the most expensive. Next is grade A medium amber, which has a more pronounced maple taste, followed by grade A dark amber. Grade B is strongest in flavor and color and is best for baking or cooking.

Get in a Pickle

Long before refrigeration had been invented, people preserved food with acid and salt. In fact, it wasn't long ago that homemade pickled meats, fish, vegetables, eggs, and fruit along with relishes, chutneys, and even vinegars filled most pantries throughout the winter. But with fewer people having time to even cook for their family, let alone preserve food, many of these foods disappeared. (I talk about resurrecting this lost art of preserving food in Chapter 15.)

With the rise of the local food movement, and a growing dissatisfaction with highly processed foods produced by big companies in faraway places, interest in these old-fashioned favorites is once again bubbling up.

Made in small batches by small, local producers usually with all-natural ingredients, these are the kinds of foods locavores seek out. Many of them have an ethnic flair to them, inspired by the Indian, Asian, and Middle Eastern populations who live nearby. Others boast a trendy twist like an interesting spice or herb. Still others are made pure and simple, the old-fashioned way.

Like all local food, stick to the rules and you can't go wrong: buy from reputable sources, ask questions regarding origin and preparation, inspect the product, and develop a relationship with the producer (if you can) before buying. Then try a few samples.

Beverages Close to Home

Like all locally prepared or processed foods, beverages mirror the foods and especially the fruits of the region. Expect to find cider where apple orchards flourish in the Northeast; citrus drinks like oranges, lemon, and lime juice in Florida and California; and cherry juices in the northern Midwest states.

Consider also what food or beverage companies began in the region. Celestial Seasonings, based in Boulder, Colorado, started its line of teas with an herbal drink culled from the wildflowers grown in the local mountains. Today, that company has gone way beyond herbal beverages, fostering a culture of tea that has spilled out into the surrounding areas and resulted in a number of teahouses, tea stores, and unique tea varieties. So while tea leaves are not a local ingredient per se, they are specific to the culture and lifestyle of the region.

The same holds true for coffee, particularly in places like Seattle, Washington, and in the Northwest. Although not grown there—Hawaii is the only state actually growing boutique coffee beans—Seattle has a strong local coffee culture, stronger than nearly any other part of the country.

Ciders and Juices

Wherever you find apples, you're likely to find apple cider. And because apples are one of those ubiquitous fruits that grow in all 50 states (thanks to Johnny Appleseed), apple cider is easy to find. Although it's more likely to appear in the fall, when apples are at or even past their prime, thanks to new storage technology (see Chapter 4), you may be able to find apple cider throughout the spring and summer, too.

The difference between apple cider and apple juice is that apple cider is simply apples that have been washed, cut, and mashed before being pressed. The liquid contains apple pulp, hence the dark brown, cloudy color. It's highly perishable, and the taste largely depends on the type of apple.

Apple juice, on the other hand, is 100 percent apple (like apple cider) except it's filtered to remove the apple pulp, which gives it a clear color. It's usually processed or pasteurized for a longer shelf life.

At local markets, you won't find apple juice, but you're likely find apple cider. The best kinds are the ones made from heritage apples or only one or two apple varieties (the farmer should know) and are simple and pure. Lately, I've found many apple ciders to be a blend of juices such as apple-cherry cider, apple-pomegranate cider, and apple-blueberry cider. This is okay as long as the extra fruit is locally grown, ideally from the same orchard, and from the real fruit. *Be sure to read the label.* Many times the apple orchard simply sends their apples to a processor to make apple cider. If the farmer isn't vigilant about what he wants, processors may add cheaper, manufacturer-type ingredients you might not want in there.

> **KEEP YOUR DISTANCE**
>
> Don't assume all ciders you buy at local markets are free of additives. Upon reading the label of apple cider from a fruit vendor at my local farmers' market, I was surprised to find artificial colors and flavors as well as some dyes listed.

In the future, other local beverages may be on the horizon. In Oregon, a long-time cranberry farmer and his family business, Vincent Family Cranberries (www. vincentcranberries.com), recently started selling local cranberry juice sweetened with agave, and a group of farmers in western New York State have built a successful industry selling Concord grape juice. Beyond juice, Pennsylvania Amish have a reputation for making local root beer and birch beer soda. Recently, HOTLIPS Soda, a company in Portland, Oregon, began making sodas flavored with juices from local seasonal fruits and berries (www.hotlipssoda.com).

Microbreweries and Brewpubs

For people who want to eat and drink locally, brewed beer or craft beers are an option worth exploring. Thanks to hundreds of dedicated brew masters, as well as an ever-growing number of home brewers, the industry has expanded greatly. Today the United States is home to more than 500 microbreweries. Brewpubs—pubs or restaurants that make their own brews—number nearly 1,000. Certain parts of the country, like Denver, for instance, have a well-established, extensive microbrewery culture. Others areas are just starting out. Either way, be on the lookout for these diamond-in-the-rough beers. Many are only known—and appreciated—by locals.

Other places you're likely to find local beer: small package stores, beer dinners, beer bars, and beer festivals.

Wet Your Whistle with Local Wines

Wine connoisseurs rejoice! Not only are local wines getting better and better, they're also growing in breadth and scope, making them a natural part of the food landscape in many areas.

Searching out these local wines has other benefits, too. First off is quality. Some of the most eclectic, quirky, and excellent wines don't stray far from the vine. Look for unusual fruit wines, merlots, Rieslings, and chardonnays using local produce. These vinos often come at bargain prices, too.

Buying local wine is a great way to reduce your carbon footprint and support the local agriculture. If you can, try to buy biodynamic organic wines.

Getting into the Spirit

If the thought of local liquor conjures up images of moonshine cooked up behind a barn, think again. Today's small mom-and-pop distilleries brew up premium products made from all kinds of fruits and grains, often sourcing high-end local ingredients and aromatics. Many take advantage of the region they live in, as does the New York–based Harvest Spirits, makers of the liquor AppleJack, which uses apples raised in Hudson Valley, or California-based Modern Spirits company, which makes Pumpkin Pie Vodka every fall featuring locally grown pumpkins.

> **A CLOSER LOOK**
>
> Many local liquor producers are known for their creative packaging. The most unique is Portland's Clear Creek Distillery's pear brandy—it has a whole pear right inside the bottle! The small pear is placed in the bottle at the orchard and it literally grows inside.

Although still a drop in the bucket compared to the mega-liquor producers, these small-batch producers are slowly gaining ground. Today these distinct liquors can be found everywhere from the Pennsylvania's Blue Ridge Mountains to Oregon's Willamette Valley. Look around your area to see what local treasures you can find.

The Least You Need to Know

- Locally prepared foods cover a wide range of both sweet and savory products.
- Not all locally prepared foods use local ingredients; some are specific to the culture of the region.
- Several states now produce their own boutique olive oils.
- Locally produced honey is better than commercial brands, and purchasing local honey can help save honey bees.
- Although ciders are the most common kind of local beverage you'll find, other local juices, sodas, beers, wines, and spirits are becoming more and more popular.

Local Food in Your Community

When deciding to eat local, one of the biggest challenges people face is where to find "local food." Luckily, this is getting easier and easier, particularly if you live in urban and suburban areas. As consumer demand grows and distribution increases, locally grown food will become more and more widely available in the American food supply system. Some of these local foods will appear in the conventional supply chain, while others will forge their own path, changing the way we buy and prepare food.

In Part 3, I discuss the many places where you can buy local food, including both traditional and nontraditional markets. We will explore farmers' markets, food festivals, fairs, church picnics, community supported agriculture (CSA), co-ops, and even supermarkets. Keep in mind, however, that these markets are continuously adapting and changing to meet demand and quality standards. Therefore, new ways of buying and finding local foods are appearing at a rapid pace.

In the final two chapters in Part 3, I cover the closest place you'll ever find local food: right in your own backyard. By starting a vegetable garden or by food foraging, fresh food is just a few steps away.

Farm-Fresh Markets

In This Chapter

- The many faces of farmers' markets
- The benefits of shopping around
- Moving beyond produce
- Smart shopping tips
- Top local hot spots

Farmers' markets are the ideal way to connect with the farmers and the foods of your region. If you've never been to a farmers' market, you'll be amazed at the variety of abundance you'll find there. Colorful veggies piled high on tables or mounded in baskets; sweet, aromatic fruits and berries; leafy green herbs still in their pots—all fresh, top-quality, and at the peak of ripeness.

For urban and suburban dwellers, farmers' markets have an added bonus: they're often the easiest and most accessible way to buy local food. Many of these markets have now moved beyond produce to provide local meat, dairy, cheese, eggs, and a host of other products.

In this chapter, I explore the different types of farmers' markets and some of the special events they offer so you can pick the one that's right for you. I also offer you some tips and tricks on how to make shopping at your farmers' market an enjoyable and successful experience—one you'll look forward to every week!

Fabulous Farmers' Markets

If you're new to eating local (or even if you're not!), farmers' markets are your best bet when it comes to finding a wide variety of local foods, particularly if you live in the city. The basic premise of a farmers' market is that the farmer or the person who specifically produces the food sells the food *directly* to you, the consumer, bypassing any middlemen like large distributors or supermarkets. The end result is you get the freshest, highest-quality product you can buy—sometimes picked right off the vine that day!—and the farmer gets money directly in his pocket.

A CLOSER LOOK

A time-honored tradition, farmers began selling their products directly to consumers in public markets during colonial times. Lancaster Central Market (centralmarketlancaster.com), the oldest continuously operating farmers' market in America, dates to 1730 in Lancaster, Pennsylvania.

The system is inherently local because the farmer can only travel so far—at most a day's worth of distance—to bring you his goods. According to a U.S. Department of Agriculture survey of farmers' markets, more than 50 percent of vendors travel less than 6 miles to get to their market. If your farmers' market is directly in the city or the suburbs, you're probably looking at a longer distance, but with only a few exceptions, most fall within the range of 50 to 100 miles. Most farmers opt to stay close to home.

Luckily, finding a farmers' market near you is getting easier and easier, thanks to the explosive growth this industry is experiencing. In 2009, more than 5,200 farmers' markets dotted the U.S. landscape, up 23 percent from the previous year and more than triple what it was in 1994. Although these numbers still represent a drop in the bucket compared to the more than 85,200 grocery and convenience stores nationwide, their popularity is testament to a trend that continues to gain momentum as more and more people value local, fresh food. Expect these markets to continue growing in the future.

What about right now? More farmers' markets mean more locally available foods produced and sold. It also means more diversity among the farmers' markets themselves. Visit several farmers' markets, and you'll quickly realize no two markets are exactly alike. Each has a different feel, different products, and sometimes even different prices. You'll find a wide range of variations.

The Marketplace

Although nationwide the average farmers' market hosts some 30 vendors, smaller operations can have as few as 6 stalls, while some of the largest ones have more than 200. Your local market can be a tiny start-up only a year or two old, or it can be a well-established venue more than 150 years old. It can be an open-air market with folding tables and makeshift tents, or it can be housed in a large warehouse or shed with 44-foot-high vaulted ceilings and terracotta tiles.

Many farmers' markets make their home in urban environments, so space is at a premium. The more established markets like those in Boston, Philadelphia, Seattle, and New York City tend to have the best spots: large public places with easy access. Newer farmers' markets take whatever they can get, in parks, parking lots, train stations, and underneath bridges or highways.

Because of their location, many of these newer farmers' markets usually set up shop only once a week, for a very specific time period. For example, during the season, my local farmers' market is open every Friday from 4 to 7 P.M. Other farmers' markets are open for business only in the morning hours from 8 A.M. to noon on Saturday or Sunday. Because these are just temporary locations, it's possible for a farmer to be at a different farmers' market every day of the week.

A CLOSER LOOK

A prescription for produce? To encourage patients to lose weight and eat healthier, some doctors are actually prescribing people to buy fruits and vegetables at farmers' markets.

Other farmers' markets housed in a more permanent setting, like the Pike Place Market in Seattle, can do business seven days a week from 10 A.M. to 6 P.M. These enclosed markets are usually open all year long, unlike the majority of outdoor farmers' markets that operate on average only about five months a year. Markets with longer growing seasons, such as those in the Southeast, can stretch out their season longer, around six or seven months. Look for most farmers' markets to start around April or May.

Winter farmers' markets, even in colder climates, and off-season markets are another option. Although not as plentiful as their summer season counterparts (in both number and size), demand for them is growing.

A Feast for Everyone

By its very nature, a farmers' market is unique. Local food varies greatly from region to region, depending on the area's climate, geography, and soil. However, even within your local region, many distinctions exist. Most farmers' markets offer organic produce, but some do not. Even in season, some farmers may opt to grow okra and kohlrabi while others grow peas and onions instead. One may plant only melons while another focuses on only berries. It pays to shop around.

The amount of diversity depends on the market and the season. Every farmers' market has a manager who takes care of running the market and working with the farmers. One of his or her many duties is to ensure the market offers a wide variety of local foods. (Some do a better job of this than others.)

More Than Just Produce

While agricultural products like fruits and vegetables are often top of mind when talking about farmers' markets, that's certainly not the only thing you'll find there. In fact, over the years, value-added products like jams, jellies, preserves, apple butter, sun-dried tomatoes, pesto, and tons of homemade baked specialties have become increasingly more prevalent. How local these products are depends on the farmers' market.

Proteins are also earning a name for themselves in these circles as local farms humanely raising cattle, sheep, pigs, or goats find a thriving market among consumers fed up with commercial, factory-processed meats. Eggs, cheese, milk, and other dairy products have also joined these ranks, as well as sustainable local seafood, as you read about in earlier chapters. As these foods become more specialized, you'll see vendors become known as the "pig guy," "fish guy," "milk man," or "lamb lady."

In an effort to drive up business, some of the larger farmers' markets have expanded to sell prepared, ready-to-eat foods like hot sandwiches or meals cooked by local restaurants. More often than not, these markets include outdoor dining areas like picnic tables or chairs to accommodate hungry shoppers. During busy times, a band or local musician might play.

Farmers' markets do more than just sell a commodity; they foster a sense of community with other like-minded locavores who care not only about the food they eat, but about the land, the environment, and the farming traditions that affect it.

KEEP YOUR DISTANCE

Not all farmers' markets sell 100 percent locally grown and raised foods. Some can offer as little as 50 percent. How committed your market is to local is specified in the vendor rules and regulations. Each market is different. To find out what your market sells, check online or ask your farmers' market manager. His contact information should be on the website, but if not send an e-mail to find out his name and get this information.

Unlike conventional supermarkets, where customers rarely speak to each other as they cruise wide aisles and fill up their carts with packaged goods, farmers' markets encourage socializing. It's one of the few places where you can find a small-town feeling in a big city and where people come to meet friends, make friends, and gather together.

Connecting not only with each other but with the food and the farmer who produced it is a uniquely satisfying experience, and many regular customers create a relationship with the farmer that goes beyond business, getting to know each others' families, swapping recipes, and sharing gardening tips. Farmers' markets are also one of the few places where you can talk to several farmers from several different farms at one time.

Finally, farmers' markets keep local food cultures alive. Walking into a market, you get an immediate sense that you belong to a specific region of the country with certain farming traditions and food customs. Along with this comes pride in one's work, one's land, and the local food it produces.

Cooking Demos and Classes

In addition to providing locally produced foods and building urban-rural communities, farmers' markets aim to educate consumers on the importance of growing, buying, and eating local food. Often this information is given away free in the form of seminars like "Meet the Farmer," gardening clinics, and information booths.

Classes are another common component and teach everything from cheese-making techniques and how to make preserves, to wine seminars and kids' cooking classes. Weekly cooking demonstrations and tastings are usually presented by local cookbook authors or chefs. Their goal is twofold: to show you how to prepare wonderful dishes using the foods at hand, and to encourage you to try new and unusual ingredients.

Other popular events hosted by farmers' markets include community festivals, food fiestas highlighting a seasonal food like tomatoes or pumpkins, children's tours, and activities and fund-raising events like dinners, breakfasts, and community yard sales. One market even has a locavore challenge!

A CLOSER LOOK

A locavore challenge encourages people to eat strictly local by taking a pledge to eat local for a set period of time, ranging anywhere from a week to a month. It usually covers a specific region such as a city or area and is sponsored by a variety of eat-local organizations. Participation is voluntary and encourages a sense of community among locavores.

To find out about these and other upcoming events, check the farmers' market website (nearly all of them have one), or better yet, get on its mailing list. Some of the larger farmers' markets send out weekly e-mail newsletters to their customers, featuring news, events, and the seasonal produce now available.

If you want to get involved with your local farmers' market, it's likely that it's always looking for volunteers to help out. Contact your farmers' market marketing manager to find if there's anything you can do.

Finding the Right Market for You

If you live in or near a major metropolitan city, chances are you have more than one farmers' market nearby and perhaps even several. If you're not sure where they are, check out LocalHarvest at localharvest.org or check out the USDA's Farmers Market Search list at apps.ams.usda.gov/FarmersMarkets.

Visit all your local farmers' markets, and just browse around. Make notes of the personality of each farmers' market and the products they sell. As with any other market or store, you'll frequent the farmers' markets that best suit your needs, and those needs can change depending on what you're looking for.

Tips for Shopping at Farmers' Markets

Shopping at a farmers' market requires an entirely different mind-set than shopping at a conventional grocery store. In fact, some of the skills you learn for shopping in standard grocery stores are exactly the opposite for shopping at farmers' markets.

For instance, for most people, shopping at a standard grocery store consists of making a list of the foods you need before you go to the store. At the store, your main goal is to find the ingredients on your list quickly and easily.

When shopping at farmers' markets, however, it's best not to make a list at all. What's more important is having a good understanding of what's in season. Knowing what grows when gives you an idea of what to expect at the market, so you can plan a menu around what's available and what's in season. This flexibility allows you to make decisions based on quality and freshness. For some people, this takes some getting used to because it means you need to approach food from a whole new perspective. Never fear, though. As you get to know the local foods in your area, this will get easier and easier for you to do.

Communicating with farmers is also key for getting the most from your farmers' market shopping experience. Most farmers are happy to talk about their crops, and many have good tips on how to prepare, store, and cook the food they sell. Many offer recipes, too. Because they actually eat the food they grow, they often have insight into how it tastes based on the weather and time of season. Strawberries at the beginning of the season may be small and tart, but later on, they may become sweeter and bigger as the season peaks.

Before You Go

Set your standards. Many people who buy local food are specifically looking for organic produce. Others may only want to buy from farms a certain distance away or in a certain state. If you have these or other similar goals, be sure to ask questions about how and where the food is grown. Some farms may be sustainable and grow their food without pesticides but are not certified organic. You have to decide what is right for you.

Unlike at conventional grocery stores where shopping with children of any age can be a challenge because of the poor food choices they often cajole you into making, taking your kids to the farmers' market is a good thing. In fact, it's encouraged! Farmers' markets not only teach kids where their food comes from, but they show kids what whole, fresh fruits and vegetables look like when they come out of the ground. In addition, it exposes them to the abundance nature has to offer. Best of all, if your child wants to buy something there, chances are it's good for them!

It's also important that you have the right attitude. Be adventurous! Try something you've never had before! Farmers' markets often have fruits and vegetables not available in your local supermarket. Furthermore, this produce may or may not be there the next week. So if you see something you're curious about, ask the farmer about it. If it's something you think you may like, give it a try. What's the worst that could happen?

> **NATIVE KNOWLEDGE**
>
> Farmers know sampling is the best way to make a sale. For this reason, many will have some produce available for you to taste. If there's something you want to try that's not out, ask for a taste. Most farmers won't refuse you.

Don't expect supermarket prices at farmers' markets. Often the prices of food sold at conventional grocery stores are artificially low, due to government subsidies or deals with large distributors. As a result, fresh food at the farmers' market may carry higher prices. But weighed against the quality, freshness, and lower food miles, they're usually worth it. Keep this in mind as you check out price tags.

Know the Basics

Unlike today's mega supermarkets, which have everything you need to purchase food right in the store, from carts to bags to ATMs, farmers' markets tend to offer fewer conveniences. It's all about the food, after all. With this in mind, there are a few things you should know before you go.

Bring your own bags and other supplies. Big, sturdy, canvas or cloth bags are best. Insulated bags are another good choice. Many farmers do have plastic or paper bags, but these are often small and flimsy. If you buy in large amounts, consider investing in a wheeled cart or wagon. If you're shopping for perishables like meat, fish, or dairy products, bring a cooler, even if you keep it in the car.

Carry cash in small bills. Not all farmers take credit or debit cards, and only a few take checks. In fact, most small operations don't take any of these, and deal only in cash. To make life easier, produce is often sold based on 50 cent or dollar amounts. The average farmers' market customer spends about $20 to $25.

Don't go on an empty stomach (unless you planned it that way!). Farmers' markets do have better choices than grocery stores for grab-and-go foods, but you don't want to spend all your time at the bakery, popcorn stand, or prepared foods stalls. If you're hungry, you also tend to overbuy, even when you're buying fresh.

Go early. Early birds often get the best selection and quality of produce. It also pays to shop early when you're buying particularly popular items like blueberries or cherries or if the farmer only has a limited supply of something you want.

Stay late. Going to the farmers' market at the end of the day has its benefits, too. At this time, farmers are usually inclined to strike deals, especially if they don't want to load up and haul all their produce back home. This is the time you may be able to bargain.

Walk the market before buying. Think of your farmers' market as a small outdoor mall. Each farmer is like a separate store with its own unique goods. Take a quick browse through the entire marketplace before you begin buying. This gives you an overview of the products each one sells.

NATIVE KNOWLEDGE

As you walk the market, keep an eye out for prices. One farmer may offer the same produce cheaper than another or offer a different variety of the same produce, which can alter taste, texture, and staying qualities.

How Much to Buy?

Buying the right amount of produce for you and your family is sometimes like walking a tightrope. You don't want to buy too much, for fear of not being able to use it all before it goes bad. But you also don't want to buy too little, because it may be another week before you can get back.

To avoid this, ask the farmer directly how long she'll have the produce you are interested in. Most times she'll give you an estimated time frame. If you don't already know, ask when peak season is and how long she'll have this item after that. For example, cherries appeared at my farmers' market in early June. But peak season isn't until a few more weeks after that. By August, the cherries will be long gone.

Plan accordingly. It may not be practical for me to buy two quarts of cherries the first time I see them, but I may buy several quarts the next week because I've had time to plan and prepare for the bulk quantity. (See Chapter 15 on saving and storing.) Remember, when it's gone, it's gone, so buy it when you can.

Another thing to keep in mind is how much you'll be cooking during the week. If you're an avid cook and plan on creating gorgeous dinners every night, be sure to buy enough to last at least for the next four or five days. Toward the end of that time, you might want to stop at another farmers' market to pick up a few more fresh items.

But if you are going to be traveling during the week or won't be home, don't stock up on fresh produce you won't use simply because you can't resist buying it. Instead, buy only a small amount you know you will use. You can always stop at the farmers' market when you return.

Spreading the Wealth

Although many farmers' markets are located in urban areas, few low-income families and individuals frequent them. The government has made serious efforts to change that with the federally funded Farmers' Market Nutrition Programs (FMNP). Established by Congress in 1992 specifically for WIC (Women, Infants, and Children) recipients, it enables families to purchase fresh, locally grown fruits and vegetables with WIC farmers' market coupons. In 2001, the government expanded the program to include low-income seniors as well.

Today, more than 70 percent of farmers' markets are involved in the programs, and the number of WIC and senior participants who bought fruit and vegetables at farmers' markets in 2009 grew to more than 3 million.

A CLOSER LOOK

In 2004, the U.S. government replaced all paper food stamp coupons with electronic benefit transfer (EBT) cards, which require a terminal to process. Few farmers' markets can accept them now, but as the technology becomes available, more and more markets will have them available.

The importance of making fresh, local produce available to everyone has sparked other groups to action, specifically a nonprofit organization called Wholesome Wave (wholesomewave.org). Funded by both the private and public sectors, Wholesome Wave is dedicated to "nourishing neighborhoods" by supporting increased production of local food for the well-being of all. To promote healthy eating, Wholesome Wave doubles the cash value of food stamps and WIC and senior coupons used at partici-pating farmers' markets nationwide.

In the Washington, D.C., metro area, where I live, more than a dozen farmers' markets participate in Wholesome Wave. The program currently reaches more than 150 markets in more than 15 states. Log on to wholesomewave.org/shoppers/find-a-location to find a participating market near you.

Another way farmers' markets spread their wealth is by *gleaning*. In biblical times, farmers would allow poor people on their fields after the harvest to glean (get) any leftovers. Today, gleaning means harvesting food that would otherwise go unused and giving this food to charity.

Many farmers' markets have gleaning programs set up with local churches, service clubs, community organizations, and food banks. How it works is simple: after market time is over, the farmers gather up the unsold produce and put it in a central location to be loaded into a truck by a local volunteer or part-time food bank employee. Then it's dropped off at the nearest community food bank to be divvied up and eventually given out directly to the people who need it most.

> **LOCAL LINGO**
>
> **Gleaning** is the act of collecting leftover crops after they've been commercially harvested. At farmers' markets, this means gathering up whatever has not been sold and giving it away to community food banks.

Destination Hot Spots

Large farmers' markets in major cities often attract thousands of visitors every week. Many of those visitors are locals shopping for the freshest, best-tasting food in the area. Others are simply tourists hoping to get a taste of the city's local flavors.

If you do have the opportunity to visit a farmers' market while you're on vacation or away from home, you won't be disappointed. Aside from finding fresh, wholesome food like fruits, artisanal cheese, and fresh baked breads, you'll also likely discover new and interesting foods native to the region. You may even be able to sample regional prepared specialties like bratwurst in Wisconsin, empanadas in Texas, and salmon burgers in Washington State.

Because of their small-town feel, farmers' markets also give you a chance to mingle with the locals, which can offer its own rewards. For instance, striking up a conversation at a picnic table at the Boulder farmers' market, I got some great recommendations for restaurants and must-see sights I would have never known otherwise. (See Appendix C for more information on must-see farmers' markets by region.)

> **NATIVE KNOWLEDGE**
>
> If you're traveling and come upon a farmers' market, skip the fresh fruit and vegetables unless you're going to eat them right away. Instead, check out the nuts, honey, jams, jellies, preserves, and baked goods available. Not only do these items last longer, but they also travel better. In some states, it's illegal to bring produce across state lines, too!

The Least You Need to Know

- Farmers' markets are a good place to find locally grown food and talk to the farmers who grew it. They're also a great place to take the kids!
- Every farmers' market is different, so explore several before you decide on what you want.
- To make the most of shopping at a farmers' market, be spontaneous and take advantage of the seasons.
- Plan your meals according to what's in season and what's available at your market.
- Because most of the produce at farmers' markets is ripe and ready to eat, only buy as much as you will use in the next five days so you won't waste any.
- Government programs encourage low-income families and seniors to frequent farmers' markets by giving out food stamps and coupons they can use there.

Food Festivals and Fairs

In This Chapter

- Finding food festivals and fairs near you
- Making the most of your festival time
- The perks of local recipe contests
- Tips for a successful outing

For people who are on a mission to eat local, attending festivals, street fairs, and picnics is like opening a hidden treasure chest. You never know what you'll find inside, but you can be sure there will be at least a few precious jewels!

Certainly, your best bets are festivals that center around a specific food or harvest time, but events celebrating religious holidays, the community, or a specific ethnic culture can also offer a peek at the local food scene.

Knowing which event to choose can be tricky, particularly when there are so many. During summer and fall, one place or another hosts some kind of festival, fair, or picnic nearly every week. The rest of the year, you can also find food festivals. In fact, search hard, and you'll find a food festival held every month of the year in every state in the country. Most of them require a little research beforehand, but even so, because many are nearby, it doesn't take much to hop in your car and drive there. After that, it's time to sit back and enjoy the ride!

Making a Find

Like farmers' markets, food festivals celebrate the foods of the region. Unlike farmers' markets, however, food festivals generally run once a year usually for just a few days, during harvest season, when the fruit or vegetable is at its peak. Most festivals run 2 or 3 days (usually on the weekend) but a few, like the 10-day National Peanut Festival in Dothan, Alabama, run much longer. Local, luscious, and often less expensive than almost anywhere else, foods sold at food festivals are definitely worth seeking out.

Most festivals are located in the region the food hails from: the Mushroom Festival in Kennett Square, Pennsylvania (mushroomfestival.org); the International Mango Festival in Coral Gables, (south) Florida (fairchildgarden.org); Poteet Strawberry Festival in Poteet, Texas (strawberryfestival.com); Lowcountry Shrimp Festival in McClellanville, South Carolina (shrimpfest.mcvl.net); and the Napa Valley Mustard Festival in Napa Valley, California (mustardfestival.org). One of the longest continuous festivals, the Napa Valley Mustard Festival hosts activities throughout the season starting in January and running through the end of March.

You may also find several of the same kind of festivals in different states. For example, there are peach festivals in Georgia, Texas, California, South Carolina, and Colorado, to name a few.

Street fairs and church picnics are also local affairs, which often get a buzz through word-of-mouth and posters hung on doors and bulletin boards throughout the community. Like festivals, these events also run once a year.

The trick is finding out about them *beforehand*. This can take some work, especially if you don't live in the community hosting it. The best advice I can give is to pick a food, preferably a food that grows in your region or a region you'd like to visit, and do an online search for food festivals specific for that food and that state. This does require some knowledge of what's in season and when it grows. On the print side, check out the event sections of local newspapers and magazines. Then ask around. You never know what type of information your friends and neighbors will come up with.

If you're still having no luck, consider contacting the tourism board or chamber of commerce in the state you're thinking of visiting. Many would be happy to provide you with details of their upcoming food festivals.

Here are a few to get you started:

International Horseradish Festival
Collinsville, Illinois
www.horseradishfestival.com

Maine Lobster Festival
Rockland, Maine
www.mainelobsterfestival.com

Dungeness Crab and Seafood Festival
Port Angeles, Washington
www.crabfestival.org

World Catfish Festival
Belzoni, Mississippi
www.catfishcapitalonline.com

California Strawberry Festival
Oxnard, California
www.strawberry-fest.org

National Cherry Festival
Traverse City, Michigan
www.cherryfestival.org

Black Walnut Festival
Spencer, West Virginia
www.wvblackwalnutfestival.org

California Avocado Festival
Carpinteria, California
www.avofest.com

Stockton Asparagus Festival
Stockton, California
www.asparagusfest.com

Mississippi Pecan Festival
Richton, Mississippi
www.mspecanfestival.com

Olathe Sweet Corn Festival
Olathe, Colorado
www.olathesweetcornfest.com

Vermont Cheesemakers Festival
Shelburne, Vermont
www.vtcheesefest.com

For more information on these and other festivals, check out *The Best Recipes from America's Food Festivals* by James O. Fraioli (Alpha Books, 2007).

> **NATIVE KNOWLEDGE**
>
> Don't just memorize the season of specific foods; rather, understand the climate they grow in. This way you'll know why blueberry festivals in the Southeast like Mississippi or North Carolina run in mid-June or early July, while in Michigan and Maine they usually appear in August.

When you do have a festival, fair, or picnic in mind, scope out its website. If it doesn't have a website, talk to someone who has been there, or call the festival or fair manager to find out about it. This will give you insight into what to expect, what to bring, and even what to wear. (If the festival is in a park area, which tends to get muddy or dusty, you might want to skip the sandals in lieu of more sturdy footwear.)

Celebrate Festival Season

Food festivals run throughout the year starting in spring and summer, but the majority of them appear in early fall. Perhaps this is because it's the end of harvest season or maybe it's because that's the way it's "always" been. In any case, be prepared to make the rounds in September.

Some festivals are small, and some are large. The best ones include four components:

- Growers selling their product directly to consumers

- A variety of whole, fresh foods—different kinds of mangoes, oranges, berries, etc.

- Value-added products like dips, spreads, relishes, and more

- Prepared, ready-to-eat foods, preferably highlighting the festival food

A perfect example of this is the Hudson Valley Garlic Festival in Saugerties, New York (hudsonvalleygarlic.com). In addition to dozens of value-added products like pickles, pestos, spice blends, and salsas (all featuring garlic), and a slew of prepared foods all with a garlic twist such as garlic pizza, garlic fries, garlic soup, and more, the festival boasts more than 50 growers selling 70+ varieties of garlic grown throughout the region.

Some festivals even teach you how to grow and harvest produce. For example, at the International Mango Festival, hosted at the Fairchild Botanical Gardens in southern Florida, attendees not only get the chance to taste, see, and buy dozens of mango varieties, mango-inspired products, and mango culinary creations, they also get the chance to purchase their own mango tree.

Others educate by offering to give attendees a tour of the farm or operation, or if that's not possible, bringing the farm to them. That's what the Mushroom Festival in Pennsylvania does in the Culinary Tent, which offers a glimpse of how various mushrooms grow (i.e., on trees or in dirt), plus shares nutritional and cooking tips. At the Kona Coffee Cultural Festival in Hawaii, visitors get the chance to try their hand at picking the Kona coffee cherries during a coffee-picking competition. At the California Strawberry Festival, you can stroll through a 12-foot-long strawberry field at the "Life of a Strawberry" exhibit.

State Fairs

On a broader scale, well-known state fairs capture the feel and flavor of a region by highlighting locally produced food. Check out the State Fair Directory (ncstatefair.com) for a list of state fairs across the country.

Some of the big ones like the Iowa State Fair not only feature local foods like corn and pork chops, they also have blue ribbon contests and agriculture and horticulture exhibits that boast the biggest locally grown tomato, melon, cucumber, etc. and the best-looking or biggest pig, steer, cow, or sheep. For city dwellers, attending these types of fairs can really be an eye-opening experience!

A Taste of ...

Exploring local food also means checking out the rich ethnic traditions of a certain region, usually through a community or city-wide event. The ethnic foods these festivals celebrate were often brought to this country by immigrants more than a century or two ago. This has done much to shape our current food culture and farming traditions. When you find them, do visit street fairs and picnics. Although not all the foods are homegrown, you're still likely to find homemade food now grown locally that originated from countries all over the world.

Church festivals, picnics, and events are another avenue worth venturing down. Much of the food made at such happenings is homemade, and some does come from local sources. One small church near where I live hosts a small picnic in the fall. While most of the food was average fare, the main fund-raiser was a booth selling apple butter. The men and ladies of the church had spent several days making the butter from apples picked from a local orchard—homemade, fresh, and local—and some jars were even still warm! This old-fashioned, cinnamon-laced apple butter was, hands down, the highlight of my trip.

A CLOSER LOOK

One of the biggest, most famous, and longest-running religious festivals in New York City is the Feast of San Gennaro (sangennaro.org), a rollicking Italian festival that fills the streets of Little Italy every year.

Other food fairs, festivals, and celebrations have their roots in Poland, Russia, Greece, China, Mexico, the Ukraine, and scores of other countries. Most of these fairs and festivals run in early fall, but you can find some sprinkled throughout spring and summer.

Recently, some cities have started to build pride and community spirit in the local food they serve by hosting special events called "Taste of … [fill in the name of the city]." To find out if you have one of these events in your city, search online. Another option is to call your chamber of commerce.

One of the biggest of these events is Taste of Chicago, (gochicago.about.com/od/tasteofchicago/p/taste_chicago.htm), which, aside from having live music from popular entertainers, offers food samples and cooking demos from more than 70 local restaurants and chefs. You can also find a Taste of Colorado (atasteofcolorado.com), a Taste of Syracuse (tasteofsyracuse.com), and a Taste of Music City, Nashville's largest food and drink festival (tasteofmusiccity.com) as well as others. Although not as popular as food festivals, which are often set outside the city, these urban events are becoming more and more common. Try to avoid "taste of …" events that strictly promote restaurants, and instead choose ones that focus on community and culture, where you're more likely to find homegrown foods.

Explore New Worlds

The best part about attending food festivals is not so much finding new foods (most of these events highlight foods well established in our culture like cherries, pecans, potatoes, etc.). Rather, it's about learning how these foods are grown and exploring the many culinary ways they can be used. Remember, the people who are cooking at these festivals have much experience with these foods, and some have been preparing and eating them for generations. Consequently, food festivals often offer a wealth of culinary ideas utilizing a specific food.

Tasting your way through the booths is the easiest way to explore new dishes and find out what you like. This works well for some of the smaller fairs, but for the larger ones where the booths number in the hundreds, this just isn't possible. Instead, take a quick browse down the food aisle and note which foods you think you'd like to check out. Pay attention to how many people are in line, and look at people's plates as they pass by. While the longest line doesn't always equate to the best food, it's a good start.

What else can you do to make the most of a food festival? Let's look at a few other ways to get the most from your visit.

Buy a Cookbook

Many of the large, long-running food festivals like the Gilroy Garlic Festival in Gilroy, California (www.gilroygarlicfestival.com), collect recipes every year and create an annual cookbook. Church picnics may also sell regional cookbooks, highlighting the foods of the area. These often have an ethnic theme such as German or Ukraine, depending on the parish's background.

Often these cookbooks are for sale at the festival or fair. Sometimes they may even have past issues available for purchase. Take a look through these cookbooks. They can be chock-full of good ideas. If you're interested in one, be sure to pick it up quickly because many times, these kinds of books are only sold at the festival and supplies are limited.

If the festival doesn't have a cookbook, sometimes it does have recipes available via other medium, such as on their website, in a brochure or pamphlet, or on a CD. Ask at the information booth if any recipes are for sale—or better yet, free! If the festival isn't organizing something, individual vendors or growers may have some ideas or recipes to share.

Be Competitive

After you've attended a festival a few times and feel comfortable going there, you may want to consider entering a culinary content. Many festivals, fairs, and even farmers' markets run cooking contests to showcase their local food. This is a great time to experiment with new recipes and perfect old ones.

Oftentimes, these contests are run far in advance of the event, usually through the website. This gives the judges time to evaluate and narrow down the entries. In some cases, only the finalists are asked to prepare their dish at the festival, which is where the winner is actually chosen. Other times, at smaller events, all the entries are prepared and showcased at the festival.

Either way, if you do enter a contest, don't expect big returns. Usually the winners are more concerned with bragging rights than actual prizes. The true reward is the many unique and interesting ways of preparing the item you will see and taste from your co-contestants.

You don't have to be a contestant to reap the benefits, either. For a small fee, many festivals or fairs will let festival attendees sample tastes from the top recipes. After the event, the winning recipe (and sometimes the runner-ups, too) are usually available to the general public either online or as a handout. If it's not, be sure to ask about it.

Planning Your Visit

Going to a festival or fair takes a bit more planning than visiting a farmers' market or farm. For one thing, most only last a day or two, which means you can't go back a week later if you forget to buy something. If you want something, be sure to buy it before you leave.

Here are some other helpful tips you should know:

Order your tickets ahead of time. Most of the bigger fairs or festivals have websites where you can buy tickets online prior to the event. Sometimes local stores also sell tickets. In addition to saving you time at the door (you don't have to waste time waiting in line), buying in advance often also saves you money, as most early bird tickets are discounted.

Bring a backpack. Fairs and festivals are walking occasions. People generally stroll up and down the central area, looking at vendor products. Seating, although available, is usually limited to dining places or special show or event seating. Having a backpack allows you to walk comfortably while still having your hands free. It's also a great place to store the products you buy. Parking is usually in a large area such as a school or lot at a location farther away, which doesn't make it easy to quickly run to the car to stow away your purchases.

KEEP YOUR DISTANCE

Going to festivals is a great way to spend a day together with the family, but going to these places isn't cheap. While buying produce here may cost less, the price of admission, parking, and gas as well as buying meals for the family all adds up. Be prepared to spend. Even if admission is free (which many of them are), it can still be an expensive day.

Carry cash. Most of these types of events only deal in cash. Cash is also preferred by the small local vendors who sell there. Some places will have ATMs available, but finding them may be difficult, so don't count on them. Better to be safe than sorry. Bring extra money.

Stay hydrated. Most festivals, fairs, and picnics are outdoor events, held during relatively warm weather, so it's important to stay hydrated. Always bring a water bottle in your backpack, even if you don't think you'll need it.

Food festivals are fun, family events that come in all sizes. Some are small local events with only a few people, while others are large, crowded extravaganzas that stretch for blocks. Choose the one you feel comfortable with. Remember, too, that while exploring new ways of using local foods is one of your goals, most important is the fact that you relax and enjoy yourself. Think of yourself as a food festival explorer going on an adventure. Even if you don't get to everything you wanted to see or do, keep in mind that there's always next year. So have fun!

The Least You Need to Know

- Food festivals, fairs, and church picnics are great places to taste and explore local food.
- Many of these events have religious, ethnic, or community themes, but food is often an important component, showcasing a local specialty.
- The cooking contests held at some festivals are a great way to expand your culinary repertoire of a local food, even if you don't choose to participate.
- A successful outing means planning ahead for tickets, money, hydration, etc.

CSAs, U-Picks, and More

In This Chapter

- A look at community supported agriculture (CSA)
- The ins and outs of U-picks
- The benefits of buying into food co-ops
- Digging into community gardens

In the broad sense of the term, *community supported agriculture* encompasses all the ways we, as a community, help farmers who produce our food. Certainly part of this support—a big part—includes buying produce, meat, dairy, eggs, and other items directly from the farmer, at farmers' markets, at farm stores, or from roadside stands, but keeping our local agriculture healthy, sustainable, and profitable goes way beyond that. This is where community supported agriculture (CSA) memberships, U-picks, food co-ops, and community gardens come in.

Each of these allows you to get more involved in the agricultural aspects of farming (even if you don't have a green thumb) and become part of the bigger community of eating local. Each one also requires a certain level of commitment.

As you read through this chapter, think about which one of these activities would best suit your personality and lifestyle. Then jump right in. Most locavores do more than one, and some are even involved in all of them. Consider it an investment in yourself, your family, and the future of your local food system. The rewards you reap are more than just great-tasting food; you'll also gain a sense of community and collaboration with your farmer, fulfillment, and satisfaction.

CSAs: Share and Share Alike

The CSA is a partnership between the grower and the consumer who purchases his or her produce. Here's how it works: early in the year, the farmer offers a certain number of "shares" of the farm to the general public based on the anticipated costs of running the farm—seed, equipment, labor, salaries, etc. Shares are paid, usually in one lump sum (some farmers now have payment plans set up), prior to planting time, generally in January or February, and cover anywhere from 20 to 30 weeks.

People who purchase a share then become members or subscribers of the CSA. A typical share consists of a box of vegetables or other products delivered to members or available for pickup each week during the growing season. The point of the CSA is that the members share the bounty of the harvest, getting local produce delivered to them every week.

Just as important as the harvest, however, is the notion of "shared risk," which means if the farmer has a bad year and the crops fail, each individual share will also be slimmer, creating a strong sense of community among members and between the farmer and the members.

Luckily, over the years, farmers have gotten much better at planning out crops and predicting yields. They also plant a wide variety of crops, so even if one fails, plenty of others are available to use as backup. For this reason, rarely will you see CSAs having problems. But you will find items will vary depending on the weather or climate, so flexibility is a must. This is also where it pays to find a CSA with experience, so if you're uncomfortable with risk, be sure to choose a CSA with a proven track record.

Shop Around

The first American CSA began in Massachusetts in 1985, and the number has grown in leaps and bounds ever since. In fewer than 10 years, by 1993, more than 400 CSAs were in operation in the United States. Today, according to data by the U.S. Department of Agriculture, more than 12,500 farms have CSA arrangements. This phenomenal growth not only means more CSAs are now available to people who want to eat local, it also means there's a lot more choices.

A CLOSER LOOK

The first CSA model was developed in Japan in 1965 and called *teikei,* which translates as "food with the farmer's face on it."

Each CSA has specifics on what type of vegetables are planted, whether it's organic or not, the number of CSA weeks and policies about vacations, refund information, etc. How the produce is packed varies, too. For instance, many CSAs pack their boxes themselves with whatever's in season. Others allow members to pick and choose, within reason, what they want. Some people are even able to leave out vegetables they don't want. Pickup is usually at a designated central spot or at the farm, but in a few cases, the food can be delivered to your home.

Most CSAs operate during the summer growing season, but due to increasing demand, many are expanding to year-round operations, offering winter CSA membership. You can also find specialized CSAs featuring specialty items like meat, fruit, cheese, and eggs.

Although almost all CSAs encourage members to visit the farm, some actually require members to spend a certain amount of time working on the farm. This is more common on the East Coast. More often, however, this is not required, but if you like getting your hands dirty, plenty of CSAs allow you to come to the farm and help out on a volunteer basis. Some farms even give discounts to those who commit to volunteer and have programs to help families or individuals who can't afford signing up but still want fresh, healthy, locally produced food.

For young farmers who are just starting out, volunteers can be crucial to their survival. The newest phenomenon, driven by the growing interest in local food, is the appearance of *crop mobs*. This is an organized group of young urban dwellers who descend on a farm to provide a few hours of free labor. In return, they usually get a free meal, a connection with the land and the food grown on it, and the satisfaction of doing a job well done. Although they are not CSA "members," they are certainly part of the spirit of community supported agriculture.

LOCAL LINGO

Crop mobs are groups of young, urban landless or wannabe farmers who volunteer at small farms on the weekend. For farmers who have limited labor resources, they can be a lifesaver.

Not all CSA memberships involve only one farm. In fact, most farms will buy from other local farms. For example, if your farm grows only produce, it can strike a deal with neighboring farms to offer eggs, dairy, cheese, or meat to CSA members.

Some CSAs are actually a collection of farms, and lately nonfarming third parties have been setting up CSA-like businesses. CSAs can be organized and set up by restaurants (for their customers), corporations (for employees—what a great benefit!), colleges (for their students), and even in hospitals (for health-care employees).

Overall, most CSAs are still small operations, but as demand increases, their size has been growing. One large CSA in Colorado has more than 3,000 members!

The bottom line: CSAs vary tremendously, so be sure to do your homework first before becoming a member. Some of the best places to start looking for CSAs are LocalHarvest (localharvest.org) or the U.S. Department of Agriculture's resource site (see Appendix B). Pick one that appeals to you and matches your values. If you can, visit the farm before you sign up, and be sure to ask around or check references.

CSAs run anywhere from $500 to $800 a summer season (about 20 weeks or so), depending on if you get a half share or whole share (a full share generally feeds a family of four for a week), so it's a big commitment. Be sure you're comfortable with your decision.

Benefits to Bank On

People who are regular CSA members love vegetables, love to cook, and love the challenge of the unknown—planning meals based on your CSA "surprise" each week. They also make the time to prepare these foods.

If this sounds like you, here are some of the benefits of CSAs you can expect:

- Ultra-fresh, tasty, local produce

- An introduction to new and unfamiliar vegetables

- Savings on time (less grocery shopping) and money (Most CSAs are less expensive than going to the farmers' market and run about $20 to $30 per week.)

- Special perks such as admission to special events at your CSA farm or first dibs on meat or egg buys

- A relationship with your farmer (Many of the larger ones communicate regularly with members via e-mail newsletters or online groups. Members are kept up-to-date on goings-on at the farm and get recipes, tips, and more.)

- A better understanding of the seasons and what grows when

In addition, you'll have U-pick opportunities. Along with the regular CSA pickup, members of my CSA were allowed to go to the farm and collect certain items—a pint of blackberries, a bag of green beans, etc.—directly from the farm, for free as a benefit of their CSA membership. This is a great way to supplement your CSA and an extra incentive to become a member.

You'll also get a chance to "glean" (see more about this in Chapter 13) the farm, also free of charge. At my CSA, the last two weekends of the season, members were allowed to have the run of the farm, meaning they could pick or glean whatever vegetables were left on any of the plants before they plowed them under and after the harvest. I came home with bags of green beans, zucchini, yellow squash, peppers, collard greens, mustard greens, beets, plus a few heads of broccoli, some cherry tomatoes, and potatoes. What a steal!

In the Know

The first time I signed up for a CSA, I was so excited about getting fresh produce from a local farm that I didn't pay attention to where it was located, so my weekly CSA trip was much farther than I thought. The next time, I chose a better location.

To help smooth out some of those bumps in the road before you hit them, here are a few tips from experienced CSA'ers:

Sign up early. This is especially true if you're in a highly populated area. All the local CSAs around me are sold out by March.

Pick a convenient time and place for pickups. If it's easy for you to get to the pickup location, you're more apt to go. It also makes your life a lot less stressful.

Remember quantity varies. Generally produce is lighter in the spring and gets heavier as the season progresses.

Produce isn't always pretty. Compared to conventional produce, CSA items can be dirty and some may have small bugs (particularly if it's organic). So plan on spending more time washing and prepping your stash.

Don't expect the CSA to meet all your produce needs. Many CSAs are light on fruit, and depending on how big your family is, often people need to buy staples like potatoes, carrots, and garlic in addition to their CSA bounty.

Be prepared for abundance. In addition to cooking more, you might also have some preserving, freezing, or canning to do.

Have a backup plan. Invariably life happens, so be sure you have a friend or neighbor you can give your CSA produce to if you can't use it one week. Some CSAs will let you skip a week and double up later.

U-Pick, U-Gain

For locavores who want a more personal connection with the land, U-pick farms may be the answer. U-pick or pick-your-own (PYO) farms allow visitors to come and harvest produce right off the vine. Farmers like this arrangement because they don't have to pick, store, or bring their produce to market to sell it. Consumers like it because they get to choose the fruit they like, right off the tree—how fresh is that?—and enjoy a day outside at the farm.

But for people who eat only a local diet, U-picks offer even more.

The U-Pick Advantage

There are many reasons why people who eat local should regularly visit a U-pick farm during harvest season, including:

U-picks save you money. Because you're eliminating a whole laundry list of middlemen, including labor, prices are lower—in some cases, as much as 25 percent less than market prices.

U-picks support local agriculture. Money spent on U-pick farms goes straight into the farmers' pocket.

U-picks tend to be organic or close to it. Ask the farmer to be sure, but many U-pick farms use sustainable and organic practices even if they aren't certified.

U-picks give you a glimpse of rural life. They teach kids living in urban areas about where their food comes from. It also shows them that the best-tasting food doesn't always look perfect.

A CLOSER LOOK

For families, U-pick farms are more than just a day in the sun. These annual events create memories and family traditions that often last a lifetime. And it's fun, too!

U-pick farms usually have a shop selling local homemade products. This shop features items made from the crops they grow—baked goods, jams or jellies, ciders, and other prepared items.

Plan Ahead

Like any family outing, planning a day at the farm takes a bit of prep work. Always call ahead. Weather conditions can alter picking calendars literally overnight. If you do still go ahead under threat of rain, be sure to have a backup plan just in case. U-pick season begins in May and lasts throughout the summer season.

Be sure, when you call, to inquire about picking containers. Many farms provide them but others do not, so be prepared.

Approach a U-pick outing like any other outdoor activity. Pack plenty of water, snacks, sun hats, sunscreen, and bug repellent. Dress in old clothes and shoes.

Learn the signs of ripeness. Knowing what a ripe fruit looks and feels like is crucial for a successful U-pick day. If you don't know what to look for, ask the farmer before you venture out.

Read the farm rules. Every farm is a bit different, and some have more relaxed rules than others. If you have small children, teach them that the plants are to be cared for and respected.

Food Co-Ops

Most food cooperative stores, or food co-ops, were formed in the 1970s, when natural and health foods were hard to come by and demand was high. Jointly owned by the customers, or "members," who shop there, these stores are democratically controlled enterprises, member-governed, and based on values of self-help, self-responsibility, equality, and solidarity.

Anyone is able to join and become a member for a small fee. As a member/owner, you have greater control over product quality and range than traditional stores. You have a say as to what the store carries and where they get it from. You also get part of the profits.

KEEP YOUR DISTANCE

Don't get food co-ops confused with stores like Costco or BJ's, which also require membership. These big-box stores are privately owned and operated "discount clubs." The annual fee they charge is in exchange for a discount on purchases.

Low-Cost Local Foods

Locally owned food co-ops provide services and goods in a way that keeps community resources in the community. Thus, these stores have a long history of buying from local and regional farms. Their strong commitment to purchasing food close to home has made them experienced leaders in the local food movement.

Providing local, high-quality foods is only one of the things food co-ops do well. Another is saving you money. Because co-ops aren't out to make huge profits for absentee stockholders or investors, their goal is to provide maximum value for customers/shareholders. They do this primarily by buying in bulk.

In addition to being better for your pocketbook, buying in bulk is also environmentally friendly because it uses less plastic packaging. Co-ops also save you time because you spend less time going back and forth to the grocery store. Finally, co-ops give you a wider array of fresh choices because some things sold in bulk are not available in smaller packages.

There are also other ways to save. Some food co-ops offer discounts off groceries for their members who volunteer at activities or events.

Co-Ops Reinvented

Food co-ops are all about creating community, promoting education, and strengthening cooperation, so as the needs of the community changes so does the co-op. Many offer cooking classes, wellness classes, and fitness classes. In the community, they work with food banks, promote local farmers, and help women and children in need.

Traditional food co-operatives are small or medium-size stores stocked with a variety of healthy, natural, local items, usually in urban neighborhoods. Membership is composed of the general public.

Lately, however, another type of co-op has been gaining ground: the farmer cooperative. While farmer cooperatives involving production distribution chains have been around for nearly 100 years, none have dealt directly with consumers.

Owned, operated, and run by the farmers of the region, this kind of co-op is a storefront operation that offers farmers the opportunity to sell their products directly to consumers, 7 days a week, 365 days a year. One of the best examples is the Centerville Market, based in Lincoln, Nebraska. This farm co-op stocks its shelves almost exclusively with products produced in Nebraska, a model for rural communities. Most people expect it will only be a matter of time before more and more of these types of stores—ideal for both farmers and consumers—start popping up across the country.

Another type of co-op making waves in the industry are co-ops without walls. These store-less food co-ops are appearing in inner cities as well as rural areas and are run like a distribution service, delivering boxes of fresh foods and other goods to local residents.

The premier one is the Oklahoma Food Cooperative (OFC). OFC has been running—without a store—since 2003. More than 2,000 members strong, customers visit the website (www.oklahomafood.coop) at the beginning of each month to see products, all of which are native to Oklahoma and primarily from small processors and farmers, and post an order. On the third Thursday of every month, all food and nonfood products are delivered to 32 pickup sites across the state. All workers are volunteers.

Inspired by the success of this store-less co-op—sales approached $1 million dollars in 2008—other states like Kansas, Texas, Michigan, and Idaho are making similar efforts. It works particularly well in rural areas.

Share the Work—Join a Community Garden

When it comes to community supported agriculture, community gardens top the list. In this type of activity, you're working side by side with other people to till the land, nourish plants, and harvest crops, all for a common goal—growing your own food.

Located on a public plot of land that's not in use, or more likely in disrepair, community gardens can be in rural communities as well as inner cities. Depending on how the garden is set up, you can have your own individual plot to plant what you want, or you can have a share, work the garden together, and enjoy the garden's bounty communally.

In addition to producing fresh, healthy food, community gardens can improve your neighborhood by revitalizing rundown areas, reducing crime, and providing volunteer opportunities for youths, keeping them out of trouble. Community gardens bring people together to work on a common cause, fostering a sense of togetherness and building bonds in the neighborhood.

Community gardens are a learning opportunity. Sometimes these are in the form of formal classes on planting and growing fruits and vegetables. More likely, however, you learn from each other and while doing so, discover what techniques are best and what works and what doesn't. So what if you don't have a green thumb? Maybe your neighbor does, and you can ask her for some advice.

Community gardens help people in need. While some gardens allow you to keep the produce, others give away their harvest to local food banks or people in the neighborhood who need it.

A well-maintained garden saves you money. Although most community gardens charge a small fee for rental space—about $50 per year for a 20×20-foot square plot—the fruits and vegetables you grow more than make up for that. According to the National Gardening Association, a plot that size, about 400 square feet, can yield anywhere from 200 to 300 pounds of produce, amounting to a considerable savings in grocery bills—at least $300. (See Chapter 12 for more details on how gardening can save you money.)

Perhaps the biggest benefit is the simplest: working in a community garden is a way to share your time, knowledge, and tools with other people who care about the earth, the environment, and the food they eat.

To find out if there's a community garden near you, check with the American Community Gardening Association (communitygarden.org).

A CLOSER LOOK

If you can't find a community garden available in your neighborhood, consider starting one at work. Company or corporate garden plots are getting more and more popular as interest in eating local increases and companies strive to offer employee perks without spending a lot of money.

If you do find a local community garden and can't get in, don't give up. With the local foods movement heating up, more and more people are looking to get closer to the land by gardening. As a result, a plot in a community garden, particularly in highly populated urban areas, has become hot property. In Washington, D.C., some people have been on a waiting list for years before being able to get a spot. Because these plots are so precious, few people are likely to give one up when they get it. So understandably, turnover is low.

What can you do if you can't get into your community garden? You could try to find another plot of land nearby and start your own community garden, but it takes a lot of time, effort, and planning to coordinate such a project. If you're not up for such a task, consider planting some vegetable plants or herbs indoors or on a deck or porch in container gardens. (For more information on gardening in the city, check out Chapter 12.)

The Least You Need to Know

- CSAs are good for people who want to eat local, like to cook, and don't have a lot of time to shop.
- CSAs come in many sizes, types, and setups, so shop around for one that fits your lifestyle.
- U-pick farms are a great way to save money, learn about how food grows, and enjoy time with your family outdoors.
- Joining a food co-op allows you to buy many local foods in bulk at discounted prices.
- People who belong to a community garden share the work as well as the bounty of the harvest.

Supermarkets and Specialty Stores

In This Chapter

- Searching for local food in the supermarket
- The importance of reading labels
- Adjusting your expectations
- Buying local when it counts

As more and more consumers clamor for locally grown food and the movement gains momentum across the country, few supermarkets can afford to ignore this trend. For small, mom-and-pop grocery stores that have a stake in the community, this is an easy transition. In fact, many have been offering some local foods all along. Lately, however, local has moved into more mainstream markets, which means large national grocery stores and even superstores have been getting into the local food act. Although still aligned with industrial large-scale agriculture, many are now promoting some local products as well.

While these programs offer a promising start, some of their principles are still a bit murky, particularly when it comes to defining exactly what a local food is. And despite good intentions and lots of marketing hype, finding these local products can be difficult. In this chapter, I help you navigate through the aisles and give you tips on how to find the real deal when it comes to eating local. I also tell you about some new programs you may be seeing in the future.

Savvy Supermarkets

Eating local is a hot trend among consumers, so it's no wonder savvy supermarkets are jumping on the bandwagon. For these stores, the problem is finding local farmers large enough to supply the store with the quantities needed. Furthermore, many large stores operate from large distribution centers, miles away, which poses another hurdle.

These large, broad-line distribution centers work on economies of scale, meaning they want large volumes of product, preferably from a small number of suppliers. Most of them also require suppliers to participate in different promotions and marketing programs. These can be expensive, costing more money than what it's worth for the farmer to sell his product.

To overcome these issues, grocery stores often deal directly with several local farmers at a time. Direct store delivery is more flexible, but it does require a good transportation system, particularly if delivering to multiple stores. Farmers also need to be savvy about pricing structures, invoicing, and ordering systems as well as post-harvest handling techniques like chilling, sorting, and grading.

Using a specialty distributor is another solution and usually has less-burdensome service agreements. They usually target more niche markets like co-ops, natural food stores, and restaurants.

Sometimes farmers band together to form marketing or produce cooperatives. Designed to improve productivity and distribution, these networks bring farm products to city or suburban markets. A good example of this is Good Natured Family Farms in Kansas City (goodnatured.net), an alliance of more than 100 farmers within 200 miles of Kansas City that sell locally sourced meat, poultry, eggs, and dairy products to supermarkets.

Entrepreneurial companies are also sprouting up, like Thousand Hills Cattle Company (thousandhillscattleco.com), which markets grass-fed beef produced by 40 farmers in Minnesota, Iowa, Illinois, and Wisconsin. The company, started by one of the farmers, processes the meat locally in Minnesota at a central location and then sells it to retailers in the area.

Because farmers are too busy working the land to take care of all the details involved in selling to bigger markets, many hire a third party to help them manage this side of the business. These people are responsible for packing and processing products to fit supermarket specification. Usually structured more like a co-op, they have the farmer's best interest in mind. In the Washington, D.C., area, Tuscarora Organic Growers (tog.coop) is one of the biggest. Based in Pennsylvania, the company delivers produce from 45 farmers to retail outlets/supermarkets and restaurants in the Baltimore–Washington metro area 12 months a year.

A CLOSER LOOK

Ingles Markets (ingles-markets.com), a 200-store supermarket chain located in six southeastern states, works directly with local farmers through Appalachian Sustainable Agricultural Project Connections (asapconnections.org), a community-based collaborative that links farmers to markets. At Ingles, local farmers are featured in store-ads, photos, podcasts, articles, and on its website.

While local farmers have to adjust to working with supermarkets, these retail stores also need to make changes. Supermarkets must "re-regionalize" the food system and begin building relationships with local suppliers. Furthermore, these relationships must be communicated to customers, as this sense of connection of farm to food is for most locavores what eating local food is all about. This requires more manpower and resources. It also demands commitment. Some stores are better at this than others. Generally, I've found that the bigger the store, the fewer local products you'll find. You may, however, find more marketing hype. Remember, there are always exceptions.

Local on a National Level

When it comes to buying local, national supermarket chains are usually the last place you'd shop at. Few stores are able to sell local products year-round—most sell it only seasonally—and what local products they do carry are few and far between, amounting to a very small percentage of their business. Change, however, is in the air, as consumer demand has been pushing these stores in a new direction. As a result, many have initiated local programs.

One of the largest and most progressive in this area is the national supermarket chain Whole Foods Market. The Austin, Texas–based chain has been making local foods a priority for the last two decades. Over the years, they have developed explicit guidelines for defining "local" in each of their distribution regions. For example, the definition of local at my Springfield, Virginia, store is 300 miles from the store or an eight-hour or less drive. This covers Pennsylvania; Virginia; parts of North Carolina, New Jersey, and Delaware; and some parts of New York. At the Whole Foods in Denver, Colorado, local means a six-hour or less drive.

Local vendors are touted on their website and blog, and during summer peak season, stores often host "local" promotions, tastings, and cooking classes. In the past, the Whole Foods has also hosted farmers' markets in their parking lots. And recently, the store has initiated a Local Producer Loan Program to help small local businesses.

> **A CLOSER LOOK**
>
> Whole Foods recently announced plans to grow a fruit and vegetable garden on 1 acre of a 6-acre plot at one of its Virginia stores. The goal is to educate consumers about the value of eating local. The store plans to rent out the rest of the land to wannabe farmers.

Now other stores are stepping up to the plate. Safeway, one of the top three grocery chains in the country, claims to get nearly a third of its produce nationwide from local/regional growers. In heavy agricultural regions like California, this figure can be even higher, at around 45 percent. Likewise, Walmart, which is Safeway's biggest competitor, aims for 20 percent of the fruits and vegetables stocked during the summer months to be local—meaning produced in the same state the store is located. Both stores are also making a big push into organics as well.

Regional Characters

Many regional stores are also jumping into the local farming scene. On a regional level, working with local farmers is much easier because of the smaller area you deal with. Much depends on the type of regional grocery store itself, including its philosophy on local, commitment to building relationships, and location in the country, for developing a win-win strategy.

Take, for example, Hannaford Supermarkets, a 171-store operation in Scarborough, Maine. Their successful "Close to Home" program connects local farms with consumers via an in-store magazine called *Close to Home*, which highlights local vendors and provides recipes to consumers. They also hired a local sourcing specialist.

To build on this program, in 2009, Hannaford launched Keep Local Farms, a broad educational program aimed at supporting local dairy farmers in New England. They're also partnering with universities and health-care providers in the local community.

Some regional stores have had local programs in place all along and are now just stepping them up or expanding them to meet demand. This is the case with Wegman's, a New York–based company with 70 stores in Pennsylvania, New York, Maryland, New Jersey, and Virginia. Twenty years ago, Wegman's started a "Locally Grown Produce" program, which now lists more than 1,200 local grower-suppliers of fruits and vegetables.

Local Champions: Small Chains and Independents

If you do go to a supermarket, small chains and independently owned operations are where you'll have the most luck finding locally grown, raised, and prepared foods. In fact, many have been sourcing local products all along, and now they're just expanding their efforts.

Size, of course, is the main reason these stores stayed close to home, and with fuel costs rising, this makes even more sense. Many pride themselves on building strong relationships with local suppliers as well as customers. Balls Food Stores, which operates 12 Hen House Markets and 17 Price Chopper stores in the Kansas City area, has a close, long-term relationship with Good Natured Family Farms, which supplies locally produced meat, poultry, dairy products, and produce. Gooseberries Fresh Food Market, an independently owned single grocery store in Burlington, Wisconsin, boasts dozens of Wisconsin-state products via "A Taste of Door County" and other programs.

How Do You Know It's Local?

How do you know if a product is local? Look for the signs. Nearly all local produce in conventional supermarkets is heavily promoted with signs, posters, placards, or banners. Sometimes stores will include the name of the farm where the produce comes from, including town and the number of miles the food traveled to get to the store.

I've also seen stores place big posters of maps of the area in the produce section. These maps pinpoint each local farm, listing the operation by name and the crops it supplies. This works particularly well if you live in a region where several states are close by. For instance, in my northern Virginia Safeway, local produce comes from farms located in Pennsylvania, Maryland, New Jersey, New York State, and Delaware.

Locally sourced prepared items like jams, jellies, or pickles may be harder to find. Occasionally, these items are stocked together, in a local section, but more often they're simply sprinkled throughout the store.

Because there's no set definition for "local," ask the store manager exactly what "local" means in that store. After all, what's local to one store may not be local to another. Some stores measure local strictly by the distance food travels, which can vary from 100 miles, to 250 miles, to 400 miles. Another store may categorize local by time, such as how long it takes to drive from the farm to the store. Still others choose to buy only within the same state.

This can vary even within store chains, as mentioned with Whole Foods. "Local" for a chain store in New Jersey can be different from "local" in a chain store in a bigger, more rural state like Oklahoma, which may have a broader definition.

Search for Seasonal Items

Most of the local items supermarkets carry are fruits and vegetables, so pay particular attention to foods sold in the produce department. The best time to look for these items is during peak summer season. Don't expect that just because the store carries local items, it's July or August, and you live in Georgia that it will be selling Georgia peaches. Read labels and signs carefully!

Also be aware that the "local season" for stores is a short one, usually much shorter than even at your local farmers' market. Thus, local plums, apples, or berries may only be available for a week or two before stores switch back to more conventional produce (likely from California) or imported brands.

Often, buying is influenced not as much by what's in season or available but by the procedures and policies in place, as well as the agriculture of the region. For instance, one national store I frequent consistently offers local meats, dairy, and eggs, yet local produce even in June and most of July (when farmers' markets are in full swing) is sparse. This year it didn't kick in until August and then it was only for one month.

KEEP YOUR DISTANCE

Signs and banners promoting "local" don't always translate into local products on the shelf. Many times these signs simply state local store philosophies or principles. Always read the fine print, and don't assume it's local unless it says so and tells you where.

Keep in mind that seasonal items can also relate to prepared products like honey, salsas, dips, and spreads. Interesting or unusual labels can tip you off that these products are local, but not always. What should you do? Read, read, read!

Remember, too, that large, one-stop-shopping stores are home to thousands of products, and local items represent only a small percentage of that mix. So don't get upset if these stores don't carry as much local produce as you expect or if they're not familiar with the origins of their food. It's only recently that they've been carrying local food at all, so think positive!

Don't Forget Dairy, Meat, and Eggs

Depending on what part of the country you live in, some supermarkets near you may carry local eggs, milk, cheese, and even meat. Generally, you're more likely to find these types of local products if you live in dairy states like Pennsylvania, New York, and Wisconsin; near Amish communities; or in cattle country like Colorado or Montana.

Here again, be sure to read the fine print on the label. This tells you specifically where (city and state) the company that produced the product resides. Sometimes only a distributor is listed. This tells you where the product was processed or shipped from, but it doesn't tell you where the actual farm is. In this case, you might want to ask a manager or the buyer, but don't be surprised if he or she doesn't know. Many managers are far removed from the buying process.

Also remember that at the supermarket level, you may be able to find out where the product comes from, but you still don't know anything about how the animal was treated or raised other than what the package label tells you. If this is a concern for you, you may want to stay away from these products or do a little more investigating on your own before you buy. Some of these places do have websites, so that could be your first research spot.

What About Price?

The prices on local produce in supermarkets can be all over the board. Because large chains buy in large quantities and set up long-term agreements with packers and distributors, conventional produce is cheap. That's not usually the case for local produce.

Due to the fact that it's more labor-intensive to produce and sold in smaller quantities, local produce usually starts off at a higher price than conventional produce. Add on the cost of shipping, marketing, and other middleman costs, and you can see why local produce is more expensive than conventional—and in some cases, often higher than that same produce sold at local farmers' markets.

On the other hand, with the rise of "local" in big businesses like Walmart, you may see prices dropping. Walmart got interested in local a few years ago, after the "local" trend had picked up steam and showed no signs of stopping. About that same time, one of the executives came upon a 1920s picture of a thriving apple orchard in a town only a few miles away from the Arkansas-based company headquarters. The find was surprising. For decades, Arkansas cash crops have consisted of only two plants: tomatoes and grapes.

Since then, Walmart has begun to resurrect these cash crops of the past, creating more diversity, stronger local agricultural regions, and even bigger markets. The result is Walmart's Heritage Agriculture Program (walmartstores.com/Sustainability/10378.aspx), an initiative designed to promote local products. The program encourages farms within a day's drive of its warehouses to grow crops for them. This drastically cuts down on the food miles.

While the Heritage Agriculture program and the sustainability index (another program designed to provide customers with more knowledge about the products they buy) are both noble endeavors, considering Walmart's past business practices and possible *greenwashing*, many people are adopting a wait-and-see attitude. Here's where time will tell.

LOCAL LINGO

Greenwashing is a deceptive marketing practice where companies put an environmentally friendly spin on their product or policies when it is actually not the case.

Quality Counts but It's Not Perfect

When it comes to buying local produce in supermarket stores, whether convention or natural ones like Whole Foods, quality is still an issue.

Unlike farmers' markets, where you can talk directly to the grower to find out about conditions of the crop, effects of weather, etc., at grocery stores, you're still several steps away from knowing exactly how that produce was grown and picked.

Plus, grocery store products and especially produce must be packaged, handled, and stored a certain way (i.e., sized in boxes). Sometimes this process isn't done correctly and damages result, affecting the quality and taste of the produce. For all these reasons, I find the quality of local produce at supermarkets inconsistent.

Unfortunately, you usually don't know the quality of your produce until after you buy it. At farmers' markets, you can taste and feel the food. At supermarkets, that's not the case. Many times they're packaged so you can't touch the produce either. So it all comes down to how comfortable you are with taking that risk.

Specialty Stores

Specialty stores—like natural food stores, health food stores, and organic stores—focus on a specific niche market. Most of these types of stores focus on healthy, natural food, and locally produced products are often a natural fit. Ask the store manager if he or she works with any local producers.

Another reason why local food may be more apt to appear in these stores is because small specialty stores tend to be more community-oriented. What better way to support the community than by selling the wares of local producers?

Let's face it, supermarkets and retail stores are a fact of life that's largely unavoidable. Even if you're a dedicated locavore, you probably won't stop shopping there. So you must be a smart shopper. Decide on what type of store you want to shop at, and seek out local foods whenever you can. Read labels, ask questions, and be flexible.

Remember, quality and price may not be exactly what you want or expect, but this is all part of the shopping experience. Take comfort in knowing that whatever you do is better than nothing. Whether you buy most of your foods local all year long, buy local only in the summer season, or buy only certain local foods, you're still making a difference.

The Least You Need to Know

- Although local food is now appearing in big supermarkets, don't expect stores to have a wide selection just yet. Most times, only seasonal items are stocked.
- What a conventional grocery store considers "local" depends on the store or even chain's policy and can vary by store and location.
- Local foods aren't any cheaper at supermarkets, and in some cases, they may be more expensive than what you'll find at local farmers' markets.
- The quality of local foods carried in supermarkets isn't necessarily any better or worse than conventional foods.
- Specialty food stores are another venue for finding local food.

The Homegrown Advantage

Chapter 12

In This Chapter

- Why start a garden?
- The ABCs of growing your own food
- Learning to compost
- Being an urban gardener
- Indoor options

What could be more local than growing your own fruits and vegetables in your own backyard? To walk outside, rummage through a few plants, and leave with an armload of produce for today's lunch or dinner means you'll feast on incredibly fresh, incredibly satisfying, and incredibly delicious meals. I've been gardening for nearly two decades, and I still get a thrill from seeing that first tomato, first zucchini, or first cucumber blossom from just a little flower.

But gardening isn't all fun. It takes time, patience, and hard work—along with a little help from Mother Nature—to nurture a plant into producing fruit. And although having a plot of fertile land is ideal, it isn't mandatory for having a successful garden. In this chapter, I teach you the basic steps of starting a food garden (that includes vegetables, fruits, berries, and herbs) and the many benefits it offers. I also discuss the numerous options for growing your own food in suburban, rural, or city neighborhoods.

No matter where you live, managing a garden can be a rewarding, meaningful, and fruitful endeavor in more ways than one. It also doesn't matter whether you've never planted a seed or you're a master gardener. When springtime rolls around, everyone's on level ground. So roll up your sleeves and get ready to get dirty!

Vegetable Gardens Gaining Ground

Although gardening has always been a favorite pastime among Americans, lately more and more people are breaking ground—literally. Vegetable gardens in particular have seen a huge rise in popularity, with good reason.

First and foremost, there's taste. The superior taste of fresh food raised in a garden is, by far, the primary motivating factor for most gardeners, followed by quality—nothing is as fresh as right out of the garden. But there's more.

Recent outbreaks of food-borne illness in produce have many people concerned about food safety. The pesticides and other chemicals used to get rid of pests or to make conventional produce grow bigger, better, and faster is also an issue. If you go organic, with no pesticides or herbicides, you don't have to worry about this when feeding your family homegrown food. Even if you do opt to use some of these products, you can control the type and the amount you use. Therefore, you know exactly what's in your food and how it was grown and handled. This is particularly important for people with young children.

Gardening also gives you the chance to spend time outdoors and keeps you active. Digging a garden is a great way to get exercise, and even weeding burns calories. It relieves stress, and for families, vegetable gardening is a perfect group activity, bringing people together for a common goal. Best of all, there are no age barriers. Everyone from the youngest toddler to the oldest teenager can still help pick, water, or weed. Many parents use gardening as a way to educate their children about where food comes from and how it grows, fostering in them an appreciation for land and labor as well as creating the next generation of locavores.

A CLOSER LOOK

According to the National Gardening Association (NGA), 41 million households grew edible foods like vegetables, fruits, berries, or herbs in 2009—that's up 14 percent from the previous year, when only 36 million households planted gardens.

Gardening allows you to grow foods you can't get elsewhere, even at farmers' markets. For instance, who knew broccoli leaves could be just as delicious as the stalk? Or that squash blossoms, a rare treat so delicate they rarely make it to market, are so easily gathered in the early morning? These are foods only a gardener can love.

A Gratifying Experience

For locavores, backyard gardening has even stronger appeal, driven by the connection between land and sustenance. You can't get any closer to food than this!

There's also a sense of getting back to basics. Whole, natural food right out of the garden requires little fussing in the kitchen and is often simply served unadorned, like fresh roasted beets with a sprinkle of thyme, grilled eggplant slices brushed with garlicky olive oil, or thick slices of tomato dressed with only a dash of salt. With a little prep, garden fare can create quick, easy, and in many cases, often a memorable meal.

Dig deeper, and you'll find people who eat local enjoy their vegetable, fruit, or herb garden for more than just what it produces. Certainly watching plants grow from tiny seedlings to full-blown vines or tall, bushy shrubs heavy with produce inspires feelings of pride and accomplishment. In fact, in this service-oriented culture, many of us jump at the chance to actually be "productive," but gardening is also the means as well as the end.

To be a successful vegetable gardener is to work alongside Mother Nature, with all her whims and unpredictable fancies, adapting and adjusting as you move ahead. It also requires you to understand the land you live on, the soil, your climate, and your seasons. For people who care about eating local, this step is crucial because it ensures a sustainable and healthy food system for years to come. It's also a challenge many people are eager to face.

Money in Your Pocket

Let's face it. Buying fresh food can be expensive. Raising your own food in a backyard garden is cheaper. In 2009, households with food gardens spent on average only $74 a year. And although yields can vary tremendously, on average, the National Gardening Association (NGA; garden.org) estimates you can produce about ½ pound of produce per square foot of garden. Most gardens run about 600 square feet so that gives you a yield of about 300 pounds of vegetables. Even for a small garden like mine, which is only about 150 square feet, this amounts to about 75 pounds of produce. At about $2 a pound, that's a cost savings of $150!

Of course, you have to add in extra costs like time, labor, and water, but even so, you're still looking at a considerable savings. Furthermore, the longer you garden, the better you get at it, so your yields will likely increase and your costs decrease the more experience you gain.

Consider, too, that for the cost of only a few dollars' worth of seeds, you can buy heirloom plants and specialty produce, like fancy mesclun mix. At markets and grocery stores, this type of produce has a much higher price tag than conventional versions. Plus, yields, particularly for gourmet greens, are high, so you may find yourself having enough to give away.

> **NATIVE KNOWLEDGE**
>
> Choose your crops wisely. Depending on where you live, some plants are more productive than others. For instance, if you live in the Northwest, chances are corn probably won't produce big yields for you, but berries, on the other hand, will thrive. Check out your local state extension service to see what grows best in your area.

Some vegetables and fruits, like asparagus, strawberries, and artichokes, have high initial investments but big payoffs down the road. Keep this in mind when you're budgeting. Remember, too, that extra produce can be frozen, canned, or dried for use later during the off season, shaving even more money off your food budget.

Backyard Gardening

For rural or suburban dwellers who have a large yard or who have access to a plot of land, backyard gardens are ideal. Where you locate your backyard garden depends on how much land you have and the lay of that land. What you plant there, when you plant it, and how much you plant are all your own personal decisions, as is how you decide to tend it. Every garden is different as it represents the individuality of the gardener.

Every garden is also different as it represents different climates, soil, and geography. It's easy to see this if you compare a garden grown in New York to one in Arizona, but subtle microclimates can exist even within short distances. This is the reason why one year my garden may flourish while my neighbor's garden only 50 feet away falters even though we both tend them regularly.

Basic Needs

Some factors you can't control or predict—frost in June, a disease that kills your basil plants, or an animal that chews down your lettuce to a stub. But all things being equal, your main goal is to have happy, healthy plants you can easily tend to. Here are a few other things to keep in mind:

Sun. The first time I planted a garden, I was so excited about having a plot of fertile land I didn't pay attention to all the nearby trees. My poor garden was shaded nearly all day, and consequently, the plants suffered terribly. Most plants grow best with six to eight hours of good sun.

Soil. Healthy soil is essential for healthy plants. If it's your first time gardening, you'll probably have to spend a good bit of time getting your soil up to snuff, especially if you live in an area with poor-quality dirt. Most gardeners treat their soil with *organic matter* like *compost* or *aged manure* and/or topsoil or potting soil. Be sure your soil has good drainage, too, so your plants aren't sitting in a soggy mess. (I talk more about soil later in this chapter.)

> **LOCAL LINGO**
>
> **Organic matter** refers to decomposed living matter. This can be plant matter—straw, wood chips, leaves, kitchen scraps, or grass clippings—or animal matter, usually in the form of manure. **Compost** is plant material that's further decomposed by microorganisms to make a rich, soil-like material. **Aged manure** is dung from cows, sheep, goats, and other animals. It must be aged (allowed to sit and rot) for several months before using.

Easy access. You need easy access to your garden so you'll be motivated to take care of it and for watering, so be sure a good water source is located nearby. Usually, having a garden you can see from your kitchen or house window or one that's only a few steps away is best. This not only makes your life easier but allows you to enjoy the pleasures of gardening, keep an eye on what's growing, and reminds you to take care of it when life gets hectic.

Think small. When it comes to gardening, bigger isn't necessarily better, especially if you're just a beginner. Start small and build on your success. Choose a size garden that's manageable—100 square feet is a good beginner plot—taking into account the work involved not only in preparing and planting your garden but also harvesting the crops. If you plant six zucchini plants, you'd better be prepared to make zucchini bread, give some away, or host zucchini dinner parties. While not every season will give you a stellar crop, this is one case where it's better to overestimate than under-estimate. This way you're ready if you do get overloaded. If you do want to expand, you may want to consider two smaller plots rather than one large one because smaller plots are easier to manage.

Consider a fence. If your garden backs up to woods or if you have a lot of wildlife in your area, you should think about putting up a fence. There's nothing worse than waking up to find all your hard work has been chewed down to a stub by a hungry animal. A fence also prevents pets or young children from walking into your garden.

Plan out everything ahead of time. Most gardeners know what they're going to plant, how much, and where they're going to plant it before they drop one seed into the ground. Do some research and talk to other gardeners before you break ground. Then sketch out your ideal garden on paper. The process will make the actual gardening go much more smoothly.

Start with the Soil

Healthy gardens start with healthy soil. All soil is made up of several different layers of organic materials. Knowing what type of soil you have helps you better manage your treatment of it. It can also influence what types of plants you choose. Ideally, you want soil with enough texture, structure, and nutrients so plant roots can grow, air can pass through, and water can drain … but not too fast.

Here are the kinds of soil you're likely to find:

Clay. Clay soil is hard and rock solid. It absorbs water very slowly, has poor drainage, and usually becomes waterlogged quickly and easily. Because it's so dense and lacks air, it's difficult for plant roots to grow. To improve clay soil, you need to break it up and add lots of organic matter, like compost, peat moss, and well-rotted leaves.

Sandy. Sandy soil is just about the opposite of clay soil. The dirt is thin and resembles sand. It lacks structure and texture. As with clay, your best solution is to add organic matter to fill in the gaps.

Chalky. Chalky soil is too alkaline and tends to have lots of stones, which allow water to drain too quickly and doesn't allow your plants to get the nutrients they need. It also may lack some essential nutrients. To this type of soil, you need to add lime to adjust the pH (if your soil is too acidic, you would need to add sulfur), organic matter to help build structure and texture, and fertilizer or nutrients to give the plants what they need to grow.

Loamy. This is the best kind of soil for gardening. It's actually a combination of sand, silt, and clay. It crumbles easily, is home to an array of soil-dwelling insects and worms, and absorbs water readily. If you're lucky enough to have loamy soil, you may only want to consider minimal treatments.

Before planting, turn your soil at a depth of 6 to 10 inches so it's light and airy. You can do this either by digging it up yourself or hiring someone to rototill it. (A rototiller is a machine that tills, or turns over, soil.)

Think About Composting

Composting is the practice of turning organic waste such as kitchen scraps, grass clippings, mulched leaves, and even manure into soil. The practice is as old as the hills, but until recently, it was mostly done by farmers in rural areas. Now many urban and suburban gardeners are doing their own composting. Not only is compost good for the soil, but it's good for the environment, too. Compost can significantly reduce your carbon footprint and waste, meaning less garbage going into landfills. Aside from that, it's easy, cheap, and becoming more and more accessible to city-dwellers and suburbanites.

In addition to the old-fashioned way of digging a hole or building a bin to let nature do her work, you can buy a number of different types of composters, ranging anywhere from $50 to $500. For urbanites, electric composters that fit under a sink are available, allowing you to compost right in your kitchen.

> **NATIVE KNOWLEDGE**
>
> People who want to compost but don't have the time or space to do it can now hire a service like the Compost Cab in Washington, D.C. (compostcab.com). For a few dollars a week, the cab will come to your house and haul off your scraps, delivering it to a local compost. In return, you can eventually get some dirt, but many people are satisfied knowing they're helping the environment and promoting sustainable agriculture.

Designing Your Garden

With the right layout, small gardens can yield big returns and large gardens can be manageable and productive, as well as a work of beauty. For most gardens, you'll need to create paths to help you maneuver your way around. This allows you to haul compost, pull weeds, and harvest your crops easily. It also reduces your chance of harming any plants or packing down the soil as you walk among the plants. Packed soil has poor drainage and aeration.

Where to plant is another consideration. Think about the size of the plants and how they grow. You may want to put tall plants in the back and smaller ones up front so they all get enough sun. Be sure to give larger plants like zucchini more space, while tall and slim plants can be nestled closer together.

When it comes to garden layout, you have several style options:

Traditional rows. In this design, plants are placed directly into the ground in a single row, usually in a flat bed. This is the most common style, but it also uses the most space because plants must be far apart.

Wide rows. Wide rows can range anywhere from 2 to 4 feet across and let you cram more plants in a small space. Each row can have several rows of plants or be staggered. Beware, however, that not all plants do well sown close together. Some do better in traditional rows.

Square-foot gardening. In this method, the garden is divided into 4-foot squares and each of the squares is further divided into 1-foot squares. Each square is designated for a specific plant, and the seeds are staggered to get the most from the small space.

Square-foot gardening is generally best for raised beds. Raised beds are mounds of dirt (about 12 inches deep) contained by four wooden boards in the shape of a square or rectangle. The beauty of a raised bed is that it doesn't require any digging, although you'll likely have to buy dirt or planting soil.

> **NATIVE KNOWLEDGE**
>
> It pays to buy good-quality gardening tools. The right tools will make your life a lot easier. They'll also last longer so you don't have to purchase new tools every season.

Organic Backyard Gardening

Organic gardens don't use pesticides, herbicides, and synthetic fertilizers. But more than what they don't do is what they do! Organic gardening uses materials and practices that enhance the natural balance of ecological systems, working in harmony to create a sustainable ecosystem. In this way, organic gardens strive to be an integrated part of the whole environmental system.

While organic gardening does have many benefits—environmentally, nutrition-wise (although there's still some debate about this), and cost-wise—it's not for everyone.

Organic gardening takes more time and more work than conventional gardening. This is mainly due to taking care of your soil, usually with homegrown compost. (Buying compost can be expensive.) You also need to learn how to organically manage pests or diseases, if they arise. Organic gardens produce lower yields, at least at first. Organic gardening requires you to think long-term. Many of these natural methods take years to achieve.

Organic gardening doesn't have to be an all-or-nothing approach. Many people use a mix of both organic and conventional methods to suit their lifestyle and budget.

What to Plant

When it comes to choosing plants for your garden, I have only two pieces of advice: grow what you like to eat, and grow plants that thrive in your region. No use planting a dozen jalapeño peppers if you don't like spicy food. On the other hand, even if you love Brussels sprouts, this cool-weather plant may not fair well if you live in the Deep South. For best results—and for an interesting dinner table—aim for a variety of edible plants.

You also want to consider succession planting, or planting different vegetables that mature at different rates in the same space. This keeps your garden productive from spring through fall. How does it work? Plant cool-weather plants like peas or spinach in the early spring. Both these vegetables harvest quickly, leaving you enough time to grow peppers or cucumbers in the same space afterward.

Another gardening method you might try is intercropping. With this space-saving technique, you plant different plants with different maturing times together. A perfect example of this is the "three sisters"—corn, beans, and squash. Native Americans planted these three vegetables together in the same hill. As the cornstalk grows, it acts as a pole for the bean vine to climb, and the squash, a low-growing plant, prevents weeds by covering the ground.

No Space? No Problem!

Millions of Americans live in apartments or condominiums where outdoor space is strictly regulated or even nonexistent. But just because you live in a city doesn't mean you can't grow your own herbs, vegetables, and even fruits. This is where container gardens come in.

Creative Container Gardening

Container gardens can be practically anything—big pots, boxes, buckets, pails, windowsill planters, or just about anything else that can hold dirt and has good drainage.

What you plant in container gardens is limited only by the size of the container and your imagination. Many people opt for herb gardens, but with a little bit of ingenuity, you can grow a variety of vegetables—think tomatoes, peppers, green beans, salad greens, carrots, and beets, to name a few—and even some fruits. Dwarf or bush varieties work best.

Container gardens are also ideal for people who want to have a vegetable garden but don't want to dig up their backyard.

For city dwellers, finding a place to put your container garden can be challenging. Many locavores, however, have come up with some surprising and creative places:

- Window ledges
- Fire escapes
- Balconies
- Rooftops (Some rooftop gardens can be pretty elaborate!)
- Front steps

A CLOSER LOOK

A popular trend in big cities, guerrilla gardening is the unauthorized cultivation of plants or vegetable crops on vacant public or private property. Many locavores see it as making good use of wasted space.

Up, Up, and Away

If you're short on space or just want to get more bang for your gardening buck, consider vertical gardening. A vertical garden is basically any vegetable, fruit, or herb plant that goes straight up (or down) from pots, baskets, or buckets. These plants can be hanging off a deck or sitting on a balcony or patio. Usually all they require is some stakes, trellises, or fences and some string to tie up the plants.

Growing vegetable plants upside down is particularly popular with tomatoes. If you check online, you can probably find dozens of tutorials instructing you how to do it. Upside-down tomato kits are even available for you to purchase.

In addition to tomatoes, here are some other vegetables you can grow upside down:

Cucumbers	Peppers
Eggplants	Potatoes
Grapes	Small melons
Green beans	Strawberries

Really, almost any plant can be trained to grow vertically with only a few exceptions such as zucchini and plants producing heavy crops like watermelon.

To really maximize space, on the top of your upside-down garden, plant shallow-growing vegetables like herbs, lettuces, and radishes.

Staying Indoors

Whether it's because of space, weather, or simply because they like to be surrounded by their own locally grown food in the comfort of their own home, many people are trying their hand at indoor gardening.

Unlike outdoor gardening, where Mother Nature usually calls the shots, when it comes to indoor gardening, you're in charge. From the lighting, to the climate, soil, and water, you provide everything for your plants. The advantage, of course, is that if you do it well, you can usually have luscious, homegrown produce and fresh herbs year-round.

Herbs have a long history of being grown indoors particularly during the wintertime, but many other plants can do well indoors, too. Because of space constraints, small plants do best, so look for dwarf varieties of most fruits and even some vegetables. Take into account the needs of the plant as well as the space it needs. For instance, tomatoes and peppers love light and heat, so they do best in a bright, sunny, warm place, while plants like Swiss chard and beets aren't so fussy.

Growing your own food can be as simple as having a few potted plants on your deck or balcony or as elaborate as a 40×40-foot garden filled to the brim with dozens of crop-bearing plants. Whatever way you choose to go, remember that having a garden can be a memorable, rewarding, and lucrative experience.

The Least You Need to Know

- Growing your own food in a backyard garden is an ideal way to eat local; save money; and enjoy fresh, quality food.
- You have many different styles of gardening available to choose from. Always aim for a wide variety of plants.
- Composting is an environmentally friendly and economical way to promote sustainable agriculture, even if you don't have a garden.
- For people who don't have access to land, container gardens offer the best solution.
- Many locavores take advantage of wild foods that grow in their region by food foraging.

Food from the Wild

In This Chapter

- The benefits of eating wild edibles
- Learning to forage in a modern world
- Discovering wild food sources
- The perks of urban gleaning

Eating local means taking advantage of the bounty of food available on the land where you live. Certainly this means the food that's domestically grown and raised on nearby farms and ranches, and of course, it's also the food you've labored over in your own garden. But what about the edible plants, seeds, nuts, tubers, and animals Mother Nature provides without any help? These wild, undomesticated foods, untouched by human hands, like huckleberries, dandelion greens, daylilies, ramps, and fiddlehead ferns, are ripe for the picking. And many locavores are including these types of foods in their diet, too, thanks to a revival of one of the oldest practices in the world—foraging.

Foraging, the art of finding and eating wild foods, does more than just provide a variety of delectable edibles growing right in your own backyard. It connects you with nature, the environment, and the seasons, not to mention the fact that you can get loads of foods you probably won't find elsewhere for free.

But foraging isn't something you can do lightly. It's not as simple as going to the market, visiting a farm, or even planting a garden. Foraging takes skill, knowledge, and experience, and a good guide to show you the ropes is an absolute requirement.

In this chapter, I discuss why foraging is enjoying a comeback (thanks to locavores), foraging etiquette, and what kinds of wild foods you can expect to find in the wild. Then I give you some tips on how to expand your foraging know-how. Finally, I cover urban gleaning, a type of domestic foraging.

You'll be surprised at how much food you can find if you just open your eyes and look around you!

Why Forage?

When I was a girl, every spring my father and grandfather would take my sister and me to the country to forage for cardunas. Like most foragers, my grandfather knew just where to go to pick these delicacies and had several special spots he frequented. If these spots were on someone's property, he would always ask the owner first if we could take the plants. Inevitably, the owner would say yes, shaking his head wondering why we'd want his weeds but still happy to get rid of them. My grandfather would smile, and we did, too, because the owner didn't know what he was missing. We loved cardunas (which I would later find out were actually the stalk of the wild burdock plant), and we couldn't imagine anyone not liking them.

> **KEEP YOUR DISTANCE**
>
> If you want to forage on someone else's land, be sure to contact the landowner first to obtain the proper permission before starting. The same holds true for public places like national and state parks. Some prohibit visitors from taking anything outside the boundaries of the park.

Like most wild edibles, the only way to get the cardunas, and many other vegetables, is by foraging. In this respect, foraging can introduce you to a wealth of new foods you wouldn't otherwise get a chance to try—and they're all right in your own backyard (or close by). Elderberries, mulberries, salal berries, wild leeks, wild garlic, purslane, wild turnip, sorrel, and garlic mustard—these are all forage finds.

If domestic or cultivated versions of these plants are available (and they usually aren't), they often pale in comparison to the wild versions. For example, years ago at a specialty market, I happened to find something labeled burdock. The vegetable had big, thick stalks that were about twice the size and thickness of a large celery stalk. It was also pale green in color. The wild burdock of my youth was dark green in color with a rosy tinge. The best ones (and most of them) were pencil-thin, like asparagus. Alas, the taste was disappointing as well—bland and mild with only a hint of the earthiness and intensity of the wild ones my grandfather picked.

If you have an adventurous palate, wild foods are something you'll want to try. Most are unusual and interesting in taste. Many have a stronger, more robust flavor and color than what you'd find in conventional markets. And because so many factors can affect sweetness, the sweetness of wild fruits can vary tremendously depending on time of year and plant—from explode-in-your-mouth wow! to only slightly sweet. On the other hand, other sensory attributes like pungency, tartness, nuttiness, lemony-ness, and others, are usually heightened as well.

In addition to their unique taste, wild edible foods are more often than not considered gourmet-quality special delicacies to be savored and enjoyed. The cardunas we picked each year were definitely a lot of work. They had to be peeled, boiled, breaded, and fried, yet every year we looked forward to them as a special treat. They were a culinary treasure we appreciated and admired—a sentiment shared by nearly all foragers about their finds.

When it comes to a healthy diet, many wild foods are nutritional standouts. This is especially true of the numerous wild greens available. The compounds that give them their distinct taste and color are often the ones that also protect us from diseases.

More Than Just the Food

Gathering food from the wild is more than just finding free food—although that does help lower the monthly food bill. For most foragers, it's an adventure in the great outdoors, a challenge that culminates with the reward of a sweet cherry or luscious green. Although most experienced foragers usually have an idea of what to expect and where to find it, there's always a thrill when something surprising happens—which it often does—like coming upon a ripe blackberry bush or fetching some wild plums when you're looking for something else.

There's also a sense of accomplishment, of pride even, when carrying your loot home. You're able to feed yourself, to be self-sufficient, even if you picked only a few things from the land that surrounds you.

Finally, foraging heightens your sense of the seasons and increases your understanding of the region. This fosters a greater respect for the land and what it produces. Unlike farmers, who work hard planting, sowing, and tending their plants to get their crop, foragers don't do anything to produce the food they get. Therefore, they see their edibles as more like a gift from nature—something to be cherished, enjoyed, and appreciated.

Rediscovering a Lost Art

Long before man learned to plant seeds or domesticate animals, he was a hunter-gatherer, searching out his food from the local forests, mountains, streams, and rivers around him. So you could say foraging is in our genes. Although we no longer forage to survive, up until just a few short decades ago, people still gathered wild edibles to supplement their food supply or celebrate a special season or delicacy. At least they could do it if they wanted to.

Today, with the advent of industrial agriculture and a food supply system far removed from the people who use it, foraging has become so foreign to most people that few people look beyond the supermarket for their food. Without the knowledge and experience of generations past, it's easy to lose faith in our instincts and ability to recognize even the most obvious edible plants. Some people, particularly city dwellers, have even become fearful of Mother Nature.

To overcome any fears, remember that gathering or foraging wild edible foods is not as crazy as it sounds. First of all, wild foods are free—an attractive incentive in the current economy. And although you can't survive on foraged food alone, it can provide a nice and very inexpensive supplement to your other produce. Second, foraging is easier than you think, if you know what to do. Spend some time with an experienced forager. He can put many of your concerns at ease. Finally, relax and enjoy nature, fresh air, the outdoors, and getting exercise. As you become more comfortable and knowledgeable about gathering foods in the wild, you'll see the potential for food everywhere.

A CLOSER LOOK

Foraging is a hot trend among foodies as well as locavores. According to epi-log on epicurious.com, foraging is one of the top 10 food trends for 2011. It's actually in the top 5.

Facts About Foraging

It doesn't matter whether you're a new forager just starting out or an experienced gatherer with years of practice under your belt, all foragers follow some golden rules, without question.

Safety First

Always be absolutely sure of a food before you eat it. If you have any doubt that a plant might not be the one you think it is, don't eat it. Better to be safe than sorry.

Get a Good Guidebook

Foraging guidebooks tell you exactly how to identify and harvest a plant and include drawings or pictures of each one. Some even tell you how to cook and store the food. A good guidebook is essential for any forager. It can be general or region specific such as plants of Minnesota, California, or New England. I recommend getting one of each. Here are some general ones:

1. *Edible Wild Plants: Wild Foods from Dirt to Plate (The Wild Food Adventure Series, Book 1)* by John Kallas (Gibbs Smith, 2010)

2. *Guide to Wild and Useful Plants* by Christopher Nyerges (Chicago Review Press, 1999)

3. *Identifying and Harvesting Edible and Medicinal Plants in Wild (and Not So Wild) Places* by Steve "Wildman" Brill and with Evelyn Dean (HarperPaperbacks, 1994)

4. *Nature's Garden: A Guide to Identifying, Harvesting, and Preparing Edible Wild Plants* by Samuel Thayer (Forager's Harvest Press, 2010)

5. *Stalking the Wild Asparagus* by Euell Gibbons (Hood, Alan C. & Company, Inc., 2005)

6. *The Forager's Harvest: A Guide to Identifying, Harvesting, and Preparing Edible Wild Plants* by Samuel Thayer (Forager's Harvest Press, 2006)

Don't Take Too Much

Don't ever harvest plants that are rare or on the endangered list. For the plants you do harvest, be sure to leave enough so the plant can thrive in the future. Most wild foods have a short season, so timing is important. To ensure you'll have a steady supply of wild foods next year, be sure to follow this forager rule: take half, and leave half.

> **NATIVE KNOWLEDGE**
>
> What should you bring on a hunt? A trowel for digging up roots, a paring knife with a cover, leather gloves, and a basket or cloth grocery bag for carrying your treasures. You also may want to include a pair of scissors or pruning shears.

The majority of the time, foragers strive to not damage or overharvest a plant, but there are a few times when this rule doesn't apply and you can and should take as much as possible. This is the case with edible invasive plants, which tend to take over everything. In this situation, you want to take as much as you want but be careful not to further spread the plant in the process. Edible invasive plants are usually common plants such as the Himalayan blackberry in the Northwest, the Japanese knotweed in the Northeast, and kudzu (otherwise known as "the vine that ate the South") in the Southern part of the United States. You can eat the leaves, flowers, and roots of kudzu.

Start Small

The first time you try a plant, only sample a small amount. Some wild plants are strong tasting and could lead to stomach upset or digestive problems in certain people. Plus, there's always a possibility of a food allergy. If the food fares well after a small taste, you can always eat more next time.

Other Points to Keep in Mind

As you begin to forage on a regular basis, you'll get to know your surroundings. You'll start to recognize signs indicating when a food is ready or almost ready to be picked—the appearance of certain flowers, cracked nuts or seeds on the ground, new shoots or growth, etc.

Be vigilant about discovering a plant's identity, and be sure all the attributes match up. Some plants have toxic lookalikes (think mushrooms) that differ by only one or two things like the shape of a leaf. Remember, too, that just because one part of a plant is edible doesn't mean the entire plant is. For example, rhubarb stalks make a great pie, but the leaves are poisonous. Tomato plants are known for their luscious fruit but the leaves are also toxic.

Season makes a difference, too. Some plants change throughout the season, producing different edible parts at different times. Take the cattail, for example. In early spring, you can cook the shoots, and later in the season, you can gather the flower or harvest its pollen. In winter, some foragers dig up the roots for soup.

Keep track of places and locations of all your forages and the foods you find there. Often you'll come upon a wild plant at the wrong time, either too early or too late in the season. Then your job is to mark the location, either on a GPS, with some type of marker like a stick or a flag, or on a map, so you can return next year or next season. And don't expect all foragers to be forthcoming with where they find their stash. Many don't like to share their secret places and may even go out of the way to hide them.

Be certain of your surroundings. Choose places that haven't been treated with chemicals, pesticides, or weed killers. If you're foraging in the forest, this isn't as likely to be the case. Sometimes, particularly in public areas, government officials will post signs or make announcements when or if they're spraying a certain land. If you live or hunt near a suburban area, this can be more tricky as the manicured lawns often require copious amounts of fertilizers and pesticides. Be sure the foods you're foraging for are pesticide-free.

KEEP YOUR DISTANCE

Beware of edible plants growing near contaminated landfills, polluted streams, conventional farms, or highways. Chances are, they're contaminated with pesticides, herbicides, or lead from car exhaust fumes. Instead, look for less-trafficked areas off the beaten path.

Finally, don't trust other animals. Just because a plant leaf, berry, or fruit has been eaten by a wild animal or bird doesn't mean it's safe for you to eat. Animals and birds have very different digestive systems from humans. You also don't know what happened to that animal after it ate the offending item. Maybe it didn't fare so well.

Get Serious: Take a Class

Food foragers take their job seriously, and rightly so. Eating the wrong plant can lead to severe and sometimes even fatal consequences. Foragers must have an in-depth knowledge of the wild foods that grow in the region. They also need to be able to recognize these foods by sight.

Taking a class from a reputable instructor teaches you where to look for wild foods. While most are found in foothills and forests, edibles can also be spotted in vacant lots, in cracks of sidewalks, and other surprising places in the city. A class will also teach you when to go out. Practiced foragers keep a close eye on the weather and the calendar.

To find a forager, take a class, or attend a tour, check with local colleges, universities, nature centers, or conservatories first to find out what's available. Many websites, blogs, and workshops online can give you information, too. Some well-known foragers travel all over the country giving tours, so don't be put off if there's no one who lives in your area. You may even want to contact the forager directly to find out if he'll be in your town.

To help you get started, check out these sites, many of which also include other foraging resources:

Eat Wild
eatwild.com

Forager's Harvest
foragersharvest.com

Foraging.com
foraging.com

Foraging with the "Wildman" (Steve Brill)
wildmanstevebrill.com

Wild Food Adventures
wildfoodadventures.com

One Man's Weed Is Another Man's ...

What kinds of wild foods are you likely to find foraging? Certainly a large part depends on what part of the country you live in. Even then, so much of what you'll find will vary. But generally, you'll find a plethora of greens or edible weeds in the spring. Many of these, such as lambsquarter, purslane, and dandelion greens, have been made popular by restaurant chefs.

Later in the summer and into the fall, you'll see roots, tubers, and bulbs, like burdock, sunchokes, and ramps; all kinds of fruits (imagine pawpaws, persimmons, or mulberries); plus nuts, seeds, and mushrooms. Berries also run rampant depending on where you live, including the more traditional blackberry, blueberry, and strawberry, as well as more unusual kinds like elderberries, cloudberries, and boysenberries.

For beginner foragers, it's best to stick with foods you feel comfortable with, like common berries, wild leeks, chives, garlic, and wild mustards and greens like purslane or dandelions. Then as you get more experience, you can look for other things.

> **NATIVE KNOWLEDGE**
>
> Use your nose. If a plant looks like a wild onion or wild garlic *and* smells like it, it should be safe to eat. The key is having *both* attributes.

You also don't want to go out alone, at least not at first, so be sure to pair up with another more experienced forager.

Cooking Wild

Last but not least, what should you do with wild foods when you have them? Some foods must be treated a certain way before they can be eaten. For instance, pokeweed must be cooked in several changes of water before eating or it will cause intestinal distress.

Dandelion weed is known for its bitterness, but if you cook it with bacon and bacon fat (as many old-fashioned dishes do), the fat masks the bitter taste. Another option is to boil the dandelions for about four or five minutes before preparing. This removes the bitterness.

Sometimes these cooking tips are incorporated in guidebooks. At other times, you may have do an online search or browse the book section of foraging.com for something. To get you started, here are a couple guidebooks that include cooking tips:

1. *Edible Wild Plants* by John Kallas (Gibbs Smith, 2010).

2. *The Foraging Gourmet* by Katie Letcher Lyle (Morris Publishing Group, 1997).

3. *The Wild Vegan Cookbook: A Forager's Culinary Guide (in the Field or in the Supermarket) to Preparing and Savoring Wild (and Not So Wild) Natural Foods* by Steve Brill (Harvard Common Press, 2010).

Consider, too, that produce isn't the only thing you can forage. Hunting and fishing is also a form of food foraging. (See Chapter 5 for more information on game.) Be sure to check with your state department for licenses and legal requirements before doing this.

Try Urban Gleaning

The main difference between food foraging and urban gleaning is that with food foraging, you're gathering from wild plants, while urban gleaning means you're collecting fruits, berries, or vegetables from domestic, cultivated plants that have already been harvested. The fruits on these plants would otherwise go to waste if they weren't gleaned. You're also gathering these crops from the city or suburbs rather than the country or the wild outdoors. (Some farmers' markets and CSAs also have gleaning programs usually to help the community or provide an extra benefit to their members, but these are not the same as urban gleaning programs.)

Urban gleaning leans toward fruit and berry trees and bushes rather than vegetables. Unintentional plants—like the watermelon or zucchini that cropped up because birds carried over some seeds from a nearby neighbor—also fall into the realm of urban gleaning.

Just Ask

Urban gleaning can be as simple as knocking on a neighbors' door and asking them if you could pick some of the fruit off their tree, or it could be a more formal, organized group of people who descend on an area. Because unharvested fruits fall on the ground and cause an unsightly mess, many private owners welcome those who are willing to clean out their fruit trees.

Over the last few years, urban fruit gleaning programs have been popping up in big cities like San Francisco and Portland as well as all over the country. Networks of fruit exchangers and urban gleaners have been growing, with the appearance of websites like Neighborhood Fruit (neighborhoodfruit.com), a national site that's dedicated to connecting fruit pickers with fruit owners in urban neighborhoods—there are currently 10,000 trees nationwide. Veggie Trader (veggietrader.com) is another. It's your place to trade, buy, and sell local homegrown produce.

Reaping Just Rewards

In some of these programs, gleaners have a specific goal in mind: to spread the wealth. Harvesters are allowed to eat their fill and some even take home a small bounty, but the lion's share is sent to local food banks, shelters, and food centers. In this way, locally grown produce is shared with the community and serves a more positive purpose.

A CLOSER LOOK

Started in 2006, the Portland Fruit Tree Project (portlandfruit.org) is one of the most active in the country and a model for others of its kind. In 2010, they picked more than 25,000 pounds of fruit that would have otherwise gone to waste. The fruit was distributed throughout the community.

There are other motivators, too, like spending a day outside, working together for the common good, and getting to meet other like-minded locavores who care about food.

They come from all walks of life and include all ages, sharing in the work and the wealth with a certain happy camaraderie. These are gleaners.

The Bottom Line

Today, food foraging is no longer part of our day-to-day living, but thanks in part to the local food movement, it's enjoying a comeback, particularly among locavores. While in the past most foraging skills were passed down within families from generation to generation, today's modern forager is more likely to start from scratch learning from nature, books, website, and experience (from other foragers).

Locavores are drawn to foraging because of the bond it forges between man and nature. There's also a sense of accomplishment and satisfaction in being able to gather food from the land around you. From a more practical perspective, foraging saves energy, protects our natural resources by protecting wildlife, and saves you money. It can also fill in the gaps between seasons. Early spring offers a wealth of foraged food before many farmers' markets are up and running.

Urban gleaning, like foraging, does all these things as well. For this reason, dedicated locavores try to incorporate both of these practices into their lifestyle as much as possible.

The Least You Need to Know

- Many locavores take advantage of wild foods that grow in their region by food foraging.
- Wild edibles are all around us and offer a diversity and variety not found elsewhere. However, it takes skill, knowledge, and experience to find them. Always use caution when foraging.
- Cooking wild edible foods can be a bit different from cooking domestically grown foods.
- Many books, websites, classes, and tours are available to teach you the ins and outs of foraging.
- Urban gleaning allows you to harvest fruit that would otherwise go to waste.

Cooking Local

Once you've got all this local food, what do you do with it? Start cooking, of course! Part 4 gives you all the tools you need to manage local meal planning. This includes cleaning and storing your local food so it's ready when you need it, creative cooking methods, and tips for coming up with exciting local menus your family will love. (To help get you started, I've gathered 25 regional recipes in one appendix—Appendix D. These dishes highlight the local foods you'll find in that area.)

Then for when the season's bounty gets overwhelming or if you want a taste of summer during fall and winter, I also explain traditional ways to save and store produce, through old-fashioned preservation techniques.

Learning how to freeze, can, dry, or preserve summer's harvest can stretch out the season and allow you to enjoy these treasures all year long. It also gives you a sense of pride and accomplishment knowing you can feed your family local foods all year long. Now what could be better than that?

Meal Management the Local Way

In This Chapter

- Making your local food last longer
- Favorite food combinations
- Creative cooking ideas
- Managing a local menu year-round

Planning and preparing meals with local foods isn't the same as making dinner from conventional supermarket products. It requires a whole new approach to the way you look at food—and even learning a few new skills.

The good news is, the hard part of your work is already done. You've gotten the freshest, highest-quality local ingredients you could find. Now it's time to turn those ingredients into a delicious, home-cooked meal. This is the fun part! It's also the most time-consuming. Locavores generally spend more time thinking about, planning, and preparing local foods than their nonlocal counterparts. Don't be put off by this. It's time well spent because you'll be consistently rewarded with fresh, healthy, great-tasting meals you'll soon be raving about to all your friends.

You'll also spend more time in the kitchen preparing and cooking these foods. The simple cooking techniques featured in this chapter help culinary novices become more confident and comfortable in the kitchen, ultimately increasing their speed and efficiency. For those who already know their way around a stove, think of it more like a refresher course that can rejuvenate and revitalize your culinary repertoire.

Perhaps the biggest challenge locavores face is coming up with creative and imaginative ways to eat seasonally throughout the year. I give you plenty of ideas for managing your mealtime menus, whether you're faced with the bounty of summer harvest or the leaner, less-familiar fruits and vegetables of the winter months. Plus, I give you lots of motivation and inspiration to get in the kitchen, get cooking, and create fantastic seasonal dinners with whatever you have on hand. You'll be surprised at how imaginative you can be!

Proper Care and Handling

Unlike conventional produce, which is bred for travel and long periods of storage, local produce is usually bought ripe, or close to it. It also doesn't come in any fancy plastic or other kinds of packaging. For this reason, you can't just throw it in the refrigerator and forget about it. On the other hand, because local food spends so little time in transit, meaning it goes from ground to your house in less than 24 hours, it can usually last longer if it's kept refrigerated.

Prep First, Use Later

As soon as you get your local food home, take a few minutes to go through it. Doing this now saves you tons of time later. If the produce is really dirty, wash it; if not, keep it unwashed until you're ready to cook with it. Remember, these foods aren't waxed or coated to extend their shelf life, so treat them gently. Rinse leafy greens, and get rid of any dead leaves or bruised or damaged pieces. Then carefully wrap and properly store everything.

> **KEEP YOUR DISTANCE**
>
> Don't store fresh-picked tomatoes in the refrigerator. Cold temperatures make their flavor fade and taste bland. If you do need to put them in the fridge to prevent them from going bad, take them out about 15 minutes before serving. Bringing them to room temperature restores some of this lost flavor.

Place leafy greens and fresh herbs in a paper towel, seal in a plastic bag or container, and put in the refrigerator so they're ready to use when you want them. Put fruits that need to ripen in a bowl on the counter. When they're ripe, you can move these foods to the refrigerator.

Most vegetables go in the refrigerator produce drawer, but some, like potatoes, onions, garlic, and sweet potatoes, do best in a cool, dry, dark pantry. Berries, grapes, and cut fruits should also go in the fridge. Be sure to keep fruits and vegetables in separate drawers. If you store them together, they can pick up off odors. You don't want your strawberries smelling or tasting like onions! For specifics on which fruits go where, visit the University of California, Davis, Postharvest Technology Research Information Center (homeorchard.ucdavis.edu/FVStorage.pdf).

Keep an Eye on Organic

When you have produce from the farmers' market, or if you belong to a community supported agriculture (CSA), take a look at each piece closely because bugs or worms like to hide in leaves or lurk in small holes. This is particularly important if you buy organic produce because pesticides aren't used to get rid of insects.

Certain vegetables may be more prone to bugs than others, too. Corn is a great example. In late summer, when the weather is hot and humid, corn often attracts worms and bugs, which crawl into the ear. I always shuck and clean my corn as soon as I bring it home. This prevents the worms from feasting on it in the fridge and also makes it easy for me to cook it quickly later.

Preservation Tips

Sometimes weather, season, and even the size of your family dictate the amount of attention you need to give a certain fruit or vegetable.

During green bean season, my CSA provided me with a 2-pound bag of these slender veggies. Upon inspection, I knew the beans wouldn't last but a few days in the refrigerator, so to extend their life, I immediately washed, cleaned, and blanched (partially cooked) the beans in boiling water for about 1 or 2 minutes and then immediately cooled them in ice water for about 30 seconds.

The extra step meant my beans could now be quickly added to dinner meals like tuna niçoise, pesto pasta, or Chinese stir-fry throughout the week. I even bagged up and froze some. Because they were already cooked, they stayed fresher longer and required only minimal prep.

Be Creative

Local cooks are inventive cooks. How else could they deal with mountains of tomatoes during tomato season or scores of peaches in July? Coming up with interesting and appetizing ways to make the same, everyday food appealing day after day (or at least until the season is over), is challenging to be sure, but it's also something you'll get better and better at doing as time goes on.

Despite what some people think, creativity in the kitchen doesn't just happen. It takes time, patience, and a willingness to try new things, not to mention a lot of experimentation and practice. Experience is definitely an advantage here. To spark your imagination and come up with your own creative recipes, try some of these tips:

- Read local food blogs and websites. These offer a ton of new ideas, and their food photography is usually fabulous. (I've listed a few of my favorites in Appendix B.)

- Browse cookbooks and food magazines in the bookstore.

- Go to the library and check out the cookbook selection.

- Visit a farmers' market. The colorful produce often inspires budding chefs.

- Take a cooking class.

- Talk to friends, neighbors, co-workers, and people in your CSA. Offer to share recipes and menu ideas.

- Watch cooking TV shows.

> **NATIVE KNOWLEDGE**
>
> Want to learn to cook but don't have time to go to a class? Do it online. Internet courses enable you to download lesson plans and watch video tutorials. Some courses even use Skype. The best part: you get to prepare a meal right in your own kitchen!

Foods That Go Together, Grow Together

When it comes to deciding what foods to pair together in meals, take a hint from Mother Nature. What grows together in a season goes together, often beautifully. Many fruits and vegetables naturally straddle seasons and may appear at different times in different climates throughout the country, so some of these foods may fall in other categories. For example, beets are typically a spring vegetable, but they can also appear in summer, fall, and even winter. Nevertheless, knowing in general what's available when is a great way to help you make some memorable culinary matches.

Spring: Spring is the season of cooking greens and leafy greens; Salads made from all types of lettuces are a mainstay during this time. Spinach is abundant, too. Dress these salads with sweet spring fruits like sweet cherries, apricots, or strawberries; fresh cow's or goat milk cheeses; and nuts, which are also at their peak.

Cooking greens like Swiss chard and collards are other big players at this time. They're delicious sautéed with green garlic (a young mild garlic plant), beets, and carrots.

Here are some other spring specialties:

- Asparagus and morel mushrooms or eggs (the season for eggs is spring, summer, and early fall)

- All types of peas—sugar snap, snow, and green—which go exceptionally well with crisp radishes or pungent green onions

- Cucumbers and tomatoes, perfect in the Spanish cold soup gazpacho

- Artichokes married with a rich fava bean or avocado dip

- Rhubarb, naturally partnered with sweet strawberries or cherries in pies, tarts, or cobblers

Summer: With so many possible combinations of wonderful vegetables during this time of year, it's hard to pin down just a few. Your best bet here is to turn to ethnic dishes and food flavor combinations specific to your region. For instance, the abundance of sweet and hot peppers, eggplant, tomatoes, and zucchini lends itself to Mediterranean dishes from Italy, Greece, Turkey, and France.

Corn, a prominent ingredient in American cooking, was one of "three sisters" (the other two are squash and beans) Native Americans planted together for hundreds of years—and still do today. Cook them together in soups, stews, and casserole-type dishes with a Southwestern flair. New Englanders and Southerners have their own favorite traditions using these foods as well, like cornbread, corn chowder, corn cakes, and savory corn pudding.

Here are some other interesting summer combinations:

- Steamed potatoes and green beans with fresh herbs

- Okra and tomatoes

- Fresh pea and corn salad tossed with lime juice

- Stone fruits like peaches and plums mixed with berries in pancakes, cakes, and tarts

- Melon salsa (melon and cilantro)

Fall: While some fall foods, like fall tomatoes, are holdovers from summer, many are not. These foods tend to be on the heavy side:

- Cauliflower and broccoli medleys

- Butternut squash baked with apples or pears

- Sweet potatoes and chestnuts

- Roasted fennel or walnuts and Brussels sprouts

- Kale and white beans

Pumpkin is another fall favorite that's just as versatile as squash. Serve it with an arugula-garlic pesto or a drizzle of honey and walnuts.

Winter: Most people aren't as comfortable with winter produce as they are with summer. But it doesn't take long to warm up to these root vegetables. Many, like rutabagas, parsnips, celery root, turnips, leeks, and cabbage, are excellent companions in soups, stews, or roasts. Hardy greens like Swiss chard, kale, and collards also make another appearance and go well with winter fruits and hard-shelled squashes, which are usually still lurking around. You may even see some winter lettuces. In states where citrus grows (California, Texas, Arizona, and Florida), winter is peak season for oranges, lemons, limes, grapefruits, kumquats, and limequats.

- Roasted carrots, parsnips, rutabagas, and squash

- Beets and blue cheese

- Shredded cabbage, leeks, and Gruyère (or any hard or semi-hard cheese)

- Mashed potatoes and turnips

- Oranges, grapefruits, and honey

From Nose to Tail

People who buy local meat, fish, or poultry often buy in bulk—meaning they purchase an individual animal or animal share, such as a $\frac{1}{2}$ or $\frac{1}{4}$ of a pig or steer or a whole fish or bird. This not only gives you high-quality, fresh meat humanely treated, it also saves you money.

But lest we forget, buying the whole animal also means *cooking* the whole animal, including parts like the heart, liver, and tongue most of us are unaccustomed to dealing with.

Luckily, utilizing all the parts of an animal is a growing trend fueled by restaurant chefs as well as local foodies. Why? Cost, of course, is the main issue. These lesser-known cuts are cheaper than big muscle cuts. But other factors just as important are generating less waste, having more respect for the animal, and being better for the environment (supports sustainable agriculture).

Flavor is also a bonus. Underutilized cuts and *offal*, like pig *trotters* or ears, beef cheeks, *tripe*, or chicken gizzards have a richer, more intense taste that for some people takes some getting used to.

LOCAL LINGO

Offal is organ meat. **Trotters** are pig feet. **Tripe** is the stomach lining, usually of a cow.

These pieces also require some culinary know-how to prepare. Many, like shanks and bones, need long cooking times to become tender, while others, like beef liver, need to be fried quickly. If you're unsure how to prepare it, ask your butcher. You may want to invest in a good cookbook on meat cookery or charcuterie (see Appendix B).

Big-Batch Cooking

Even if you don't have a big family, it pays to cook up big batches of food during harvest time in the summer and early fall. This way, you can cook once and eat twice or even three times later on in the week. This saves you time and money; reduces waste because you don't have to throw out any unused food; and if you eat half and freeze half, it can even build a nice supply of food for later in the year.

Doubling or even tripling up recipes is probably the best way to make big batches. To make the time go by faster, invite a few friends over to help. You can socialize and cook at the same time. And if they bring different food to prepare, you can all share in the results.

Invest in Some Stock

Soups, stocks, and sauces are standard staples in the locavore kitchen. Soups in particular are extremely versatile and great for using up leftovers. One woman told me that once a week, the night before her CSA box arrived, she would make soup with the previous week's CSA ingredients. She would then immediately freeze it. So far, she had more than a half dozen soups stashed away. She told me that this way not only are she and her husband eating well all summer, but she could also enjoy the fruits of her labor through most of the winter as well.

Go-To Recipes

Go-to recipes are simple, quick family favorites you can turn to during busy nights or when you don't have a dinner planned. People who eat local shy away from fast food, convenience foods, and frozen dinners, so the best thing to do is create your own "fast" food made from local food.

One way to do this is to learn some basic cooking techniques:

Baking. A dry-heat cooking method where food is surrounded by hot air. In baking, food is cooked uncovered in an oven. Baking generally applies to breads, cookies, pies, cakes, and casseroles.

Braising. To cook in a small amount of liquid. Sometimes foods will be browned before braising, like a pot roast. Braising can be done in the oven or on top of the stove.

Broiling. Cooking at very high heat, usually from an overhead source, for a short period of time.

Grilling. A dry-heat method where food is cooked over intense heat, like a barbecue. This could be via gas, electric, or burning coals or flames. Almost any food can be grilled—vegetables, meats, poultry, fish, and more.

Roasting. Similar to baking, roasting applies to meat, poultry, game, and vegetables.

Sautéing. Cooking food in a small amount of butter, oil, or fat, usually on top of the stove. This is the most versatile and easiest of all the cooking methods.

Steaming. Cooking a food, covered, over boiling water in a basket or a rack. Steaming cooks food quickly and retains more nutrients than boiling.

Stewing. Stewing is similar to braising except you tend to use more liquid and the pieces of food (meat or vegetables) are cut into small pieces.

Once you've mastered these basics, you can prepare nearly any vegetable or even some fruits. Then they can be easily tossed into a salad; made into a side for grilled meats or fish; or served on top of rice, pasta, or other grains like quinoa for a main dish.

Next, think about the foods you and your family love to eat. If you like pasta, you can develop some pasta recipes, have a once-a-week pizza night, or make fried rice or

Asian-influenced stir-fry dishes. The key is to have a recipe with only a few ingredients that can be adapted to go with a wide variety of fresh herbs and vegetables and can be pulled together quickly.

You also might want to hone in on one vegetable and then think of many ways to prepare it. For instance, this summer I had a wealth of beet greens, so I sautéed them with garlic and onion and kept them in the fridge. I used them in risotto, in soup, as a topping for an egg and cheese sandwich, on pizza, and with pasta.

Nature's Way

Everything in nature has a natural cycle and rhythm, and our eating patterns are no exception. Unfortunately, as we've gotten farther and farther away from our food supply and where and how food is grown, we've also gotten farther away from this natural cycle.

As you start eating local and more in line with the patterns of nature, you'll once again realign with the seasons of nature. For example, most people tend to eat smaller amounts of lighter foods during the hot summer weather. In the winter, on the other hand, we tend to eat heavier, more caloric foods, mostly because our body needs to spend more energy keeping warm.

The kinds of food you eat also changes when you follow a local diet. Although meat is plentiful during the fall and winter, it's only occasionally eaten during spring and summer. This is so young calves, kids, and piglets have a chance to mature and reproduce, generating a sustainable and continuous lifecycle.

A CLOSER LOOK

Dairy products like cheese also follow a natural cycle. Fresh cheeses are typically more plentiful in spring and summer when fresh milk and green grass are abundant. Later on in the fall and winter, stronger, hard cheeses appear. These have aged throughout the spring and summer. Of those, the most popular winter cheeses are blue cheeses.

Much of our food during spring, summer, and early fall comes from a plant-based diet. We eat lower on the food chain, which helps the environment, promotes diverse agriculture, and improves local ranching practices.

Year-Round Local Menus

Eating local year-round is certainly possible in most parts of this country, but it does take more thought and planning to follow this diet, particularly during the off season, than nonlocal eating.

Once you do become adjusted to a locavore lifestyle, however, it's hard to go back to more conventional eating. As you begin to get accustomed to nature's food cycle, you begin to look forward to the riches each new season brings. It's this expectation that makes the rewards of fresh, local food even sweeter.

Remember, too, that local eating is seldom stagnant. In fact, no matter how long you've been eating local, each year often brings some new culinary discovery. Certainly, if you want an orange or grapefruit, by all means buy one, but with the wealth of foodstuffs available in your region, you may find yourself wishing for that orange less and less.

The Least You Need to Know

- Take care of your local foods as soon as you bring them home and they'll last longer in storage.
- Eat with the seasons, preparing culinary creations with foods that grow together in the garden.
- Preparing underutilized cuts of meat and organ meats is one way locavores can eat local, stretch their food budget, and create sustainable food systems.
- Big-batch recipes are an ideal way to use up locally grown food and can be used in a variety of ways.
- Stocks, soups, and sauces are a great way to use seasonal produce when the produce bin is overflowing.

Chapter 15

Saving and Storing

In This Chapter

- An introduction to freezing
- Canning basics
- Making preserves, pickles, and relishes
- Discovering drying methods
- Cool storage options

Preserving or "putting up" foods for the winter is just as much a part of eating local as getting to know your farmer. There's something about the experience of standing in a hot kitchen and making strawberry jam or pickling cucumbers with locally grown produce that immediately and inexplicably reconnects you to the land and the food it provides.

Knowing you and your family will enjoy these seasonal foods later in the year makes doing this work all the more meaningful. But many benefits go beyond the personal satisfaction of feeding your family. Preserving foods yourself means you know exactly what's in the food you feed to your family. You can rest assured it's free of chemicals, additives, and unwanted preservatives.

If you grow your own food, or even if you don't, storing foods for the winter is the best way to use up foods that would otherwise go to waste. This is particularly true when there's an abundant harvest.

The food you preserve yourself tastes better, too. Perhaps this is because you have more control over what spices and flavoring ingredients you add, but more likely, it's because you start out with fresh, high-quality local ingredients in the first place.

There are many different ways of "putting up" food, and entire books have been written about each one. In this chapter, I'm going to touch on several of these methods to give you a taste of what's involved. If you want to learn more about a specific technique, visit the U.S. Department of Agriculture's (USDA) National Center for Home Preservation Center (uga.edu/nchfp), buy an in-depth book on the subject, or take a class.

Making Friends with Your Freezer

Freezing is the easiest and quickest way to preserve food. It also keeps flavor, color, and nutrient content better than any other method, making it closer to fresh than canned or dried.

But it's not for all foods. The majority of fruits; vegetables; and raw meats, fish, and poultry freeze well. Eggs; fried foods; many dairy products like milk, cheese, cream and mayonnaise; and certain fruits and vegetables, namely lettuces, cucumbers, apricots, watermelon, and cabbage don't fare so well, mostly due to changes in texture and quality after thawing.

And remember, freezing takes some planning ahead. You'll need to spend a little time in prep or processing for storage, but you'll also need a day or up to two for thawing.

Facts About Freezing

Freezing foods at low temperatures, 0°F or below, stops microorganisms like bacteria, yeasts, and molds from growing, but it doesn't kill them. Once the temperature rises, like during thawing, these microbes become active again and can cause food spoilage. This is why it's so important to thaw frozen foods properly.

There are three safe ways to thaw foods:

- In the refrigerator
- In cold water
- In the microwave

In the refrigerator is the best method, but it also takes the longest, and you must remember to pull out your frozen food at least a day or two in advance. Cold water works more quickly, but it does require you to be on hand to change the water frequently. It can be messy, too. Microwaving is the least-preferred method because it doesn't defrost evenly and may affect quality. Still, it works in a pinch.

Freezing also slows down, but does not stop, the natural enzyme activity of foods. Enzymes in fruits and vegetables control the ripening process and can cause some light-colored fruits to turn brown. Enzymes can give some foods, including meat and fish, an off flavor, and over time, they can significantly decrease quality. For this reason, the USDA recommends most foods be frozen for only a few months to no longer than a year.

> **NATIVE KNOWLEDGE**
>
> To ensure that your freezer remains below 0°F when adding a new batch of food, set your freezer control to –10°F. That way, the new foods freeze faster and don't affect the already-frozen foods.

Basic Essentials

When it comes to freezing food, the biggest and most expensive investment is the freezer itself. Not only do you need a good-quality working freezer, you also need the space to put it somewhere. And a freezer requires a continuous power supply, which will increase your household energy usage. Also know that if there's an extended power outage, frozen food must be cooked up quickly or thrown out.

You also need freezer bags, wrap, and containers to corral your food. Freezer bags and containers are specifically made for freezing, so they're more heavy-duty and seal better. Properly packaging frozen foods keeps them fresher longer and reduces the chances of freezer burn. Freezer burn is caused by the presence of air. In this case, the air draws moisture from the food, causing the outside ice crystals to evaporate, and resulting in a food that becomes dry and cracked. So be sure to remove as much air as possible when sealing bags.

If using containers for sauces, soups, or any type of liquid, leave some space between the food and the lid because liquids expand when they freeze. How much space you leave depends on the food being frozen; a range between ¼ and ½ inch should be fine.

If you're freezing nonliquid foods, always pack them tightly together in airtight containers.

Be sure to have labels and pens or markers nearby so you can clearly label and date each item. Write clearly and large enough so you can see it. The last thing you want are smudged labels you can't decipher. On the other hand, be sure the labels can be easily removed or washed off after the food is eaten so you can re-use containers without having to worry about having the wrong label on it.

How to Freeze

To help retain their vivid color, taste, and texture, most vegetables should be blanched and cooled before freezing. Blanching is briefly cooking (usually only a few minutes, depending on the vegetable) in boiling water, and cooling quickly in cold water. Exceptions to this rule are onions, peppers, and leeks, which can be frozen raw.

Fruits are rarely blanched. Berries and grapes are probably the easiest to freeze. Simply lay them out on a single layer on a baking sheet, and freeze. When they're frozen, transfer them to a sealable freezer bag, and label. This keeps the berries from sticking together.

Other fruits like peaches, plums, or pears are usually frozen in a sugar syrup, which helps them retain texture and quality. To keep fruits from turning brown, you can add citric acid, lemon juice, or ascorbic acid.

Meat, fish, and poultry should be cut into portion sizes, double wrapped with freezer paper, sealed tightly in an airtight freezer bag, and labeled.

Although most people store herbs in their dry form, freezing actually retains better color and flavor—and it's easy! To freeze fresh herbs, finely chop in a food processor and add a small amount of either water or oil. Spoon the mixture into ice cube trays, and freeze. When frozen, place frozen herbs in freezer bags, seal, and label.

NATIVE KNOWLEDGE

Keep your freezer full. A well-stocked freezer requires less energy to maintain and ensures all your food stays frozen solid.

Labeling is essential for keeping track of what you have in the freezer and worth repeating in this section. Clearly identify and date all food before you freeze it. Some people even keep an inventory list on the front of the freezer so they know what goes in and comes out. This takes more work but is worth it in the long run.

Yes, You Can Can

Canning was first invented by a Frenchman in 1811 as a way to keep food fresh for Napoleon Bonaparte's soldiers. Since then, much has changed in the canning world, but the basic principles remain the same: food is sealed in an airtight jar and then heated to destroy microorganisms that cause food to spoil. The airtight seal keeps organisms out and the food safe.

The beauty of this method is that once it's done, or "processed," canned foods need no special treatment. They do not need to be refrigerated (or frozen for that matter). They should, however, be stored on a shelf in a dark, cool place. (Cellars are great for this!) Kept this way, canned food can last for a year or more. Plus, they're ready to use immediately, because they require no thawing or cooking. Many people can in the summer and then give away the canned goodies as homemade gifts during the holidays. Once opened, canned food is just like any other perishable item and should be refrigerated.

Canning comes with some downsides, too. Because canning involves heating foods to high temperatures for a certain period of time, some taste and texture changes take place. There even may be some color changes. Light-colored fruit tends to turn dark. Dipping the fruit into ascorbic acid (vitamin C) or other commercial preparations before canning can prevent this from happening.

Canning also results in the loss of certain vitamins like A, C, thiamine, and riboflavin. And although it's possible to can without adding extra sugar and salt, most recipes do call for some, so if this is something you're watching, beware. For example, fruits are generally prepared with a sugar syrup, but you can make them with unsweetened fruit juice instead or even use a sugar substitute like Splenda. When it comes to salt, tomatoes, vegetables, meat, poultry, and seafood can be prepared without it because it's only used for flavoring, not food safety.

Canning is a long process. Most home-canners spend a full day or more on the task, and each step must be followed exactly—no short cuts here. This is imperative because improperly processed food can lead to spoiled food, not to mention a lot of wasted time. It can also foster the growth of bacteria called *Clostridium botulinum*, which thrives in anaerobic, or oxygenless, environments like airtight containers. This bacteria produces a poisonous toxin resulting in botulism. Fortunately, *Clostridium botulinum* cannot grow in the presence of acids like vinegar and lemon juice.

Having the Right Equipment

If you want to start canning, you've got to have good canning equipment. This is essential. First off, you need a large supply of canning jars, lids, and metal rings. Sometimes called Mason jars, these come in a variety of shapes and sizes. They're specially made to withstand long bouts in boiling water, so they're sturdier than regular commercial glass jars. They also have special seals.

You also need a canner. This is the pot in which you "process" or boil your canned products. There are basically two types:

- Boiling water canner or water bath canner

- Pressure canner

A boiling water canner is a large aluminum or stainless-steel pot with a lid, handles, and a removable rack inside that holds the jars in place and keeps them from touching the bottom of the pan. This is the most common for home use.

This kind of canner only reaches temperatures of boiling water (212°F), so it's best suited for high-acid foods. High-acid foods are most fruits, a few vegetables, and pickles. Canning low-acid foods with a water bath canner is *not* recommended because heat-resistant bacteria can still grow in this environment. (High-acid foods prevent this bacteria from growing.) Low-acid foods are most vegetables (like green beans), meats, and seafood.

Pressure canners (not to be confused with pressure cookers) are also a large pot, probably about 16 quarts or bigger, with a jar rack, dial or weighted gauge, automatic vent cover lock, safety fuse, and tightly fitting lid. Steam pressure increases temperature, thus pressure canners can reach higher temperatures than water bath canners, about 240°F to 250°F. For this reason, they're essential for processing low-acid foods (and getting rid of heat-resistant bacteria). They can also process high-acid foods.

Other tools you need include a jar lifter, tongs, and canning funnel.

KEEP YOUR DISTANCE

Where you live makes a difference when it comes to canning. General canning instructions you'll find are based for those canning at sea level, but if you live at a higher altitude, you must make adjustments. If using a water bath canner, the higher the altitude, the longer you need to process your products. For a pressure canner, higher altitude means increasing pressure.

Following the Rules

To give you an idea of exactly what's involved in canning, here's a quick guide, minus the details (which vary depending on what you're processing):

1. *Prepare your food.* This can be as simple as cutting and peeling the raw ingredient, or it can require cooking the food with different seasonings or making a simple sugar syrup (like for fruits).

2. *Clean and sterilize the canning jars, lids, and rings.* Jars, lids, and rings are usually held in hot water until they're ready to use.

3. *Fill the canning jars.* Jars need to be filled to the top, but not overfilled. Food naturally expands, so it's important you leave headspace between the top of the food and the bottom of the lid. This space varies depending on what type of food you're canning. Other things to think about: removing all air bubbles and making sure seals are properly applied.

4. *Processing the can.* This means placing the sealed jars in a boiling water bath or pressure canner and tightly covering for the prescribed amount of time. Lids will pull down when they're sealed, slightly concave.

When done, remove the jars from the canner and leave them to cool undisturbed at room temperature. You may hear a distinctive "ping" as the seal sets.

If the jar fails to seal, remove the lid and check for tiny nicks. If necessary, change the jar. You can reprocess within 24 hours, or you can simply store in the refrigerator, but it must be eaten within a few days.

Sweet Treats: Preserves

When it comes to preserving foods, fruits are always a favorite. Perhaps it's because most fruits have such a short season and it's only natural we try to extend it. More likely, however, is the fact that nothing can bring back the fresh taste of summer like a sweet peach compote or intense strawberry jam.

Sweet fruit spreads contain four essential ingredients:

- Fruit
- Sugar
- Pectin
- Acid (such as lemon juice)

They can be canned, frozen (freezer jam), or stored in the refrigerator for immediate use.

The best fruits should be ripe but not over-ripe. In fact, for this case, slightly under-ripe fruit works even better because it's filled with pectin. Pectin is the substance that causes liquids to thicken and gel and makes for a good spread. As fruits ripen, pectin disappears.

A CLOSER LOOK

Apples are an excellent source of pectin, so they're often included in making preserves, jams, or jellies. Some people even make homemade pectin using apples. Store-bought pectin comes in liquid or powdered form. Types of pectin vary in strength, so they're not interchangeable in recipes.

Which sweet fruit spread you choose to make usually depends on the abundance of the harvest. If peaches are having a good run, my shelves fill up with peach preserves. If blackberry bushes are overflowing, it's blackberry preserves. Choose whatever works for your region.

Whether you decide to make jelly, jam, or preserves, you only need four basic ingredients:

Fruit. Nearly any type of fruit can be used to make these sweet treats. Use perfectly ripe fruit, and remember the better the fruit the better the jam. Use under-ripe fruit, and your jam will be dry and have poor flavor. Use over-ripe fruit, and your jam will be too soft and not set properly. Always wash fruit first.

Sugar. This is the main ingredient and how much you need largely depends on the type of fruit and its sweetness level. Tart fruits need more sugar than sweeter ones. Before you add the sugar, you must have fruit cooked down first in water or its own juices; otherwise, the fruit will get hard. If you're making jelly, you'll strain the fruit and just use the juice is used. If you're not making jelly, you can leave in the fruit pieces.

Pectin. Pectin is naturally occurring in all fruits and is responsible for the gelling of jams and jellies. With certain fruits, you may be able to get by without adding in extra pectin, but it does take a long time. Most fruits, however, do require that extra boost. How much you use depends on the fruit.

Acid. Acid is required for pectin to form a gel. Commercial pectin products contain acid, but you may need to add more, usually in the form of lemon juice or other citrus fruit.

For more information on making jellies, jams, and preserves look up some books in the library on making jams and jellies, or check out *The Complete Idiot's Guide to Preserving Food* by Karen Brees (Alpha Books, 2009).

Pickles, Relishes, and Fermented Foods

Pickling preserves fruits or vegetables in a vinegar-salt solution. (The acid prevents the growth of microorganisms.) A small amount of sugar is also added, mostly for texture and firmness.

> **LOCAL LINGO**
>
> **Pickling** is the act of preserving a low-acid food in a solution of acid and salt. A wide variety of foods can be pickled, namely cucumbers, beets, other vegetables, and meats.

Relishes are basically bite-size pickles. While pickles are large pieces usually in their whole form—think pickled eggs, pickled beets, pickled cucumbers, etc.—relished are chopped into small pieces. They can be cooked or raw, and specialties can appear throughout the year, such as Indian summer corn relish, orange apple relish in the fall, and cranberry ginger relish in winter. Both pickles and relishes run the gamut when it comes to flavor, and can be spicy, sweet, sour, mild, or hot depending on what spices you add.

Canning pickles and relishes enables you to enjoy them throughout the winter and spring season. It also gives their flavors a chance to meld and develop.

Fermented foods are most familiar to us as sauerkraut, Korean kimchi, soy sauce, and vinegar. Like pickled foods, they use an acid environment to keep undesirable microorganisms at bay. This time, however, "good" microorganisms like yeast, mold, or bacteria do the work, converting sugar and carbohydrates to alcohol and carbon dioxide and "fermenting" the food. Most of these foods involve a brine, or saltwater solution, and are simple to make. Sauerkraut, for instance, has only two ingredients: cabbage and salt. The key to fermented food success is in the proper process (it must be weighted down) and time. Fermentation doesn't happen overnight. Most foods require several weeks and sometimes even months to transform.

Drying Out

Drying is probably the oldest and simplest way to preserve food, dating thousands of years to the Middle East, when fish, olives, and figs dried naturally, courtesy of the hot sun and dry climate.

Dehydrating removes 85 to 95 percent of a food's moisture, and because most fruits and vegetables are composed of water, drying results in a much smaller, more compact, and much denser food. Drying also concentrates the flavor along with the sugars and calories. In fact, dried produce can have as much as four or five times the calories, ounce for ounce, as fresh. So remember to eat small amounts!

Drying foods may also incur some nutrient losses, particularly for heat-sensitive vitamin C. On the other hand, dried fruits are much higher in fiber than the fresh versions.

Dried foods are also lightweight, portable, and easy to store, taking up much less space than other preserved foods. While dried fruits and meats like jerky can easily be eaten out of hand, vegetables generally need to be rehydrated before they're cooked, so they're best suited for soups, stews, and casseroles.

A CLOSER LOOK

Make your own homemade fruit roll-ups! Also called fruit leather, these chewy snacks can be made by pouring fruit purée on a flat baking sheet and drying.

You also may have to do some pretreatments before you dry, such as blanching vegetables or dipping cut fruits into a solution of lime or lemon juice or ascorbic acid to prevent them from browning.

If you're drying foods outside, you'll have to protect against insects and air pollution. People who live in hot, dry climates like those in the West and Southwest are more apt to use the drying method for food preservation. Here are a few ways it's done:

- *Air drying* uses air circulation, not the sun's warmth, to remove moisture.

- *Sun drying* uses the sun's heat to extract moisture.

- *Solar drying* is similar to sun drying except you use a specific structure with ventilation and reflectors to intensify the sun's heat.

- *Oven drying* is done indoors, so climate doesn't matter.

- *In a food dehydrator*, a freestanding electric unit that controls temperature and humidity is used.

Rah, Rah Root Cellars

Long before refrigeration existed, people stored their food underground in root cellars. Traditional root cellars were simply large holes dug into the side of a hill and lined with bricks, stones or concrete. They had dirt floors and good air circulation. It is possible to build your own root cellar inside, in the basement, or aboveground, but it takes a lot of work.

Root cellars take advantage of the earth's natural coolness and keep foods cool enough so they don't deteriorate but not so cold that they freeze. Done right, root cellars essentially act like a refrigerator, without electricity, and hold foods between 40°F and 55°F during summer and above freezing (34°F to 40°F) during winter.

Apples are far and away the most common fruit root cellared, and properly stored, they can last throughout the winter and spring season. Next come pears, citrus, and grapes. Vegetables tend to be the hardier winter varieties. These include potatoes, cabbage, beets, carrots, rutabagas, Brussels sprouts, cauliflower, onions, leeks, parsnips, pumpkins, and squash. It's also possible to root cellar celery, green tomatoes, and peppers.

For best results, be sure all fruits and vegetables to be root cellared are not bruised, cut, or diseased; are picked at maturity (not over-ripe or under-ripe); and don't have large clumps of dirt on them.

> **NATIVE KNOWLEDGE**
>
> You don't have to clean vegetables to be root cellared, but do knock off most of the dirt.

Certain vegetables keep better if they're "cured." In this case, *cured* means letting them sit out for several days or weeks, after harvest, to develop a thick skin or rind. Potatoes, sweet potatoes, pumpkin, onions, garlic, and winter squashes keep best cured.

Salting and Smoking

Salting and smoking preserve food by removing moisture and drying out foods. Smoking has the extra benefit of adding heat.

Although vegetables can be salted, the most commonly salted foods are meats or fish like salt pork, herring, or mackerel. The process usually involves either soaking the meat or fish in brine or packing it in dry salt.

Smoking generally follows salting and can be cold or hot. Cold-smoked food is held over smoking chips of wood at low temperature (70°F to 120°F) for a long period of time. Hot smoking uses higher temperatures. Hot-smoked food is more prevalent than cold-smoked food, particularly for fresh food. Salmon is probably the easiest and most common food to smoke—both hot and cold. But you can also smoke beef, chicken, pork, and some vegetables.

The Least You Need to Know

- Many people like freezing because it's fast and simple. All it requires is space for a freezer, good freezer containers, and some preplanning for thawing food.
- Canning is an excellent way to preserve food, as long as you follow all the proper steps.
- Jams, jellies, pickles, and relishes are the most popular kinds of foods preserved from local harvests.
- Drying food is another convenient way to preserve a bounty.
- Root cellars are a good way to make fruits like apples and sturdy vegetables like potatoes, beets, and cabbage last throughout the winter months and into early spring.

Living a Local Lifestyle

Locavores believe in eating local because it's the right thing to do. They also know local foods taste better and are fresher than conventional produce, which often takes days to get to you. That's why most people who eat local think of it as a lifestyle rather than just something they do at home. The final part of the book shows you how to live like a locavore by finding and choosing local food outside of the local marketplace and your own kitchen. Find out how to buy local when dining out, and discover how local food has impacted chefs and the foodservice community. You learn what local means to restaurants and how these establishments are catering to locavore customers.

The last chapter brings eating local to the next level by showing you how to advocate for these foods in schools and in your community. I discuss ways you can drum up interest in local food in all these areas plus become a part of the dynamic and exciting local food community online via blogs, websites, and social media. So get ready to get connected the local way!

Dining Out, Dining Local

In This Chapter

- What "local" means to chefs
- Getting from farm to fork
- What to expect on the menu
- Advantages of eating out local
- *Garden-fresh, farmstead,* and other key terms to look for

Although chefs have been shopping at farmers' markets and working with farmers for decades, it wasn't until recently that the local food movement really picked up steam in foodservice. Now there's no stopping it.

According to the National Restaurant Association's What's Hot in 2011 survey, in which 1,500 chefs across the country were asked to rank 214 items according to importance, locally grown meats and seafood and locally grown produce are the top two most important trends facing chefs today. Eighty-six percent of the chefs named these two trends as number one—they tied for first place. A close second, with 84 percent of the vote, was sustainability. On the consumer side, demand is also up. Seventy percent of adults say they're more likely to visit a restaurant that offers locally produced food.

Everywhere you turn, foodservice operations are serving up locally sourced menu items, meals, or promotions. As a result, locavores now have more ways to support local agriculture and more choices when dining out.

Nevertheless, "local" means different things to different people. In this chapter, you discover exactly what chefs mean by buying local, what you can expect to see on menus, and why choosing locally grown foods are to your advantage. With so many options, there's no reason why you can't dine out, dine local, and dine well, whenever you like!

Restaurants Go Local

Why has offering local food in restaurants become so popular? The fact that more people are clamoring for these home-grown goodies is certainly a factor, but so is the growing number of locavore chefs. These dedicated professionals believe in buying local because it's the right thing to do for local economies, for the environment, and for their patrons. Others want a deeper connection between the land and the food that's harvested from it. Many are interested in saving small farms and forming fair market agreements.

All, however, agree on one thing: the quality and taste of conventional foods often can't compare to their fresh, local counterparts. Indeed, quality and taste are driving forces for chefs seeking out local products.

Consequently, what started in a few high-end, independent restaurants on the coasts has now become a full-fledged, industry-wide trend cutting across all foodservice segments. Even mid-scale restaurants, casual dining operations, chains, and fast-food places are in on the local movement. Experts predict buying local will eventually become standard practice among foodservice professionals.

A CLOSER LOOK

Eating local is more than just food; it also carries over to water. At Restaurant Eve in Alexandria, Virginia (restauranteve.com), the chef nixed bottled and imported water, opting instead for purified tap water. Now he offers customers self-bottled still and sparkling water free of charge.

Farm-to-Fork Operations

For many chefs, shopping at farmers' markets is the first step toward finding local food. Others begin with a small herb garden because they're easy to maintain, don't require much space, and can provide the restaurant with a good supply of fresh herbs with little effort. Planting a small garden on a plot of land nearby consisting of a combination of vegetables and herbs is another way chefs can initiate a local program. Some even opt for rooftop gardens.

But what started out small is now growing into a major movement in the foodservice industry. An increasing number of chefs are now going *hyperlocal*, growing their restaurant's produce right on site, harvesting honey from beehives on the rooftop, or managing the raising and butchering of their own meat.

> **LOCAL LINGO**
>
> **Hyperlocal** chefs try to serve food as local as they can. This means growing, raising, or harvesting as much food as they can onsite, near the restaurant or kitchen. More and more chefs are going hyperlocal.

At the same time more chefs are going hyperlocal, there's also a movement to move beyond this first step. By buying their own land and growing their own ingredients, they essentially have their own farm. This gives them the control of growing what they want, especially ingredients they may not be able to get elsewhere. Plus, it gives them the shortest distance from farm to table.

The chef or owner could simply buy the land directly and own it himself. Or he could form a partnership or co-operative with friends or other chefs. Or the chef/owner could buy land and then lease it to farmers, buying the harvest at fair market value— a practice made popular by Blue Hill Farm in New York (bluehillfarm.com).

Over the last 10 years, Blue Hill Farm has become a model of stewardship for the local movement among chefs and restaurateurs. Their chef-farmer partnership encompasses Blue Hill Farm in Barrington, Massachusetts, Blue Hill at Stone Barns Agricultural and Educational Center (an 80-acre working farm and restaurant), and Blue Hill Café, both in Westchester, New York, as well as Blue Hill restaurant in New York City.

All the restaurants have seasonal menus based on the produce and livestock supplied by the two farms (in Massachusetts and New York). According to Chef Dan Barber, less than 20 percent of their ingredients hail from outside the New York region. And what the restaurant doesn't use (about a third of the food the farms produce), is sold at local farmers' markets or to other local restaurants. A family-run operation, the farms and the restaurants are owned by Barber and his brother.

Creating a Partnership

Both farming and cooking are a big undertaking and require gargantuan amounts of time, commitment, and cash. For this reason, most chefs take a middle-of-the-road approach, opting to leave the farming to the farmer, and instead forge strong bonds with local farmers. Often this means more than just setting up contracts to buy a certain amount of meat, produce, eggs, or dairy. Chefs committed to the success of the local farm spend time working at or visiting the farm. They may arrange for certain plants to be grown specifically for them, guaranteeing a buy back, and some even go so far as to buy seeds. Others have special cheeses, cured meats, or sausages produced just for them.

Rather than thinking of them simply as a supplier, locavore chefs treat farmers more like a partner. Developing this partnership is a win-win situation for everyone.

Foodservice Foragers

Buying local in foodservice operations often means working with several different farms. Juggling these different vendors is more time-consuming than dealing with a traditional supplier, but nearly all chefs feel it's worth it. This works for small, independent operations, but if the restaurant does a large volume or there are multiple units, sourcing local can be complicated. That's why some places are now hiring sourcing managers specifically for handling local and sustainable products.

Sometimes known as food foragers, these full-time local food procurers seek out unique local ingredients, develop relationships with farmers, and visit farms. How much local food procurement managers purchase depends on the operation.

For instance, for big chain operations like Chipotle, being a food forager means covering a large region like the Mid-Atlantic and is more about logistics and reliability than buying unusual ingredients. For another, the job may entail roaming the countryside with a true food "forager" and collecting wild edibles. Either way, the goal—supporting local agriculture, local economies, humanely raised animals, and environmentally sound farming practices—is the same.

A CLOSER LOOK

Leading players among multichain units sourcing local foods include Denver, Colorado–based Chipotle; Burgerville, a burger chain headquartered in Vancouver, Washington; and Eat'n Park, a family-dining chain out of Pittsburgh, Pennsylvania.

Great Expectations

What kinds of food you find on the menu of a restaurant serving locally sourced ingredients depends largely on the type of restaurant it is, where it's located, and how committed it is to serving local (the restaurant's food philosophy).

Any kind of restaurant—Italian, Indian, Chinese—can use some local ingredients, but the ones that buy the majority of their ingredients local tend to focus on more American home-style or regional dishes.

What's on the Menu?

Compared to conventional chefs, locally oriented chefs have to be more creative and flexible with their dishes as seasons change frequently and quantities fluctuate. Many have begun reviving old-fashioned preserving techniques like canning; freezing; drying; and putting up jams, jellies, butters, and pickles on a regular basis. These foods later show up on the menu, usually in the off season. Here's what you're likely to find:

Local produce. Most restaurants celebrate the season by highlighting a specific local ingredient, which varies depending on what part of the country you're in. Some of these items may only be available to foodservice operators; others may be around only for a short time.

During the season, this item usually appears throughout the menu, but once it's gone, it's gone. On the other hand, abundance breeds culinary creativity, so when in season, you can usually find it in many forms. For example, when peaches are in, you're likely to see peach jam, peach chutney, peach mustard, and peach butter on the menu, in addition to peach desserts and peach entrées.

A CLOSER LOOK

To encourage their chefs to buy local, Loews Hotels created an "Adopt-a-Farmer" program, which mandates that chefs use food from at least one local farmer within a 100-mile radius. The program, which runs in all 17 locations, encourages chefs to create seasonal and regional menu items.

Local cheese and dairy. Local cheeses are always a big draw on restaurant menus, and although particularly popular in dairy states like New York, Wisconsin, and California, nearly every region has its own artisan cheesemakers. Most of the local cheeses used are highlighted on cheese platters, but more and more chefs are serving them up on burgers, sandwiches, pastas, and more. Some restaurants even go so far as to use local ice cream, milk, and other dairy products.

Local meats and seafood. Restaurants touting local pork, beef, and turkey are often using heritage or rare breeds. Although on the expensive side, ordering these meats helps save these animals from becoming extinct. It also gives you the chance to taste something you aren't likely to get elsewhere. (Many heritage meats are not sold in the consumer market.)

Local fresh seafood is another menu find. Although most common in coastal areas, a large number of rivers and lakes throughout the country also boast thriving fish populations, and chefs are quick to take advantage of this. Remember, too, that most seafood is seasonal and not always consistently available, so if you see it on the menu, grab it quickly. It may not be there next time.

Regional beverages. Almost any restaurant focusing on serving food grown close to home will include a variety of local wines and beers on their menu. Restaurants are also increasingly adding handcrafted, small-batch spirits to this list. The flavor of these high-quality, artisan spirits really shines.

Local beverages can also come in the form of juices or shakes prepared from local fruits such as berry drinks in the Pacific Northwest or tropical or citrus drinks in Florida. Burgerville, a burger chain based in Vancouver, Washington, sells seasonal shakes made with local pumpkin, hazelnuts, or blackberries.

The Local Advantage

Aside from getting great-tasting, sustainable food, buying local food when dining out has other advantages. Let's look at a few reasons why dining out and dining local makes sense for everyone.

Eating local while eating out …

- Supports restaurants that are buying local.

- Lets you try certain local foods you couldn't find elsewhere, as some local products are only sold to foodservice operations.

- Allows you to taste products. For instance, if you wanted to try a locally produced gin, you would have to buy the entire bottle, but at a restaurant you can order just a drink.

- Creates a culinary experience. Many people shy away from buying local foods because they don't know what to do with them at home. At a restaurant, you can take comfort in knowing a knowledgeable chef, familiar with the food, is preparing your meal.

- Offers a wide variety of prepared local foods in one place. Take, for example, a cheese platter featuring four different locally produced cheeses. It offers a great way to try new or unusual cheeses. Buying each one of these cheeses separately can be expensive.

Bottom line: it's easier and cheaper to buy it in a restaurant!

Not 100 Percent

While restaurants committed to supporting their local communities strive to buy as many local products as possible, few restaurants go 100 percent. Why? Price is one factor. Sometimes local products are priced out of a restaurant's budget; other times, market forces and small quantity logistics make them inappropriately high.

Time is another factor. It takes time to source products, go to farmers' markets, and find local products. Restaurants need the resources to do this. This includes both manpower and cash flow. And because local products don't have a well-developed distribution system, getting the product to the restaurant can be a logistical nightmare. Luckily, this is changing as demand increases.

> **NATIVE KNOWLEDGE**
>
> Chefs Collaborative (chefscollaborative.org) is a nonprofit organization dedicated to connecting chefs to a local sustainable food system. They also promote chef advocacy, education, and collaboration with the broader food community.

Finally, there's the case of availability. Sometimes certain products restaurants need just don't exist locally. Dried beans or peas, rice, and sugar are such items. These are standard staples at many restaurants, but they're not locally grown in many parts of the country. While sunny Southern California may have plenty to offer, northern Minnesota in winter may not.

Take for example, the communications giant Google's employee eatery Café 150, named so because it serves food only from a 150-mile radius from the company's Mountain View, California, headquarters—400 purely local meals a day. Mountain

View sits in the Salinas Valley food shed, a wealthy agricultural region loaded with ranches, fisheries, and farms. The café also has the backing of a successful company with deep pockets and unlimited resources. Could this concept work someplace else in the country? Probably not.

Quantity can also be a deterrent. Large restaurants especially require large amounts of ingredients. Some local products just can't be mass produced.

Finally, there's the issue of reliability. Many restaurants want a consistent, regular local food supply, and while many farmers will plan for these lean times, sometimes things happen. Some restaurants are better at coping with Mother Nature's fluctuations than others. Small, independent restaurants can often substitute a product when it doesn't come through. Large foodservice operations, on the other hand, like chains and multiunits, usually cannot.

Local Tip-Offs

Most restaurant menus use the term "local" to identify their local products, but other marketing descriptors can also help you pinpoint local foods:

- Name and town of the farm product originated from
- *Grown in* [state]
- *Grown in* [region]
- *Fresh*
- *Foraged, wild*
- *Farmers' market*
- *Seasonal*
- *Homemade*
- *Farmstead*
- *Garden-fresh*
- *Handcrafted*

Some of these terms don't guarantee a local product, but they do signify a high-quality ingredient or meal and are definitely worth asking about.

KEEP YOUR DISTANCE

According to Mintel Menu Insights, the top four ingredient menu descriptors on restaurant menus in 2009 were *fresh, homemade, seasonal,* and *freshly made.* All signal better freshness and flavor, but they don't necessarily mean local.

Special Events and Local Promotions

Sometimes restaurants feature local items in special promotions. Often these promotions are seasonal and so are only offered for a limited time. They usually center around one familiar crop like strawberries or asparagus. The restaurant prepares several dishes—usually an appetizer, one or two entrées, and a few sides—highlighting this produce.

Restaurants also spotlight a certain farm or producer, describing who the farmer is, what she does, and where she's located. This gives a more personal face to your food and is becoming more and more common in the foodservice industry. Many chefs like to do this with cheesemakers. Again, the product is then featured in several dishes.

Often restaurants will host special local dinners. These can be food-centric such as a potato dinner in Maine or a crab fest in Maryland, or they can include a variety of local ingredients like a Chesapeake Bay or New England Dinner. Some restaurants even prepare "50-mile" or "100-mile" dinners.

On the Road

What about when you're traveling? Dedicated locavores will seek out local food wherever they go. It's exciting to discover new and interesting foods, and the foods you do find taste better and brighter when they're grown nearby.

Finding these foods does take some legwork. Some, like avocados in California or oranges in Florida, are easy to spot; others aren't so obvious, like mangoes in Hawaii. Before you go, search online to get an idea of local flavors in the area where you're heading.

Once there, keep your eyes open for food finds. For instance, you can't miss the tons of signs for cheese in Wisconsin or wine in Napa Valley, California. Peruse restaurant menus for local foods or meals, ask locals about popular local dishes, and if you can, visit a farmers' market.

Roadside stands are another good way to get a feel for the region's local fruits and vegetables and may be a good option if you're on a road trip.

KEEP YOUR DISTANCE

If you do travel abroad or at home, be sure to check out regulations regarding food importation or transfer. This applies even when crossing state lines. Certain foods are not allowed to be taken out of their home state.

Although locavores prefer to eat food grown in their own food shed, many have no qualms about bringing local food back from places they've visited. I knew of one locavore who lived in New York, but upon a visit to family in California, returned with two bottles of "local" olive oil.

For chefs who go local, it's all about the food. These chefs choose local products because they're fresh, high quality, reliable, consistent, and available. They also feel good about supporting local communities, local farmers, and local businesses, not to mention keeping their customers happy. To fill this need, many are coming up with more and more creative ways to bring local foods into their establishment and ultimately to their clientele. It's a trend we'll definitely be seeing more of in the future.

The Least You Need to Know

- Thanks to growing consumer demand and a strong locavore movement, local foods are getting easier to find when dining out.
- Many restaurants now offer local produce, meats, poultry, seafood, dairy, and alcohols on their menu.
- Most restaurants are not 100 percent local, but many are getting closer!
- When dining out, look for local foods featured on menus, seasonal promotions, or special dinner events.
- Even when traveling far from home, locavores still often search out local food.

Fostering a Community

In This Chapter

- Farm-to-school initiatives
- Teaching kids through food
- Creating a local community
- Making online connections with other locavores

Living like a locavore means more than just buying and eating locally produced food. It also means being part of a larger community that values sustainable agriculture; healthy, fresh foods; and eco-friendly environmental practices. As such, many people feel a responsibility to promote local foods in their schools, businesses, and neighborhoods.

Efforts to increase the availability of local foods, especially in the school system, have been underway for a long time. Although the process is slow, the achievements are worthwhile. This chapter gives you tips on how to foster a local community in elementary schools, colleges, and universities as well as encourage local foods where you live and work.

I also discuss ways to connect with the lively locavore community online. As the local food movement grows, you'll see more and more of these networks blossoming across the country.

Bringing Local Foods to Schools

Parents have a vested interest in bringing local food into the school foodservice system, not only because it's the right thing to do, but because putting fresh, healthy, locally grown fruits and vegetables on the menu means children will eat more of them and be healthier. Considering that more than one third of our nation's children are obese or overweight, good nutrition is an important and timely issue. Research shows adding farm-fresh, local food to school menus increases school meal participation and results in kids eating more fruits and vegetables in general (on average nearly a half serving more per day) both at home and at school.

For farmers, schools open up new and lucrative markets that can keep businesses afloat at a time when there are fewer market outlets for family farms. Introducing kids to farming and teaching them about what farmers do gets students excited about the industry and encourages young people to consider farming as a potential career path. This brings new life to the industry. It also links farmers to their local communities, building strong economic and social bonds.

The basic premise of farm-to-school programs is to unite K–12 schools and local farms, with the goal of serving healthy meals in school cafeterias; improving student nutrition; providing agriculture, health, and nutrition education opportunities; and supporting local and regional farmers. (There are also farm-to-college programs designed for higher education institutions, which I talk about later in this chapter.)

Each farm-to-school program is shaped by its unique region, the local agriculture of the area, and school resources, so programs are as varied as the communities they serve. Nearly all include an educational component, but their main focus is to provide children with access to local, healthy food while benefiting communities and local farmers.

A CLOSER LOOK

Farm-to-school programs are popping up all over the United States. Currently more than 2,200 programs are in place in 45 states, serving 8,944 schools and 2,100 school districts.

Elementary, My Dear

How much and what local foods are served at elementary, junior, and high schools depends as much on the community and location of the school as it does on the school policies and distribution system. For example, in northern Florida, Georgia, Alabama, and Mississippi, a farmer cooperative supplies foods like collard greens, sweet potatoes, okra, and black-eyed peas to more than 1 million students in local schools. In New Hampshire, local foods served in schools are more likely to include a variety of apples (more than just Red Delicious and McIntosh), apple cider, berries, and honey.

Growing seasons also influence local food availability as temperate climates yield an abundance of produce throughout most of the year while colder climates depend more on preservation techniques to get them through the winter.

Unlike other foodservice institutions, schools must follow strict federal procedures regarding how they obtain their food. They are also required to follow specific nutritional guidelines for menu planning. Because of these regulations and the fact that schools need large quantities of food, the biggest challenge for most schools is the transportation and delivery of local items. Nevertheless, schools can get local food a number of ways:

- Buy directly from individual farmers
- Work with a farmer cooperative
- Purchase regional products at a farmers' market
- Order locally grown through a traditional wholesaler

Finding the right local farmers can also take some time, particularly if you don't live in an agricultural region. These farming operations have to be large enough to supply the school system, yet still be part of the local food network. Some small schools are a good fit with small farms, but larger schools tend to use more mid-size farming operations. These operations usually provide a range of produce and also have to be flexible enough to deal with school policies and procedures.

Once procured, however, local foods almost always do well in schools. On menus, they're usually highlighted on elaborate salad bars, in addition to being featured in everyday lunch, breakfast, or snack meals. To drum up interest, foodservice operators run special events or promotions such as Harvest of the Month or theme days.

Colleges and Universities

Like elementary and high schools, colleges and universities often face an uphill battle when implementing local food programs in their foodservice departments. Luckily, these farm-to-college programs often have something the K–12 schools lack—student advocates.

The number of young people concerned about environmentally friendly, sustainable, and humanely raised food is growing rapidly. As a result, student networks promoting local food are making waves across the country. One such group called *Real Food Challenge* is made up of college student groups across the country. The Real Food Challenge aims to create a sustainable food system by promoting local, organic, and fair trade foods through grassroots efforts in the college community.

LOCAL LINGO

The **Real Food Challenge** (www.realfoodchallenge.org) is both a campaign and network. Its goal is to have 20 percent of all food purchased by colleges and universities (about $1 billion of the $4 billion budget) redirected to real food. Real food is local, organic, whole, natural food. Currently 300 universities are involved with the program.

Interest among foodservice managers is also on the rise. In addition to keeping customers happy, foodservice managers cite high-quality food; lower environmental impact; and support for local economies, communities, and farmers as other reasons to go local.

Programs are unique to the institution and range from one-day-long events to regular everyday offerings on menus. Some schools are incredibly creative. Programs include hosting special local dinners, days, or special events; increasing the number of vegetarian items offered with local produce; working with agricultural students on local initiatives; and nurturing gardens that provide foodservice with locally grown produce.

Educational Opportunities and More

Aside from providing students with healthy, locally grown produce, meats, and dairy, focusing on a local food program offers students in all grades many educational opportunities. First and foremost is the chance to teach students about how food grows and where it comes from. This is usually done by field trips to the farm and farmer presentations.

Agricultural education is only one part of the curriculum students learn about. Many teachers plan nutrition education activities around local foods related to seasonality, menu planning, and health. Students often learn how to cook and prepare the food, which teaches them basic culinary skills and food science principles.

More progressive schools have even gone so far as to plant school vegetable gardens. In addition to teaching students about science, nutrition, the life cycle, and the environment, gardens encourage physical activity and social skills by having students work together to complete real tasks. As an added bonus, these gardens introduce students to new foods and improve attitudes toward eating fruits and vegetables.

A CLOSER LOOK

Founded in 1995 by California chef Alice Waters, the Edible Schoolyard (edibleschoolyard.org) applies skills learned in traditional math, science, and humanities classes to organic gardening while also teaching about the value of fresh foods and nourishment.

Education doesn't stop at the student level. Parent involvement and outreach programs based on local food can encourage healthy eating behaviors at home as well. To this end, one farm-fresh school program in Chicago created a CSA-type service with weekly deliveries of fresh produce baskets available to parents at an affordable price.

Fund-raising activities are another outlet local foods can tap into, and some schools are even using local foods to generate revenue for their department. This was the case in New Hampshire when the foodservice director marketed a Sports Nutrition Meal Program to athletes and sports teams using local foods at a small cost. Once proven to be a success, the meals generated a steady revenue stream.

Understanding the Hurdles

Despite the positive benefits of adding local foods to school foodservice, getting local programs up and running is, more often than not, a long, slow process filled with many frustrating roadblocks, not the least of which is dealing with lots of red tape and an extensive school bureaucracy usually unwilling to change.

Here are just a few of the problems you could run across and some solutions to overcome them:

Problem: Little support for bringing local foods into schools. You may even have people actively opposing this action.

Solution: Build a team of individuals who support your goal. Research successful school programs, and communicate their positive outcomes.

Problem: Kids won't eat the food.

Solution: Include tastings and culinary demos in the local food program. Get kids excited about food, and get them involved in the program.

Problem: Too expensive.

Solution: Many farmers are willing to negotiate prices. Another option is to start small and buy seasonally. Consider, too, that many local school programs report increased participation and reduced waste, which balances out any cost increases.

Problem: No kitchen equipment or skilled labor.

Solution: Some schools have worked out deals where the produce is peeled, cut, and packaged at the farm, reducing labor at the school. Others have completely revamped menus to adapt to their labor skills and resources. Another option is to create training programs.

What You Can Do

As a concerned parent or locavore advocate, there's plenty you can do to promote local food and healthy eating in your school system. In fact, although many local food programs are generated from the "top down," several have been organized from the "bottom up," initiated by parents or farmers.

Here are just a few ways you can make a difference:

- Eat lunch with your kids! Visit the lunchroom and experience what your kids are eating.

- Join your school's nutrition and/or wellness committee.

- Be a local food advocate, and promote local foods whenever you can. Talk about it positively to whoever will listen.

- Volunteer to help with your school's garden, if they have one. If they don't have one, try to get one started. Visit Better School Food (betterschoolfood.org) and Kids Gardening (kidsgardening.com) for tips on how to get one going.

- Learn about healthy foods, and serve these foods to your family.

- Reach out to other parents to discuss issues and concerns. Present your findings to the nutrition committee or the PTA.

- If you have your own garden, see if you can donate your locally grown produce to your school foodservice. Some schools can accept local food donations.

- Join healthy, local school lunch advocacy and support groups online like Better School Food and Fed Up with Lunch: The School Lunch Project (fedupwithschoollunch.blogspot.com).

NATIVE KNOWLEDGE

Similar to the Peace Corps except with food, Food Corps (food-corps.org) places volunteers for one-year appointments at schools across the country with the goal of building farm-to-school supply chains, expanding local food systems, developing healthy eating curriculum based on local food, and planting and tending school food gardens.

In Your Neighborhood

Local food advocates are passionate about the food they buy or grow. That's why they're often more than happy to introduce others to local food.

One of the best ways to do this is to have people actually taste and experience local food. Here are some of the ways you can do this:

- Cook a big batch recipe using local ingredients, and share it with your neighbors or co-workers.

- Experiment with different dishes, and let neighbors try them.

- Give away vegetables from your garden.

- Host a potluck dinner.

- Start up a buyers' club for meat, dairy, or poultry.

- Organize a monthly cooking club focusing on local, seasonal ingredients.

- Exchange (seasonal) recipes.

- Talk up local food.

Another option is to attend a farm dinner. Beware, however, that these dinners are pretty pricey, running upward of $200 per person for one meal. To find out if any farm dinners are open near you, search "farm dinners" online or check out Outstanding in the Field (outstandinginthefield.com), a group that travels around the country organizing farm dinners.

> **A CLOSER LOOK**
>
> Farm dinners are high-end, restaurant-quality meals served at the farm. Offered only once or twice a year, these dinners help build the local community by allowing locavores to interact with each other and the farmers who host the event. In addition to great food, diners also get a tour of the farm.

Get Connected

The number of people who eat local is growing in leaps and bounds. Many are located in big cities and sprawling suburbs all over the country. And although locavores cut across all ages and ethnic backgrounds, they do tend to be a computer-savvy crowd. As a result, people who eat local boast a vibrant and active online community.

Local foods are a hot topic on blogs, websites, Facebook pages, and Twitter accounts. This makes it easy to find practically anything you want to know about eating local online. Everything from struggles of people just beginning to eat local to articles from seasoned pros are just a few clicks away. (Check out Appendix B for a list of websites you can visit.)

You'll also find how-to guides on everything from starting a garden to finding a CSA, blogs describing the trials and tribulations of eating local during different seasons and in different climates, where to find local foods, eat local challenges, and a multitude of local recipes using seasonal ingredients so you can learn how to prepare local foods.

For people who want to become part of this bigger community, social media is the way to go. Start a blog; make a post; set up a Facebook or Twitter account. Connecting with other people who care about what they eat gives you a sense of belonging and a feeling that we're all in this together. You can also develop long-lasting friendships and bonds with other locavores.

Like most things, the best way to get started is to jump right in with both feet!

The Least You Need to Know

- Farm-to-school programs improve school lunches, increase fruit and vegetable consumption, and promote healthy eating behaviors at home.

- Incorporating local food into the curriculum teaches students about agriculture, science, nutrition, and health.

- School gardens introduce students to new foods and promote life skills like working together and responsibility.

- Local food advocates are passionate about spreading the word and promote local eating at schools, in the workplace, and in their neighborhood.

- The Internet is a great way to connect to other locavores, find information on local foods near you, and look up recipes to prepare your local harvest.

Glossary

aged manure Dung from cows, sheep, goats, and other animals. It must be aged (allowed to sit and rot) for several months or more before using. It's then mixed into the soil to enrich/supplement it. Manure that's not aged long enough will make the soil too acidic and burn the plant roots.

American Livestock Breed Conservancy This nonprofit organization is devoted to protecting more than 180 breeds of livestock and poultry from extinction. It also works to repopulate and grow these endangered species.

artisanal Products that are handcrafted by skilled workers, usually using traditional methods.

biodiversity Refers to all the variety of life in a certain region. This includes species diversity, such as plant and animal variety; genetic diversity, the variety of genes in individual organisms; and ecological diversity, the kinds of habitats, biological communities, and ecosystems that exist there.

biodynamic farming A holistic and balanced approach to farming developed in the 1920s that takes into account the soil, living organisms, and the weather of the farm. It uses chemical-free farming techniques.

blanching Briefly partially cooking a food in hot water. Blanching is generally followed by shocking, or dropping the food in an ice bath right after blanching. This prevents the food from further cooking.

brine A saltwater solution used to preserve food. Brine is usually used with chicken.

buyers' club A group of individuals usually based in a metropolitan area that strikes up a deal with a producer to regularly buy local meat, produce, chicken, etc., which is delivered directly from the farm to a central location (usually a buyers' club host's house). Because they buy large quantities, pricing is usually better.

carbon footprint   A measure of the impact of our activities on the environment, and particularly climate change, as it relates to the amount of greenhouse gases produced in our day-to-day lives through burning fossil fuels for electricity, heating, transportation, etc.

certified organic   A label given to food produced without synthetic fertilizers, herbicides, and pesticides (natural ones are allowed), sewage sludge, genetic engineering, or irradiation. For animals, this means raised without growth hormones or antibiotics, fed only organic feed without animal by-products, and having access to the outdoors.

charcuterie   The art of salting, smoking, and curing meat, usually pork.

chefs collaborative   A nonprofit organization dedicated to connecting chefs to a local sustainable food system. The group also promotes chef advocacy, education, and collaboration with the broader food community.

colony collapse disorder   A phenomenon in which the bees in a colony disappear or die. The cause is unknown, but experts suspect pesticides or pollen from genetically modified plants may play a role.

community garden   Usually located on a public plot of land, a community garden brings local individuals together to work for a common goal—a garden. The harvest can be divided among the community (and the workers) or given to a local food bank.

community supported agriculture (CSA)   A community of individuals who pledge support (usually a dollar amount) to a farm operation. Members are called shareholders because they share in the risks and benefits of food production. In return, they receive a share of the farm's bounty.

compost   Plant material that's further decomposed by microorganisms to make a rich, soil-like material.

concentrated animal feeding operations (CAFOs)   Large factory farms containing a minimum of 1,000 cattle, 2,500 hogs, or 125,000 chickens, all in one space usually the size of a few football fields, where the animals have little or no access to the outdoors.

container gardening   A small, contained garden made in practically anything—big pots, boxes, buckets, pails, windowsill planters, or just about anything else that can hold dirt and has good drainage. Herbs work well in container gardens.

controlled atmosphere cold storage   A storage method, commonly used for apples, using low temperatures in an airtight room with most of the oxygen removed. This creates an environment that puts apples into hibernation for the winter and prevents them from deteriorating.

deglazing   A culinary term that means to stir a liquid in a sauté pan, dissolving caramelized bits of food from the bottom of the pan into the liquid. It's often done after cooking meat, fish, or poultry. The liquid is highly flavored and usually used as a base for a sauce. A pan can be deglazed with water, wine, or stock.

dehydrator   A free-standing electrical unit that controls temperature and humidity. The purpose of a dehydrator is to remove all the moisture from foods so they'll be preserved.

economies of scale   This relates to the size of the operation. Basically the bigger the production output, the less it costs to produce each unit.

environmentally friendly   A way of farming, living, etc. using techniques or practices that don't harm the earth's natural resources and may even protect it.

farm-to-college   Programs that allow schools, specifically colleges and universities, to use local food in their foodservice systems.

farm-to-fork operations   Restaurants that prepare food bought directly from a local farm or grown in a local garden.

farm-to-school programs   Programs that allow K–12 schools to use local food in their foodservice systems.

farmers' market   A public market, usually outdoors, where farmers and other vendors sell their products directly to consumers.

farmstead cheese   Cheese made on a farm using milk produced only on that farm.

food co-ops   Stores owned by the consumer "members" who frequent them. Food co-ops are a great place to find local food.

food miles   The distance food travels from where it's grown to where it's ultimately purchased or eaten by consumers.

foodborne illness   An illness caused by eating or drinking food or beverages contaminated with bacteria, parasites, or viruses resulting from improper processing, storage, handling, or cooking.

foodshed   A local region or area that supplies food to a specific population base or urban center.

foraged food   Food that grows naturally and is gathered from the wild; not domesticated.

free-range   A term usually used to refer to poultry. It means the animal has access to the outdoors. Also called free-roaming.

freezer burn   Pale, dry spots that develop when moisture evaporates on frozen food that's improperly or inadequately wrapped or packaged.

genetic diversity   The genetic variation within a population or species. Genetic diversity is one aspect of biodiversity.

gleaning   When a farmer allows people to collect his leftover crops at the end of the season after the crops have already been commercially harvested. Pickers can keep the gleaned food or give it to food banks, schools, or local community centers. Gleaning programs are popping up across the country.

grain-finished   The practice of giving animals grain the few months before slaughter to fatten them up. Unfortunately, this practice changes the composition of the meat, and many of the healthy aspects of grass-fed beef are reduced or negated when this is done.

grass-fed animals   An animal that's consumed only its mother's milk, grass, and forage its entire life.

greenhouse gases   Gases that trap heat in the earth's atmosphere and thus contribute to global warming. They include carbon dioxide, water vapor, nitrous oxide, methane, hydrofluorocarbons (HFCs), perfluorocarbons (PFCs), and sulfur hexafluoride. These gases come from burning fossil fuels for electricity, heat, driving, land-use, agriculture, and almost all human activities.

greenwashing   A deceptive practice some companies use involving "spinning" their products and policies as being environmentally friendly when an in-depth investigation proves these claims to be false.

guerrilla gardening   A popular trend in big cities involving the unauthorized cultivation of plants or vegetable crops on vacant public or private property. Many locavores see it as making good use of wasted space.

heirloom plants   Any garden plant (fruit, vegetable, grain, or bean) that has a history of being passed down within a family. They are unique in that they're genetically distinct from commercial plants mass-produced by industrial agriculture. Many heirloom plants are locally grown.

heritage breeds   Traditional animal breeds raised by farmers. These animals developed traits that made them particularly well adapted to local environmental conditions. These are the animal equivalent of heirloom plants.

high tunnels   A less-expensive alternative to a greenhouse that uses clear plastic to protect plants from harsh weather conditions. Unlike hoop houses, high tunnels are not high enough for a person to stand up inside. They may or may not be heated.

homogenization   The mechanical treatment of milk so the fat globules are evenly dispersed throughout. Homogenization also extends the milk's shelf life.

hoop houses   An experimental and less-expensive alternative to a greenhouse. Hoop houses are simply clear plastic stretched over large hoops. They're high enough for a person to stand up inside, and they may or may not be heated.

hyperlocal   One step further than local, hyperlocal restaurants grow their own produce on-site or manage the raising and butchering of their own meat.

intercropping   A space-saving technique allowing you to grow different plants with different maturing times together. A perfect example of this is the "three sisters"— corn, beans, and squash, which the Native Americans planted together in the same hill.

jams   A sweet fruit gel made with a fruit's pulp in addition to its juice.

jelly   A sweet fruit gel made with strained fruit juice.

Know Your Farmer, Know Your Food   A program initiated by the U.S. Department of Agriculture to promote local foods by encouraging consumers to get to know their local farmers.

legumes   Edible seeds grown in pods. Dried and fresh beans, dried peas, and lentils are legumes. Peanuts, although classified as nuts, are technically legumes.

local food   Food grown or raised in the region where you live. "Local" can be defined according to region, state, or distance.

local food movement   A trend to buy and consume mostly local food. It also reminds you to think about where food comes from and how it gets from the farm to your plate.

local products   Processed foods that are locally prepared, usually by artisans, and usually handcrafted, and sold at local markets. They do not necessarily use local ingredients.

locavore   A person committed to eating as much local food as possible, with locally grown being defined as within a 50-, 100-, or 150-mile radius.

marbling   Whitish streaks of fat found between the muscle of meat in steaks and roasts. Marbling increases the meat's tenderness—and fat content.

membrillo   A Spanish term that refers specifically to quince paste. In the United States, it's sometimes used to signify any fruit and nut paste, often locally prepared.

microbreweries   Breweries that produce a small amount of beer. Microbreweries often sell only local, handcrafted beers.

minimally processed foods   Foods whose physical or chemical properties have been slightly altered but the food's nutritional value has not changed.

monocrop farms   Farms that only grow a single crop. These are usually large, conventional operations.

monounsaturated fat   Liquid at room temperature, monounsaturated fats have only one double bond. They can be found in avocados, sesame seeds, peanuts, and vegetable oils such as olive, canola, sesame and peanut.

noncertified organic   A farm that grows or raises livestock or produce (and dairy) using organic practices but is not certified by U.S. regulatory agencies. Farmers do this to save time (certification requires a lot of paperwork), money, and hassle.

offal   Organ meats.

omega-3 fatty acid   A type of polyunsaturated fat essential for our well-being. They're found in fatty fish like salmon, tuna, sardines, mackerel, and shellfish and help protect us against heart disease, inflammation, and other chronic illness.

organic matter   Decomposed living matter. In plants, this can be straw, wood chips, leaves, kitchen scraps, or grass clippings. In animals, this usually means manure.

organic meat Meat raised free of antibiotics, hormones, and additives. It must also be fed organic feed that's 100 percent vegetarian.

pasteurization The process of heating milk to high temperatures for a certain period of time to kill harmful bacteria that may reside there.

pectin A gelatin-like substance obtained from certain fruits, like apples, used to thicken jams and jellies.

phytochemicals Biologically active plant compounds believed to protect you from illness and promote optimal health. They give fruits, vegetables, beans, and grain their distinct characteristics.

pickling The act of preserving a food by fermenting it in a saltwater solution. Pickling can preserve perishable foods for months. Also known as brining or corning.

polyunsaturated fats Fats that are liquid at room temperature and have more than one double bond in their makeup. Polyunsaturated fats are found in vegetable oils like soybean, corn, and safflower, fatty fish like salmon, and some nuts and seeds like walnuts and sunflower seeds.

pon hoss A traditional Amish dish made with pork scraps, organ meats, broth, and flour. This dish was created so no part of the animal was wasted.

preserves A sweet fruit gel make with whole fruit or large fruit pieces added to the fruit gel (unlike jelly, which just uses the juice).

processed food Food that's been altered to change its physical, chemical, microbiological, or sensory properties. Usually some part of the food—fiber, nutrients, etc.—has been removed.

pulses Dried legumes. Legumes can be both dried and fresh, but pulses are only dried. Pulses include dried peas and lentils, which are a cousin to the bean.

phytochemicals The plant compounds that give fruits, vegetables, and grains their distinctive colors, textures, and flavors. In the body, phytochemicals provide no calories but are biologically active and believed to protect you from disease and promote overall good health.

raised beds A method of planting used in square-foot gardening in which mounds of dirt (about 12 inches deep) are enclosed by four wooden boards in the shape of a square or rectangle. No digging required!

raw milk   Milk that's not been pasteurized, homogenized, or processed in any way.

real food challenge   A national student movement advocating a just and sustainable food system (serving real food), at colleges and universities across the country.

relishes   Preserved, pickled foods cut in bite-size pieces.

root cellar   Either above- or underground structures designed to keep temperatures cool, around 40°F to 50°F, used to store vegetables and fruits for the winter.

rototiller   A machine that tills, or turns over, soil.

salting   The process of surrounding a food with salt or salt mixed with sugar and spices. The salt dries out the food, inhibits bacterial growth, and adds flavor.

saturated fats   Solid at room temperature, these fats are mainly found in animals and animal products like meat and cheese. They also appear in plants such as coconut oil, palm and palm kernel oil, and cocoa butter. Diets high in saturated fats increase risk of heart disease and other chronic illnesses.

Slow Food USA   The U.S. branch of an international organization dedicated to preserving old-world foods and food traditions and reconnecting Americans with the plants, animals, and people that produce our food. More than 200 chapters operate in the United States.

smoking (food)   A method of preserving and flavoring foods by exposing it to smoke. In cold smoked foods, the foods are not fully cooked, while in hot smoked food, they are.

succession planting   The efficient practice of planting different vegetables that mature at different rates in the same space. This enables you to keep your land productive from spring through fall.

sustainable agriculture   Agriculture that protects and replenishes the earth's natural resources and integrates socially and environmentally friendly farm practices.

sweet potatoes   Long, elongated tubers that taper at the end and have a moist orange, yellow, or white-colored flesh. They're especially popular in the South. *See also* yams.

tripe   A stomach lining, usually of a cow.

trotters   Pig's feet.

U-pick farms Farms where customers can come and pick the fruit or vegetable right off the vine. U-picks are often cheaper than other local food because the farm doesn't have the added cost of labor.

ultrapasteurization The process of heating milk at extra-high temperatures (at or above 280°F) for about two seconds. This milk stays good for a longer period of time and does not need to be refrigerated. However, taste is affected.

ultraprocessed foods Foods composed of a combination of processed foods containing little if any unprocessed or minimally processed foods. Usually high in empty calories like sugar, fat, and salt, these foods lack nutritional value.

umami The fifth taste sensation that gives food a savory richness or meatiness, caused by ultraprocessed foods. Found in meats and fermented foods like cheese, rich stocks, soy sauce, shellfish, wine, mushrooms, and tomatoes as well as foods containing monosodium glutamate.

unprocessed foods Foods in their whole, natural state that have not been changed physically or chemically.

urban gleaning The practice of collecting fruits, berries, or vegetables that would otherwise go to waste from plants, trees, or bushes in urban neighborhoods.

vegan A person who eats only plant foods and omits all animal and animal products, including cheese, butter, and yogurt, from her diet.

vertical gardening A method of growing vegetables or herbs vertically from upright structures such as fences, trellises, or walls.

Weston A. Price Foundation A nonprofit organization that promotes a diet of whole, natural, unprocessed foods based on traditional diets of primitive, nonindustrialized people based on research from Dr. Price, a dentist and nutrition researcher who lived during the 1920s.

Wholesome Wave A nonprofit organization dedicated to increasing the availability of healthy local produce to lower-income neighborhoods and individuals.

yams Dry-fleshed sweet potatoes. True yams (called boniato) are from a tropical plant native to Latin America. Hundreds of varieties of sweet potatoes range in size, color, and taste. Look for hard-to-find-heirlooms like Hayman, Porto Rico, Covington and O'Henry. *See also* sweet potatoes.

Resources

Locavores have a multitude of resources to call upon to find out about almost any aspect of living and eating local. Here are just a few of the many out there. I've broken them down into books and websites.

Books

These books cover a wide range of topics. Some of them are more in-depth, while others are general. If you want to dig deeper on a given topic, plenty of other resources are available. I would start at your local public library first and then look online.

Lifestyle

Lifestyle books include the broad category of living and eating local. Usually they'll discuss the local lifestyle or diet. Because local is so specific to the region where you live, many have a certain bias. For instance, you can often tell if an author is a city or rural dweller and where they're from—East Coast, West Coast, the South, etc. Other books focus on the politics of eating local or sustainability.

Bendrick, Lou. *Eat Where You Live: How to Find and Enjoy Fantastic Local and Sustainable Food No Matter Where You Live.* Seattle, WA: Skipstone Press, 2008.

Cotler, Amy. *The Locavore Way: Discover and Enjoy the Pleasures of Locally Grown Food.* North Adams, MA: Storey Publishing, 2009.

Geagan, Kate. *Go Green Get Lean.* Emmaus, PA: Rodale Press, 2009.

Halweil, Brian. *Eat Here: Homegrown Pleasures in a Global Supermarket.* New York City: W.W. Norton & Company, 2004.

Kingsolver, Barbara. *Animal, Vegetable, Miracle: A Year of Food Life.* New York City: HarperPerennial, 2008.

Meredith, Leda. *The Locavore's Handbook: The Busy Person's Guide to Eating Local on a Budget.* Guilford, CT: Lyons Press, 2010.

Nabhan, Gary Paul. *Coming Home to Eat: The Pleasure and Politics of Local Food.* New York City: W.W. Norton & Company, 2009

Newgent, Jackie. *Big Green Cookbook.* Hoboken, NJ: John Wiley and Sons 2009.

Nestle, Marion. *What to Eat.* New York City: North Point Press, 2007.

Petrini, Carl. *Slow Food Nation: Why Our Food Should Be Good, Clean, and Fair.* New York City: Rizzoli Ex Libris, 2007.

Pollan, Michael. *In Defense of Food: An Eater's Manifesto.* New York City: Penguin, 2009.

Smith, Alisa, and J. B. Mackinnon. *Plenty: Eating Locally on the 100-Mile Diet.* New York City: Clarkson Potter, 2008.

Food Books

Food books include cookbooks as well as ingredient-specific books about a certain food like fish or mushrooms. Most of them contain recipes.

Bittman, Mark. *Fish: The Complete Guide to Buying and Cooking.* New York City: Wiley, 1999.

Brill, Steve. *The Wild Vegan Cookbook: A Forager's Culinary Guide (in the Field or in the Supermarket) to Preparing and Savoring Wild (and Not So Wild) Natural Foods.* Boston, MA: Harvard Common Press, 2010.

Ehlers, Steve, and Jeanette Hurt. *The Complete Idiot's Guide to Cheeses of the World.* Indianapolis: Alpha Books, 2008.

Fraioli, James O. *The Best Recipes from America's Food Festivals.* Indianapolis: Alpha Books, 2007.

Fletcher, Janet. *Fresh from the Farmers' Market (Reissue): Year-Round Recipes for the Pick of the Crop.* San Francisco: Chronicle Books. 2008.

Frank, Lois Ellen. *Foods of the Southwest Indian Nations.* Berkeley, CA: Ten Speed Press, 2002.

Green, Aliza. *Field Guide to Seafood: How to Identify, Select, and Prepare Virtually Every Fish and Shellfish at the Market.* Philadelphia: Quirk Books, 2007.

Gresco, Taras. *Bottomfeeder: How to Eat Ethically in a World of Vanishing Seafood.* New York City: Bloomsbury, USA, 2009.

Henderson, Fergus. *The Whole Beast: Nose to Tail Eating.* New York City: Ecco, 2004.

Letcher Lyle, Katie. *The Foraging Gourmet.* Augusta, GA: Morris Publishing Group, 1997.

Madison, Deborah. *Local Flavors: Cooking and Eating from America's Farmers' Markets.* New York City: Clarkson Potter, 2008.

Mendelson, Anne. *Milk: The Surprising Story of Milk Through the Ages.* New York City: Alfred Knopf, 2008.

Nabhan, Gary Paul, and Deborah Madison. *Renewing America's Food Traditions Saving and Savoring the Continent's Most Endangered Foods.* White River Junction, VT: Chelsea Green, 2008.

Opton, Gene, and Nancy Hughes. *Honey: A Connoisseur's Guide with Recipes.* Berkeley, CA: Ten Speed Press, 2000.

Ryder, Tracey, and Carole Topalian. *Edible: A Celebration of Local Foods.* New York City: Wiley, 2010.

How-To

How-to books are exactly what they sound like—books about how to do something. These instructional books teach you everything from how to can to raising peppers.

Bowman, Darian Price, and Carl A. Price. *The Complete Idiot's Guide to Vegetable Gardening.* Indianapolis: Alpha Books, 2009.

Brees, Karen K., Ph.D. *The Complete Idiot's Guide to Preserving Food.* Indianapolis: Alpha Books, 2009.

Brill, Steve "Wildman," and Evelyn Dean. *Identifying and Harvesting Edible and Medicinal Plants in Wild (and Not So Wild) Places.* New York City: HarperPaperbacks, 1994.

Bubel, Mike, and Nancy Bubel. *Root Cellaring: Natural Cold Storage of Fruits and Vegetables.* North Adams, MA: Storey Publishing, 1991.

Costenbader, Carol W. *The Big Book of Preserving the Harvest: 150 Recipes for Freezing, Canning, Drying and Pickling Fruits and Vegetables.* North Adams, MA: Storey Publishing, 2002.

Cutler, Davis Karen. Burpee: *The Complete Vegetable and Herb Gardener: A Guide to Growing Your Garden Organically.* New York City: Macmillian, 1997.

Gibbons, Euell. *Stalking the Wild Asparagus.* Chambersburg, PA: Hood, Alan C. & Company, Inc., 2005.

Gussow, Joan. *This Organic Life: Confessions of a Suburban Homesteader.* White River Junction, VT: Chelsea Green, 2002.

Kallas, John. *Edible Wild Plants: Wild Foods from Dirt to Plate (The Wild Food Adventure Series, Book 1).* Layton, UT: Gibbs Smith, 2010.

Maxwell, Steve, Jennifer MacKenzie, and Len Churchill. *The Complete Root Cellar Book: Building Plans, Uses and 100 Recipes.* Toronto, Ontario: Robert Rose, 2010.

Meyer, Mary Clemens, and Susanna Meyer. *Saving the Seasons: How to Can, Freeze and Dry Almost Anything.* Scottdale, PA: Herald Press, 2010.

Nyerges, Christopher. *Guide to Wild and Useful Plants.* Chicago: Chicago Review Press, 1999.

Ruhlman, Michael, and Brian Polcyn. *Charcuterie: The Craft of Salting, Smoking, and Curing.* New York City: W.W. Norton, 2005.

Smith, Edward C. *The Vegetable Gardener's Bible (10th Anniversary Edition).* North Adams, MA: Storey Books, 2000.

Thayer, Samuel. *Nature's Garden: A Guide to Identifying, Harvesting, and Preparing Edible Wild Plants.* Cleveland, NY: Forager's Harvest Press, 2010.

———. *The Forager's Harvest: A Guide to Identifying, Harvesting, and Preparing Edible Wild Plants.* Cleveland, NY: Forager's Harvest Press, 2006.

Topp, Ellie, and Margaret Howard. *The Complete Book of Small-Batch Preserving.* Tonawanda, NY: Firefly Books, 2007.

Websites

Hundreds of websites talk about local issues. Here are just a few of the ones discussed in this book.

American Community Gardening Association
www.communitygarden.org

American Farmland Trust
www.farmland.org

American Grassfed Association
www.americangrassfed.org

American Livestock Breeds Conservancy
www.albc-usa.org

Appalachian Sustainable Agricultural Project
www.asapconnections.org

Better School Food
www.betterschoolfood.org
www.betterschoolfood.com

Biodynamic Farming and Gardening Association
www.biodynamics.com

Chefs Collaborative
www.chefscollaborative.org

Community Food Security Coalition
www.foodsecurity.org

Compost Cab
www.compostcab.com

The Daily Green
www.thedailygreen.com

DrinkLocalWine.com
www.drinklocalwine.com

Eat Local (Natural Resources Defense Council)
www.simplesteps.org/eat-local
www.nrdc.org

Eat Local, America!
www.eatlocalamerica.coop

Eat Local Challenge
www.eatlocalchallenge.com

Eat Well Guide
www.eatwellguide.org

Eatwild
www.eatwild.com

Edible Communities Magazines
www.ediblecommunities.com

Edible Schoolyard
www.edibleschoolyard.org

Farm to School
www.farmtoschool.org

Farmers Market Coalition
www.farmersmarketcoalition.org

Feast of San Gennaro in New York City
www.sangennaro.org

Fed Up with Lunch: The School Lunch Project
www.fedupwithschoollunch.blogspot.com

The Food Project
www.thefoodproject.org

FoodCorps
www.food-corps.org

FoodRoutes
www.foodroutes.com

Food Foraging
www.foraging.com

Forager's Harvest by Samuel Thayer
www.foragersharvest.com

Foraging with the "Wildman"—Steve Brill, urban forager based in New York City
www.wildmanstevebrill.com

Gilroy Garlic Festival
www.gilroygarlicfestival.com

Good Natured Family Farms
www.goodnatured.net

Green City Market—Chicago
chicagogreencitymarket.org

GreenPeople—Buy Green, Sell Green, Be Green
www.greenpeople.org

Heritage Foods USA (food distributor)
www.heritagefoodsusa.com

Honey Locator
www.honeylocator.com

HOTLIPS Soda
www.hotlipssoda.com

Hyperlocavore: A Yardsharing Community
www.hyperlocavore.com

Ingles Markets
ingles-markets.com

KidsGardening.org
www.kidsgardening.org

Know Your Farmer, Know Your Food
www.usda.gov/knowyourfarmer

Leopold Center for Sustainable Agriculture—Iowa State
www.leopold.iastate.edu/research/marketing.htm

LocalHarvest
www.localharvest.org

Maple Creek Farm
maplecreekfarm.net

Monastery Mustard
www.monasterymustard.com

Monterey Bay Aquarium Seafood Watch
www.montereybayaquarium.org/cr/seafoodwatch.aspx

National Association of Farmers' Market Nutrition Programs
www.nafmnp.org

National Center for Home Food Preservation
www.uga.edu/nchfp

National Cooperative Grocers Association
www.ncga.coop

National Council of Farmer Cooperatives
www.ncfc.org

National Gardening Association
www.garden.org

National Lentil Festival
www.lentilfest.com

Neighborhood Fruit
www.neighborhoodfruit.com

Northeast Organic Wheat consortium
growseed.org/now.html

Northern Grain Growers Association
www.northerngraingrowers.org

Oklahoma Food Cooperative
www.oklahomafood.coop

Outstanding in the Field—Traveling Farm Dinners
www.outstandinginthefield.com

PickYourOwn.org
www.pickyourown.org

Polyface, Inc.
polyfacefarms.com

Portland Fruit Tree Project
portlandfruit.org

Real Food Challenge
www.realfoodchallenge.org

Real Milk Campaign
www.realmilk.com

Real Raw Milk Facts
www.realrawmilkfacts.com

Seed Savers Exchange
www.seedsavers.org

Slow Food USA
www.slowfoodusa.org

Southern Exposure Seed Exchange Heritage Harvest Festival
www.heritageharvestfestival.com

Sustainable Table
www.sustainabletable.org/issues/eatlocal

Taste of Chicago
gochicago.about.com/od/tasteofchicago/p/taste_chicago.htm

Taste of Colorado
atasteofcolorado.com

Taste of Music City
tasteofmusiccity.com

Taste of Syracuse
tasteofsyracuse.com

Thousand Hills Cattle Company
www.thousandhillscattleco.com

Tuscarora Organic Growers
www.tog.coop

University of California, Davis, Postharvest Technology Research Information Center
homeorchard.ucdavis.edu/fvstorage.pdf

USDA Agricultural Service—Farmers' Market Search Listing
apps.ams.usda.gov/FarmersMarkets

USDA Community Supported Agriculture
www.nal.usda.gov/afsic/pubs/csa/csa.shtml

USDA Cooperative Extension System Offices
www.csrees.usda.gov/Extension

USDA Dietary Guidelines
health.gov/dietaryguidelines

Vegetable Gardener
www.vegetablegardener.com

Veggie Trader
www.veggietrader.com

Vincent Family Cranberries
www.vincentcranberries.com

Whole Foods
wholefoodsmarket.com

Wholesome Wave
www.wholesomewave.org

Wild Food Adventures—Foraging Tours
www.wildfoodadventures.com

Worldwatch Institute
www.worldwatch.org

Eating Local by Region

People who eat local eat close to the land they live on. This means they support local farmers, sustainable agriculture, and humanely raised animals. But this *doesn't* mean they eat the same thing. Each region has its own unique foodshed, and the kinds of local food you'll find varies greatly from place to place. Even within regions, differences in climate and soil, as well as culture, significantly affect the type of local foods you'll find.

In this appendix, I've divided the United States into distinct regions and then broken down each region accordingly. I've discussed climate and geography, listed the foods native to each area, included some farmers' markets where you're likely to find local food, and offered some regional dishes using some of these foods.

Although nearly all regions grow typical American produce, I've tried to pick things specifically unique to the area. Also remember that certain foods may spill over within areas and regions. For instance, wheat can be grown in New England, parts of the Mid-Atlantic states, and as far south as Maryland, but it doesn't fare well farther south than that. This list is by no means comprehensive, but it should give you a good idea of interesting foods available in different places.

Northeast: New England

New England consists of six states: Maine, Vermont, New Hampshire, Massachusetts, Rhode Island, and Connecticut. All border the Atlantic Ocean except for Vermont, so you can expect seafood to play a prominent role in their food culture. New Englanders also maintain a strong cultural identity, which is expressed in their food traditions as well.

Climate and Geography

The New England states have four very distinct seasons:

- Harsh, cold, long winters

- Cool, crisp, colorful autumns

- Warm, humid, short summers

- Gentle, breezy springs

Due to the weather, there's a fairly short growing season and usually a long, late harvest of cool-weather crops.

The geography includes long rolling hills, mountains, and jagged coastline. The soil, particularly in the northern part, tends to be thin and rocky, but plenty of fertile pockets can be found around this region's river valleys and mountains. Notable agricultural regions include the Green Mountains of Vermont, Pioneer Valley in Western Massachusetts, and the White Mountains of New Hampshire. Seafood and fisheries dominate Cape Cod and the surrounding shores, while dairy farms populate much of the countryside inland. This makes for a diverse range of agriculture and an abundance of wild game and seafood (in coastal areas) and livestock.

Native Foods

Native foods center around seafood and cool-weather crops like apples and cabbage. In addition, there's dairy (Vermont is a big dairy state), potatoes (supplied by Maine), and maple syrup (found throughout New England).

Here are some native foods you're likely to find in this area:

Apple cider

Apples (all varieties)

Asparagus

Blueberries

Broccoli

Cabbage

Cauliflower

Cheese (fresh and aged goat and cow's milk cheese)

Clams

Cod

Crab

Cranberries

Dairy products

Fiddlehead ferns

Gooseberries

Honey

Lobster

Maple syrup

Mushrooms

Oysters

Pumpkins

Ramps

Raspberries

Squash

Tomatoes

Turkey

Wheat

Wild leeks

Local Farmers' Markets

Here are some of the local farmers' markets you'll want to check out:

Brunswick Farmers' Market
Brunswick, Maine
brunswickfarmersmarket.com

Capital City Farmers' Market
Montpelier, Vermont
montpelierfarmersmarket.com

Coventry Farmers' Market
Coventry, Connecticut
coventryfarmersmarket.com

Downtown Providence Farmers' Market
Providence, Rhode Island
farmfreshri.org
This site lists all the local farmers' markets in the state in addition to U-picks, CSAs, and farm stands plus profiles of nearly 50 local farmers.

Haymarket Farmers' Market
Boston, Massachusetts
boston-discovery-guide.com/haymarket-boston.html

Ethnic Influences

In New England, ethnic influences come from a variety of peoples. There's no denying the influence of the English settlers along with the Native Americans. The later European immigrants from Italy, Germany, France, Portugal, Scotland, and Ireland also made their mark.

Regional Dishes

Regional dishes reflect the flavor as well as the ethnicity of the region. Here you can tell the strongest influence comes from Native Americans and the English pilgrims:

Boiled dinner. Corned beef with beets, parsnips, carrots, potatoes, and horseradish cream.

Boston baked beans. Small dried white beans cooked with molasses, sugar, onion, and salt pork.

Broiled Boston scrod. There's no fish named scrod, so usually this refers to young cod, but it can also be haddock, Pollack, or hake. The fish is simply broiled with a buttered crumb topping.

New England clam chowder. A thick, cream-based "white" chowder made with potatoes, onions, bacon, and clams.

Steamed lobster. Steamed lobster simply served with melted butter and a wedge of lemon.

Succotash. A classic New England dish made with baby lima beans, corn, and a touch of cream and sugar.

Northeast: Mid-Atlantic States

The Mid-Atlantic states cover the rest of the northeast, and although the exact definition may vary, here I've included New York, New Jersey, Delaware, Pennsylvania, Maryland, and Washington, D.C., in the list. Northern Virginia is actually more like a Northern state in climate, population, and politics so I've counted parts of it as well. Like New England, the Mid-Atlantic states rely on the ocean to supply them with an abundance of seafood. But this area is also rich in agriculture, which provides a wealth of produce and livestock.

Climate and Geography

The climate of the Mid-Atlantic states is similar to New England, except the winters are milder and the summers are longer and hotter. In addition to the coast, this part of the country boasts fertile land, including rivers, valleys, and hills. The most fruitful agricultural areas in this region include the Allegheny Mountains in western Pennsylvania, the Hudson River Valley in New York, and the Chesapeake Bay area in Maryland.

Native Foods

The Mid-Atlantic states boast a great diversity of food and foodsheds. Pennsylvania produces a wide range of vegetables and is well known for its stone fruits like peaches, plums, apricots, and plumcots. It's also the center of the mushroom industry. The Hudson Valley in New York has a reputation for producing great cheese as well as its grapes, garlic, and apples. Small dairies can be found throughout the region, too. New Jersey is home to many farms and famous for its tomato, pepper, and eggplant production along with blueberries and cranberries. The Chesapeake Bay supplies blue crab, oysters, clams, rockfish, and perch.

Here are some native foods you're likely to find in this area:

Apple cider	Beets
Apples (all varieties)	Blue crab
Arugula	Blueberries
Asparagus	Broccoli rabe
Basil	Cantaloupes

Cheese (especially cheddar;
cow's milk, goat, and sheep
milk cheese)

Cherries

Chicken

Cucumbers

Grapes

Kohlrabi

Leafy greens (Swiss chard,
broccoli rabe, kale, and mustard
greens)

Lettuces (all kinds)

Mushrooms

Nettles

Oysters

Perch

Rockfish

Strawberries

Summer squash

Tomatoes (all kinds)

Watermelon

Zucchini

Local Farmers' Markets

The Mid-Atlantic states have some of the oldest and largest farmers' markets in the country, like Lancaster Central Market in Pennsylvania. In the heart of Amish country, this indoor market is the oldest continuously operating farmers' market in the country, hosting about 60 vendors. Here are some others:

Bethesda Central Farm Market
Bethesda, Maryland
bethesdacentralfarmmarket.com

City Farmer's Market
Wooster's Square
New Haven, Connecticut
cityseed.org/city_markets/markets/wooster/index.shtml

FRESHFARM Markets DuPont Circle
Dupont Circle, Washington, D.C.
freshfarmmarket.org/markets/dupont_circle.html

Greenmarket Union Square
New York City, New York
grownyc.org/greenmarket

Ithaca Farmers' Market
Ithaca, New York
ithacamarket.com

Lancaster Central Market
Lancaster, Pennsylvania
centralmarketlancaster.com

Ethnic Influences

The Mid-Atlantic states were settled by a wider range of people than New England, including the Dutch, Swedes, English, Quakers, and Amish. They were also influenced by a great many Eastern and Western European countries.

Regional Dishes

Because of the great diversity, regional dishes vary greatly among states. Here's just a small sampling:

Apple crumble. Apples baked with a crumb made from butter, flour, and sugar. Nuts and oats are sometimes added.

Manhattan clam chowder. A tomato-based clam chowder.

Maryland crab cakes. Blue crabmeat mixed with bread or breadcrumbs and seasoning, usually Old Bay, and baked or fried.

Maryland oyster stew. A rich stew of oysters and cream.

Pennsylvania Dutch chicken potpie. A type of chicken stew with squares of dough cooked in the broth with the chicken.

Tomato pie. A type of pizza made with tomatoes and no cheese.

Southeast: The South

The South stretches from Virginia to Georgia (I cover Florida and Louisiana later) and as far west as Kentucky, Tennessee, and parts of Arkansas. The Southeast is bordered on the west by the Appalachian Mountains.

Climate and Geography

The climate in the Southeast ranges greatly from having all four seasons and mild, but cold winters in the northern parts like Virginia, West Virginia, and Kentucky, to having a very warm climate with little or no winter in places like Georgia, Mississippi, and Alabama. Compared to the rest of the United States, the climate is uniquely warm and wet with high humidity. The geography and foodsheds of the area are a diverse lot and include the South Carolina Low Country, the Blue Ridge Mountains, the Piedmont Region of North Carolina, and the Mississippi Delta region.

The weather is mild year-round, so harvest season is long and in some cases, such as with sweet potatoes and collard greens, can last all year.

Native Foods

Native foods center around pork (pigs are prevalent in this area) seafood, rice, cooking greens like collards, and all types of beans—fresh, shell, and dried. Crowder peas, black-eyed peas, and green beans are common. The long growing season offers a wealth of different types of vegetables.

Here are some native foods you're likely to find in this area:

Barbecue (pork)

Black-eyed peas and other fresh field peas

Cabbage

Collard greens

Corn

Crab (soft and hard shell)

Cucumbers

Game meats (squirrel, rabbit, deer, and raccoon)

Green beans

Lettuces (all varieties)

Lima beans and other fresh shelling beans

Melons (all varieties)

Mustard greens

Okra

Oysters

Peaches

Peanuts

Pecans (Georgia)

Peppers

Pole beans

Pork

Rice

Sesame seeds

Shrimp

Sorghum molasses

Sweet potatoes

Tomatoes (green and creole)

Turnip greens

Watermelon

Local Farmers' Markets

Due to the warm weather, many farmers' markets have an extended season, and more and more are staying open all year long. Here is a sample of what you will find:

Charleston Farmers' Market
Marion Square, Downtown Charleston, South Carolina
charlestoncvb.com/visitors/events_news/charleston-events/21st_annual_charleston_farmers_market_-5667

Durham Farmers' Market
Durham, North Carolina
durhamfarmersmarket.com

Forsyth Farmers' Market
Savannah, Georgia
forsythfarmersmarket.org

Memphis Farmers' Market
Memphis, Tennessee
memphisfarmersmarket.org

The Pepper Place Saturday Market
Birmingham, Alabama
pepperplacemarket.com

Ethnic Influences

Many of the culinary traditions of the South were influenced by the African culture. The people in the Appalachians and the Great Smoky Mountains were also affected by immigrants from Ireland, Scotland, and England in addition to the Native Americans.

Regional Dishes

Regional dishes tend to be rich in flavor and highly seasoned. Many meats and stews are slow cooked over an open pit or barbecue. Vegetables in the cuisine, especially greens, are plentiful.

Burgoo. A thick meat and vegetable stew from Kentucky typically made with game meat such as squirrel or rabbit and vegetables like corn, lima beans, okra, potatoes, tomatoes, carrots, and celery.

Fried green tomatoes. Green tomatoes coated with cornmeal, breaded, and fried.

Fried pie. A fruit-filled, half-moon-shaped deep-fried pie popular in Tennessee.

Memphis-style barbecue. Slow-cooked pork with a tomato-based barbecue sauce that's thin, sweet, and vinegary.

Mess o'greens. Cooked greens like collards simmered slowly (about 45 minutes to an hour) with salt pork or a ham hock. Turnip, kale, mustard, and spinach can also be used.

Stewed okra. Okra cooked with tomatoes and peppers with a touch of sugar.

Sweet potato pie. A Southern custard-style pie made of sweet potatoes, usually served at Thanksgiving.

Southeast: Louisiana and the Gulf

Because of its distinct geography and history, Louisiana has a unique culture and cuisine distinct from the rest of the South.

Climate and Geography

Louisiana borders the Gulf of Mexico on one side and the Mississippi River on the other. What makes it unusual is the number of swamplands and low-lying areas that produce a multitude of natural navigable waterways. These navigable waterways are home to a wealth of animals, plants, birds, and fish that provide sustenance for the region. The climate is humid and subtropical with hot summers and winters that rarely drop below freezing in the southern part of the state. These swampy lands are ideal for growing rice and boast a variety of seafood and game. Hot-weather plants producing tomatoes, sweet peppers, eggplant, and squashes thrive here.

Native Foods

Louisiana cuisine is divided into two camps: Cajun and Creole. Creole is more "citi-fied" cooking with influences from Africa and Europe (mainly France, Spain, and Portugal). Cajun originated in the Bayou and surrounding countryside, and although it's based on French cuisine, it's considered more provincial and rustic. Major components of Louisiana cuisine include shrimp, crawfish, rice, tomatoes, onions, peppers, okra, and collard greens.

Here are some native foods you're likely to find in this area:

Andouille sausage

Black-eyed peas and other fresh field peas

Cabbage

Catfish

Collard greens

Corn

Crab (soft and hard shell)

Crawfish

Cucumbers

Eggplant (all varieties)

Green beans

Lettuces (all varieties)

Lima beans and other fresh shelling beans

Mirlitons (a type of squash vegetable)

Melons (all varieties)

Mustard greens

Okra

Oysters

Peaches

Peppers

Pole beans

Pork

Rice

Shrimp

Sweet potatoes

Tomatoes (green and Creole)

Turnip greens

Watermelon

Local Farmers' Markets

In Louisiana farmers' markets come in all shapes and sizes and populate the state. Many are small, catering to just a few rural towns. You can find bigger ones in the city. Here are some to look for:

Covington Farmers' Market
Covington, Louisiana
covingtonfarmersmarket.org

Crescent City Farmers' Market
New Orleans, Louisiana
crescentcityfarmersmarket.org

Red Stick Farmer's Market
Baton Rouge, Louisiana
redstickfarmersmarket.org

Ethnic Influences

Much of Louisiana's cuisine was formed by the Acadians (people of French Canadian descent). These Acadians eventually settled in the country and became known as Cajuns. People in the city have more European roots (French and Spanish) again inspired by African and Caribbean cultures.

Regional Dishes

Regional dishes tend to be a mixture of French and African cuisine. Creole cooking tends to be more sophisticated and complicated, while Cajun is simpler and less involved.

Etoufée. A dark-colored Cajun stew traditionally made with crawfish and vegetables and served over rice.

Gumbo. A thick soup or stew thickened with filé powder (sassafras leaves) and usually served with rice. It usually contains seafood and pork or sausage.

Jambalaya. A spicy Creole rice dish made with sausage, chicken, and seafood. Countless variations are possible with the meat and seafood.

Pralines. A candy confection made of sugar, pecans, cream, and butter.

Red beans and rice. Well-seasoned small red beans simmered for hours and served over rice. The dish is typically served on Mondays.

Southeast: Florida

Florida is the southernmost state in the Union. Its warm, humid climate and fertile soil have made it a major agricultural force in this country.

Climate and Geography

Florida is the only mainland state bordered on two sides by the ocean. It has a warm, subtropical climate and sandy soil, which make it a good place for growing tropical fruits. Much of this country's tomato, avocado, citrus, and strawberry crops come from Florida. It can be very costly if a hurricane strikes, which it usually does during hurricane season each year. Peanuts are also grown in the northern part of the state.

Native Foods

Florida features a number of tropical and subtropical fruits along with seafood and many hot-weather vegetables like Swiss chard and sweet potatoes.

Here are some native foods you're likely to find in this area:

Alligator	Mangoes
Avocados	Melons (all varieties)
Cabbage	Okra
Cherimoyas	Oranges
Coconuts	Oysters
Corn	Peaches
Crowder peas	Peanuts
Cucumbers	Peppers
Dried peas and beans	Plantains
Eggplant	Pole beans
Grapefruits	Pork
Green beans	Pummelos
Guavas	Rice
Hearts of palm (also called swamp cabbage)	Shrimp
Kumquats	Stone crab
Lemons	Sweet potatoes
Lettuces (all varieties)	Tangerines
Limequats	Tomatoes (green and Creole)
Limes	Watermelon
Lobsters	Yucca or cassava

Local Farmers' Markets

Farmers' markets are a common sight in Florida, driven by the Latino community particularly in the South. Here are some you're likely to find:

Beaches Green Market and Community Garden
Jarboe Park, Neptune Beach, Florida
beacheslocalfoodnetwork.web.officelive.com/default.aspx

St. Petersburg Saturday Morning Market
St. Petersburg, Florida
saturdaymorningmarket.com

Tampa Downtown Market
Tampa, Florida
tampadowntownmarket.com

Ethnic Influences

Florida cuisine is a blend of many different cultures but strongest from the Latinos. Specifically dominant are Cuban-, Puerto Rican-, and Caribbean-inspired dishes. Because of its reliance on tropical fruits and spices, Florida cuisine is often referred to as *Floribbean cuisine.*

Regional Dishes

In the north, regional dishes have more of a southern flair, while in the south, it's based more on island cuisine. Here are just a few of the many dishes you'll find:

Arroz con pollo. A chicken and rice dish with roots in Spain and Latin America. There are many variations.

Black beans and rice. Steamed white rice served with black beans cooked with cumin and garlic.

Fried alligator. Small nuggets of alligator battered and deep-fried to a golden brown.

Fried plantains. Made with "Maduros," the name for ripe plantains, these are sliced lengthwise and twice fried until brown and crispy.

Key lime pie. Custard pie flavored with the juice from Key limes (a small, tart, intensely flavored lime).

Orange and avocado salad. A Cuban-influenced salad of avocado and Valencia oranges with lime and cilantro.

Tostones. Fried plantains made from the green (unripe) plantain.

Midwest: Great Lakes Region

The Midwest includes the Finger Lakes region of Wisconsin, Michigan, Ohio, Illinois, and Minnesota.

Climate and Geography

Here there are distinct seasons, where winters are cold and summers are warm. If you live near the Great Lakes, you have to deal with a constant Arctic wind. Despite this cold weather and having a shorter growing season than the South, the Midwest has fertile soil, plentiful water, and a long agricultural history.

In addition to corn, the Great Lakes region is well known for dairy farming. It's also ideal for growing fruit trees, cherries, and berries. This land is well suited for raising hogs and even some heritage breed cattle and bison. Minnesota, another dairy state known for its poultry, eggs, and meat, even has an official grain: wild rice.

Native Foods

Native foods tend to be hardy so they can withstand the cold climate. These include root vegetables and cabbage (sauerkraut is big), potatoes, meat, dairy, and cheeses. Although apples thrive in the Northeast, some can be found in the cooler climates of the Midwest. Cherries and certain berries thrive in this climate as well.

Here are some native foods you're likely to find in this area:

Apples (all kinds)	Black English walnuts
Apricots	Bratwurst
Asian bitter melon	Butternuts
Bacon	Carrots
Beets	Cheese (all varieties)
Berries (all varieties)	Cherries (all varieties, sweet and tart)

Crabapples	Persimmons
Crappie (fish)	Plums
Eggs	Potatoes
Frankfurters	Pumpkin
Ham	Rutabagas
Hickory nuts	Sassafras root
Kale	Sausages
Maple syrup	Sweet corn
Milk	Turnips
Onions	Whitefish
Pawpaw fruit	Wild rice
Perogies	

Local Farmers' Markets

This area is so rich in agricultural traditions, so extensive farmers' markets fill the region, including the Dane County Farmers' Market, which is the largest in the country.

Chicago Green City Market
Chicago, Illinois
chicagogreencitymarket.org

Cleveland West Side Market
Cleveland, Ohio
www.westsidemarket.org

Dane County Farmers' Market on the Square
Madison, Wisconsin
dcfm.org

Downtown St. Paul Farmers' Market (Lowertown district)
St. Paul, Minnesota
stpaulfarmersmarket.com

Flint Farmers' Market
Flint, Michigan
flintfarmersmarket.com

Ethnic Influences

All these people have made their mark on the cuisine of the Great Lakes Regions: Central and Eastern Europeans, Germans, Swedish, Scandinavians, Italians, Polish, and Ukrainian. Of the new immigrants, the Hmong people from Southeast Asia (Laos), have been most instrumental in reviving local agriculture and farmers' markets.

Regional Dishes

The foods in this region center around cheese and meats, while vegetables take their cue from German and Swiss traditions.

Bratwurst and sauerkraut. Mild German sausage and fermented cabbage.

Fried cheese curds. Young cheese that's breaded and fried, particularly popular in restaurants.

Lefse. A Norwegian flatbread (similar to a tortilla) made with potatoes, milk, and flour and cooked on a griddle.

Perogies. A boiled or baked dumpling consisting of dough filled with potatoes, vegetables, or meat.

Walleye fish. A mild lake fish usually served battered and fried.

Wild rice soup. A cream-based soup featuring wild rice with carrots, celery, onions or peas, and other vegetables. Sausage may or may not be included.

Midwest: Corn Belt and the Northern Plains

Other parts of the Midwest include the corn belt states of Iowa, Indiana, Arkansas, and Missouri and the Northern Plains, North Dakota, South Dakota, Kansas, and Nebraska.

Climate and Geography

Often called America's Breadbasket, states like Iowa and Indiana have steep hills, deep valleys, and many lakes. The land is ideal for growing corn, soybeans, and oats. Farther west, the vast open spaces of the Great Plains also bode well for wheat. Corn is a major crop there, too. Weather-wise, the summers are warm, spring and autumn are moderate, while winters are cold and snowy. Here cattle, pigs, and chickens have found a home on the range, and livestock is another major industry.

Native Foods

Like other parts of the Midwest, native foods are heavy on the meats and cold storage–type vegetables. In the summer, corn and wheat dominate, supplemented with a few warm-weather crops like tomatoes, zucchini, and peppers. Lake fish like whitefish, perch, and walleye are also common.

Here are some native foods you're likely to find in this area:

Beef	Onions
Beets	Parsnips
Bison	Pawpaw
Black English walnuts	Pears
Butternuts	Perch
Carrots	Persimmons
Celery	Pheasant
Chestnuts	Plums
Chokecherries	Popcorn, corn
Dried corn	Potatoes
Eggs	Rutabagas
Elk	Sausages
Frankfurters	Soybeans
Ham	Sunflower seeds
Hickory nuts	Sweet corn
Morel mushrooms	Turnips
Northern pike fish	Walleye

Local Farmers' Markets

Farmers' markets are not as common in parts of these states as they are in other areas. Also, much of the agriculture is focused on industrial crops—corn, soybeans, and wheat—so little is left for diversified crops. Nevertheless, locally grown foods are growing. Here are a few places you will find them:

> **Bloomington Community Farmers' Market**
> Bloomington, Indiana
> bloomington.in.gov/farmersmarket

> **Downtown Lawrence Farmers' Market**
> Lawrence, Kansas
> lawrencefarmersmarket.com

> **North Prairie Farmers' Markets**
> Northwest North Dakota
> northprairiefarmersmarket.com
> *Operates farmers' markets in eight communities in northwest North Dakota.*

> **Old Cheney Road Farmers' Market**
> Lincoln, Nebraska
> oldcheneyroadfarmersmarket.com

> **Sioux Empire Farmers' Market**
> Sioux Falls, South Dakota
> downtownsiouxfalls.com/events-calendar/Sioux-Empire-Farmers-Market

Ethnic Influences

Many of the people who live in this part of the country are of Scottish, Scandinavian, German, Swedish, and Norwegian descent. The Native American tribes living on this land have also significantly shaped the food traditions.

Regional Dishes

Most of the dishes in this region are hearty, stick-to-your-ribs soups and stews. Corn in a variety of forms and especially dried plays a prominent role in the cuisine, as does the influence of the Scots and Norwegians who settled in this region. Game is also popular.

Corn relish. Yellow corn, vinegar, and sugar flavored with red pepper, celery, and onion, usually served with grilled meats.

Dried corn soup. Dried corn soaked overnight and cooked for several hours, usually with salt pork, wild turnips, and carrots.

Kuchen. A German coffeecake filled with fruit and nuts and baked with a sour cream topping.

Roasted pheasant. Pheasant roasted and usually served with rice or potatoes.

Venison barley stew. Venison stewed with barley and winter vegetables like carrots, potatoes, and celery.

Wojapi. A thick berry custard made from chokecherries.

Southwest: Texas

The second-largest state in the Union, by both area and population, Texas features several major metropolitan cities—Houston, Dallas-Fort Worth, San Antonio, and Austin, the state capital. It also features a diversity unmatched by other states.

Climate and Geography

As a region, Texas resembles both the South and the Southwest. Although associated with the dry Southwest desert, actually only 10 percent of Texas is desert. Most of the land is or was formerly prairies, grasslands, forests, or coastlines. The eastern parts of Texas are most like the South, with coastal swamps and piney woods, and as you move west, you'll find rolling plains—which get extremely hot in the summer, often reaching over 100°F—and rugged hills. In the west, you'll find desert and mountains.

Agriculturally, Texas grows almost any fruit or vegetable that grows in a temperate or semitropical climate. Grains like wheat and corn grow in the north and west while citrus and other semitropical fruits and vegetables flourish in the south and along the coastline. Texas Hill Country in central Texas is probably one of the most productive areas, but irrigation in the west has also produced some fertile land.

Native Foods

Along the coast seafood is important, but inland Texas has a hankering for beef (thanks to a big cattle industry) and large game animals. Fruits and vegetables range from pears, peaches, figs, and dates to corn, pumpkins, potatoes, squash, and hot and sweet peppers.

Here are some native foods you're likely to find in this area:

Antelope	Masa (cornmeal)
Beef	Muskmelons
Beets	Olive oil
Bison/buffalo	Onions (Texas sweets)
Black kale	Pears
Black persimmons	Pecans
Blue corn	Potatoes
Broccoli	Prickly pear cactus
Butter beans, speckled butter beans	Purple-hulled peas
Cactus (nopales)	Quail
Chile peppers (all varieties, but especially jalapeño)	Rabbit
Cilantro	Radishes
Corn	Red grapefruit (several varieties)
Dried beans (pinto beans and lima beans)	Shoepeg corn
Elk	Squash
Figs	Texas red grapefruit
Flat-head cabbage	Texas star banana
Goat (cabrito)	Tomatillos
Goat cheese	Tortillas
Honeydew melons	Watercress
Jujube (red dates)	Watermelon
Lamb	Wine
Lola queen peaches and other varieties	Yucca
	Zucchini
	Zucchini blossoms

Local Farmers' Markets

There are wonderful farmers' markets in the state of Texas and plenty of them, too. The state's national farmers' market director lists more than 80. Here's a small sampling:

Cowtown Farmers' Market
Fort Worth, Texas
cowtownfarmersmarket.com

The Dallas Farmers' Market
Dallas, Texas
dallasfarmersmarket.org

Pearl Farmers' Market
San Antonio, Texas
pearlfarmersmarket.com

SFC (Sustainable Food Center) Farmers' Market
Austin, Texas
sfcfarmersmarket.org
This features three Austin farmers' markets.

Sunset Valley Farmers' Market
Sunset Valley, Texas (near Austin)
bartoncreekfarmersmarket.org
This is also called Barton Creek Farmers' Market.

Ethnic Influences

Spaniards were the first to settle Texas and so have had the most influence on the cuisine, followed by the Mexicans and Native Americans. Later, immigrants from Ireland, Scotland, Germany, China, and Italy also put their stamp on the culinary culture.

Regional Dishes

Texas is best known for its blending of typical Texas and Mexican ingredients, giving us Tex-Mex dishes. Many of its dishes also developed from the nomadic cowboy culture and cooking in a Dutch Oven over an open fire. Here are just a few dishes:

Chicken-fried steak. Steak coated with seasoned flour and pan-fried.

Chili. Unlike other chilies, Texas chili contains no beans, only beef or pork in a rich stew, and tomatoes may or may not be present.

Fajitas. Grilled beef served with a flour or corn tortilla, peppers, and onions, usually accompanied by salsa, sour cream, and guacamole.

Peach cobbler. Peaches baked with a biscuit-like topping, traditionally prepared for cowboys in a Dutch oven.

Pecan pie. Sweet pie made up of sugar, corn syrup, and pecans.

Tamales. Masa (a corn-based dough) filled with meat, cheese, and chiles or other vegetables. Comes from Mexico.

Southwest: Other Southwestern States

This area includes Colorado, Arizona, New Mexico, and Oklahoma.

Climate and Geography

Although most of the land in the Southwest is sprawling desert and arid or semi-arid land, geographic diversity can still be found in the northern mountain regions, plateaus or mesas (flatlands), and deep canyons and valleys. Verdant areas include the Rio Grande Valley in New Mexico, North Fork Valley in Colorado, and parts of Arizona and Oklahoma. Temperature fluctuates to extremes from highs over 100°F during the day to lows at night hitting below 0°F. This is also a very dry region with little humidity. Most rainfall occurs during monsoon (high winds and heavy rains) season in late summer. In addition, farms must deal with high altitudes.

Due to the characteristics of the land and the harsh weather, farming can be challenging. And although traditional produce is still grown with irrigation, local foods are unlike any others.

Native Foods

Native foods consist of those grown in the valleys and near the mountains, which are more traditional like apples, tomatoes, and squash (more traditional) to desert varieties like mesquite, tepary beans, and cactus. These plants must be able to tolerate extreme heat, dry conditions, and cool nights. I've included both kinds.

Here are some native foods you're likely to find in this area:

Acorn flour or acorn nuts

Antelope

Beef

Bison/buffalo

Black kale

Cactus (nopales)

Cheese (goat and sheep milk cheese)

Chile peppers (all varieties)

Cholla buds

Cilantro

Dried beans (pinto and lima beans)

Dried corn

Elk

Game (all varieties)

Goat

Indian fry bread

Lamb

Lavender

Masa (cornmeal)

Mesquite and mesquite flour

Moose

Muskmelons

Olive oil

Pears

Pecans

Pinon nuts

Pistachios

Posole (hulled cooked corn kernels; also known as hominy)

Prickly pears

Quail

Quinoa

Rabbit

Rainbow trout

Rattlesnake

Squash (all varieties)

Tepary beans

Tomatillos

Venison

White sweet corn

Wines

Yak meat

Zucchini

Zucchini blossoms

Local Farmers' Markets

Some of the states in this region are just beginning to develop local food systems for consumers. In these areas, several farmers' markets are listed on community or state websites, which promote locally grown products. Here are a few:

Arizona Community Farmers' Markets
Phoenix–Scottsdale, Arizona
arizonafarmersmarkets.com
This site lists information on 10 farmers' markets in the Phoenix and Scottsdale, Arizona, area.

Boulder Farmers' Market
Boulder, Colorado
boulderfarmers.org

Metro Denver Farmers' Market
throughout metro Denver
denverfarmersmarket.com
This site lists six locations in the Denver metro area.

OK-Grown
throughout Oklahoma
okgrown.com/markets
Shows you farmers' markets throughout Oklahoma.

Santa Fe Farmers' Market
Santa Fe, New Mexico
santafefarmersmarket.com

Ethnic Influences

Like the rest of the Southwest, these states have strong ties to Hispanic and especially Mexican American culture and cuisine. Native Americans also play a role. Lately there's been an influx of Asian immigrants from China, Japan, and Southeast Asia, which has also been changing the cuisine.

Regional Dishes

Unlike Texas cuisine and Tex-Mex cooking, the dishes in this region are characterized by large New Mexican green chiles and chili sauces. Game is also important.

Bizcochito or biscochito. A butter-based cookie flavored with anise and cinnamon. It's considered Mexico's state cookie.

Carne adovada. Meat, usually pork, marinated in a red chile sauce dressed with vinegar, oregano, and other spices.

Chile verde. A green stew slow cooked with tomatillos, New Mexico green chiles (Hatch or others), and pork shoulder (the meat is optional).

Empanadas. A sweet fruit or savory meat turnover.

Rocky mountain oysters. Also called prairie oysters, these are bull testicles breaded and deep-fried.

The Northwest: Pacific Northwest

These northern states border the Pacific Ocean and include Washington State, Oregon, and Alaska.

Climate and Geography

This region comprises lush, extensive forests; several mountain ranges; and broad plateaus that can be arid or semi-arid. Climate varies, too, from wet, mild, cool temperatures near the coast to colder weather in the mountains and drier weather east of the mountains. The two most important agricultural regions are Washington's Yakima Valley and Willamette Valley in Oregon. The Northwest's mild climate and ample rainfall makes for good crops, particularly fruits, earning it the name "Fruit Bowl of the Nation."

Alaska is extremely dry and cold in the north, but it has more moderate temperatures in the lowlands. The southeastern part of Alaska is damp and rainy and has moderate temperatures, a bit colder than the lowlands. It's known for its extraordinary seafood, especially salmon and crab, and a multitude of berries. Long summer days produce oversize, mutant vegetables like a 23-foot corn stalk, 5-pound parsnips, 80-pound cabbages, and 1,000-pound pumpkins.

Native Foods

Fresh seafood and especially salmon, mussels, oysters, and crab make up a large portion of the diet in this part of the country. Game meats, mushrooms, berries, small fruits, potatoes, and wild greens are also a big part of the cuisine.

Here are some native foods you're likely to find in this area:

Apples (all varieties)	Kohlrabi
Apricots	Leafy greens (Swiss chard and kale)
Basil	
Beer	Lingonberries
Blackberries	Marionberries
Blueberries	Mussels
Broccoli	Nectarines
Carrots	Onions (Walla Wallas)
Cheese (fresh and aged cow's, goat, and sheep milk)	Oysters
	Parsley
Cherries	Peaches
Chokecherries	Pears
Clams	Plums
Cranberries	Pluots
Distilled spirits (vodka and gin)	Potatoes
Dungeness crab	Poultry
Edamame	Pumpkins
Eggs	Rapini
Fiddleheads	Salmon
Garlic scapes	Smelt
Gooseberries	Stinging nettles
Grapes	Sunchokes
Green garlic	Wild mushrooms
Hazelnuts (also called filberts)	Wine
Huckleberries	Yogurt

Local Farmers' Markets

Oregon and Washington State have some of the best-known farmers' markets in the country. Here's where they are:

> **Ballard Farmers' Market**
> Seattle, Washington
> ballardfarmersmarket.wordpress.com
>
> **Bellingham Farmers' Market at Depot Market Square**
> Bellingham, Washington
> bellinghamfarmers.org
>
> **Hillsboro Farmers' Market**
> Hillsboro, Oregon
> hillsboromarkets.org
>
> **Pike Place Market**
> Seattle, Washington
> pikeplacemarket.org
>
> **Portland State University Farmers' Market**
> Portland, Oregon
> portlandfarmersmarket.org

Ethnic Influences

While much of our culinary knowledge about the foods of this region comes from Native Americans, Asian populations from Japan, China, Korea, and Southeast Asia have also shaped this cuisine.

Regional Dishes

Regional dishes are simple and take advantage of the bounty of the land, highlighting seafood, mushrooms, berries, and apples.

> *Alaskan sourdough pancakes with salmonberries.* Sourdough pancakes topped with wild Alaskan berries.
>
> *Crab Louie salad.* Dungeness crabmeat served over top of lettuce, tomatoes, hard-cooked eggs, and sweet peppers. Topped with a Thousand Island–type dressing.

Hunters chicken. Pan-fried chicken in a rich mushroom sauce

Northwest apple candy (aplets). A chewy candy made of apple, apple juice, sugar, gelatin, and walnuts.

Oregon blackberry pie. Blackberries cooked in sweet pastry dough

The Northwest: Landlocked Northwestern States

Also considered part of the Northwest although not bordered by an ocean are Montana, Idaho, and Wyoming.

Climate and Geography

The mountain states in the northwest alternate between high mountains and wide expanses of flat land. These vast areas make the region ideal for raising cattle and sheep. Climate is cold in the winter (with periodic cold waves) and warm in the summer. The growing season is short, but the soil is dark and fertile.

Native Foods

Regional foods are hearty and filling; emphasis is on game, berries, fruit, and lake fish.

Here are some native foods you're likely to find in this area:

Apples (all varieties)	Distilled spirits (vodka and gin)
Beef	Eggs
Beer	Elk
Bison/buffalo	Garlic scapes
Blackberries	Goat cheese
Buffaloberry	Green garlic
Cabbage	Hazelnuts (also called filberts)
Cherries	Honey
Chokecherries	Huckleberries

Indian fry bread

Lingonberries

Marionberries

Moose

Nectarines

Oats

Peaches

Pears

Plums

Pork

Potatoes (Idaho)

Poultry

Pumpkins

Rapini

Stinging nettles

Sunchokes

Trout (rainbow, brook, brown, and lake)

Venison (roasts, jerky, and sausage)

Wild mushrooms

Wine

Yogurt

Local Farmers' Markets

Although not as extensive as the ones on the east and west coasts, farmers' markets in these rural states are growing steadily. Here are a few to check out:

Emmett Farmers' Market
Emmett, Idaho
emmettfarmersmarket.com

Idaho Farmers' Market Directory
throughout Idaho
www.farmersmarketonline.com/fm/Idaho.htm
www.visitidaho.org/assets/docs/farmersmarketbrochure.pdf
Check here for all the websites for the state's farmers' markets.

Missoula Farmers' Market
Missoula, Montana
missoulafarmersmarket.com

Wyoming Farmers' Market Association
Cheyenne, Wyoming and the surrounding area
wyomingfarmersmarkets.org

Ethnic Influences

Much of the cuisine in this region was influenced by the Norwegians, Swedes, Scandinavians, and Scots who settled here.

Regional Dishes

These robust dishes reflect the local foods along with the Native American, Scandinavian, and Scottish heritage of the area, like Scottish oats and cream of wheat and roasted game meats.

Cherry dumplings. Sweet dough dumpling cooked in a cherry syrup. Dumplings are served with a cherry syrup sauce.

Huckleberry cake. White cake with huckleberries throughout.

Pan-fried trout. Usually served with mushrooms and green onions

Pine nut–crusted goat cheese. Locally produced goat cheese coated with pine nuts.

Venison roast with apples and sage. Venison meat roasted and surrounded by apples and sage.

The West: California, Utah, and Nevada

After Alaska and Texas, California is the third-largest state in the Union. Utah and Nevada are also included in this section and although known for their rocky terrain and arid deserts, do have some fertile land.

Climate and Geography

California's climate is much like that of the Mediterranean. It has warm sunshine, moderate temperatures, and rain, mainly in the northern part of the state during the winter months. The geography includes beaches and a long coastline, snow-capped mountains, forests in the north, and desert (Death Valley) to the west.

Both Utah and Nevada are dry, arid, and semi-arid states. Nevada, the most arid state in the Union, is home to the Mojave Desert while Utah is noted for its mountain ranges, canyons (Bryce), red rocks, and sandstone. Here, high altitude produces weather extremes, cold winters, and hot summers.

Native Foods

Native foods encompass the lush, fertile produce, dairy, seafood, and meats of California and the San Joaquin Valley with the stark desert cuisine of the western states. Fertile areas include certain valleys such as Snake River Valley in Utah.

Here are some native foods you're likely to find in this area:

Apples (all varieties)

Almonds

Apricots

Artichokes

Artisan baked breads

Arugula

Asparagus

Avocados

Beef

Broccoli

Cheese (fresh and aged goat, sheep, and cow) and dairy products

Chicken

Citrus (all varieties)

Dates

Figs

Herbs, fresh

Game (elk, moose, and deer)

Garlic

Grapes

Huckleberries

Kale

Lamb

Leafy greens (spinach, Swiss chard, and kale)

Lettuces (all varieties)

Mandarin oranges

Mangoes

Meyer lemons

Morel mushrooms

Mustard plant and seeds

Nettles

Olive oil

Olives

Pea greens

Peppers

Persimmons

Pistachios

Plantains

Plums

Pomegranates

Prunes

Salami

Seafood (all varieties from the Pacific Ocean)

Strawberries

Sweet potatoes

Tomatoes

Turkey

Walnuts

Local Farmers' Markets

There are many local farmers markets in this region. Here are a few:

Davis Farmers' Market
Davis, California
davisfarmersmarket.org

Downtown Salt Lake City Farmers' Market
Salt Lake City, Utah
downtownslc.org/events/farmers-market/?from=FarmersMarketOnline

Farmers' Market Online
throughout Nevada
farmersmarketonline.com/fm/Nevada.htm
A listing of farmers' markets in state.

Ferry Plaza Farmers' Market
San Francisco, California
ferrybuildingmarketplace.com/farmers_market.php

Monterey Bay Farmers' Market
Monterey Bay, California
montereybayfarmers.org

Ethnic Influences

California was originally settled by the Spaniards. Later, the Gold Rush and the expansion of the railroad brought Chinese, Japanese, Thai, Filipinos, Mexicans, and Italians. Utah has a large Mormon population with ancestry primarily from England, Scandinavia, and Germany. Nevada is similar to Utah.

Regional Dishes

California is known for its light, healthy cuisine with an emphasis on fruits, vegetables, and seafood. Utah and Nevada have more rustic food.

Cioppino. An Italian tomato-based seafood dish with mussels, crab, and finfish.

Cobb salad. A salad with hard-cooked eggs, bacon, chicken, and avocado with Roquefort or blue cheese dressing.

Fish taco. White fish in corn or flour tortilla with a cabbage slaw dressing.

Fried scones. A biscuit-like fruit-studded fried bread dough.

Lamb soup. A tomato-based brothy soup with lamb meatballs flavored with thyme, mint, and sage.

Seared scallops with fava beans, bacon, and mint. Scallops tossed with crispy bacon; local, whole fava beans; and fresh mint.

The West: Hawaii

The only island state, Hawaii has a very distinct culinary culture shaped by its many inhabitants.

Climate and Geography

Geographically, Hawaii stretches 1,500 miles and includes 8 mainland islands and several smaller islands. The climate is tropical, and the temperature is uniform throughout the year, averaging about 75°F. Volcanic soil also makes for good growing conditions, but land is limited, so agriculture is on a small scale. Tropical fruits and nuts grow best.

Native Foods

Earliest Hawaiian inhabitants relied primarily on seafood, and fish is still a big part of the diet today. Later, Europeans (Spanish and English), Japanese, Chinese, Polynesians, Koreans, Filipinos, and South Americans (from Brazil) introduced many other foods like pork, rice, tomatoes, salt cod, and potatoes.

Here are some native foods you're likely to find in this area:

Bananas

Beef

Bitter melon

Breadfruit

Cheeses (local)

Chocolate

Coconut

Coffee

Dragon fruit

Eggplant (all kinds)

Finfish (mahi-mahi, tuna, blue marlin, and dozens of others)

Herbs, fresh (rosemary, bay leaves, and more)

Honey

Jicama

Kiwi

Leafy greens like mustard

Lettuces (all varieties)

Lychees

Macadamia nuts

Mangoes

Maui onions

Okra

Passion fruit

Peppers

Pineapple

Plantains

Pork

Radishes

Shellfish (crab, shrimp, mullet, and more)

Sugarcane

Sweet potatoes

Taro root (poi)

Tomatoes

Yams

Local Farmers' Markets

Local farmers' markets of the area include the following:

Haleiwa Farmers' Market
Haleiwa, Oahu, Hawaii
haleiwafarmersmarket.com

Hawaiian Farmers' Markets Online
throughout Hawaii
farmersmarketonline.com/fm/Hawaii.htm
A listing of all the farmers' markets in Hawaii.

Ethnic Influences

Over the years, the cuisine has been shaped and reinvented by several cultures, including Japanese, Polynesians, Koreans, Filipinos, Portuguese, Hmongs, Spanish, Mexicans, and Italians.

Regional Dishes

Regional dishes include tropical ingredients usually with an Asian twist:

Laulau. Steamed fish or pork wrapped in taro leaves.

Macadamia nut bread. Bread made with macadamia nuts.

Pineapple pork roast. Pork cooked with fresh pineapple.

Poi. Mashed taro root.

Favorite Regional Recipes

Every region of this country has its own collection of local recipes, garnered from its own native foods. Sometimes these foods, like potatoes, criss-cross the country, appearing in many guises and transforming themselves based on the ethnic heritage of the people who live and work on the land. Compare potatoes cooked in clam chowder in New England to the potato pancakes prepared by the Scandinavians in Minnesota.

At other times, foods are indigenous to only a certain part of the country, shaping the cuisine of the area. Such is the case with okra or crawfish, which is not likely to appear in any northern dishes but plays a prominent role in the cuisine of the South.

In this appendix, I share 25 recipes that represent the culinary culture and spirit of a specific region or state influenced by the people who live there. Due to ideal growing conditions and economic forces, the foods I've chosen have become synonymous with a certain place or culture. And while many foods can fall into this category, I've tried to pick the most well-known and readily available ones. This also doesn't mean these foods aren't available elsewhere. They are. So, for example, although corn may grow abundantly throughout many states, it's in Iowa where the crop really flourishes and where corn dishes are most famous.

Keep in mind that these recipes are but the tip of the iceberg, and more than one food can define a region and more than one dish can define a food. (For more information on which foods grow where and the culinary creations these native foods gave rise to, check out Appendix C.) The recipes here are meant to give you a taste of some of the foods you'll find in these regions. They're meant to inspire and motivate you to explore new culinary paths, so if there's a dish or food you really like, feel free to dig deeper into the cuisine of the region. Otherwise, move on to something else.

The culinary traditions of this country are as wide and varied as the very foods we produce. There's always something for everyone!

Northeast and New England

The Northeastern shoreline covers several states and varies greatly in geography and climate. Many culinary treasures are unique to this region. Let's look at a few.

Wild Blueberry Muffins

Sweet, wild blueberries are more intensely flavored than regular blueberries. In these tender muffins, they add a burst of color as well as taste. Perfect for a light breakfast or snack.

Yield:	Prep time:	Cook time:	Serving size:
12 muffins	15 minutes	20 minutes	1 muffin

2 cups unbleached, all-purpose flour, 1 TB. removed	1 cup whole or reduced-fat milk
4 tsp. baking powder	1 large egg, beaten
1 tsp. salt	¼ cup vegetable oil
6 TB. sugar	1 cup fresh or frozen wild blueberries

1. Preheat the oven to 425°F. Line a 12-cup muffin tin with paper liners, and spray the paper liners with cooking spray.

2. In a large bowl, whisk together unbleached all-purpose flour, baking powder, salt, and sugar.

3. In a medium bowl, beat milk, egg, and vegetable oil. Mixture should be well-blended but not foamy.

4. Create a well in the center of flour mixture in the large bowl. Add liquid all at once, and stir with a wooden spoon 15 to 20 strokes or until just mixed.

5. In small bowl, mix blueberries with remaining 1 tablespoon flour, coating well. Gently fold blueberries into batter mixture.

6. Fill muffin cups about ¾ cup full. Bake muffins for 15 to 18 minutes or until top springs back from touch. Cool on wire racks.

Variation: Use 1 cup whole-wheat flour in place of the unbleached all-purpose flour called for.

> **NATIVE KNOWLEDGE**
>
> One of only three berries native to North America, wild blueberries are smaller and more intensely sweet tasting than regular domestic blueberries. They grow best in cool climates and are cultivated in Maine and Canada during six weeks of August and early September. They're highly perishable, so they rarely make it outside of local markets. If you live up north, get them while you can!

Pennsylvania Dutch Chow-Chow

Chow-chow is a sweet 'n' sour vegetable relish that can be made with almost any type of vegetable—green beans, hot peppers, corn, onion, or cucumber. Although it's meant to be sour, you can adjust the sugar to make it sweeter if you like. It's best with starchy foods or meat.

Yield:	Prep time:	Cook time:	Serving size:
4 cups	1 day in advance	10 minutes	¼ cup

1½ cups chopped green tomatoes	2 garlic cloves, finely chopped
1 cup sweet chopped red pepper	¼ cup kosher salt
1½ cups chopped cabbage	1½ cups white vinegar
1 cup chopped onion (about 1 medium)	1¼ cups sugar
1 cup chopped cauliflower	1 tsp. celery seed
1 cup chopped carrots	1 tsp. ground mustard
½ cup chopped celery	½ tsp. ground turmeric

1. In a large plastic or glass bowl (it must be nonreactive, so no metal), combine green tomatoes, red pepper, cabbage, onion, cauliflower, carrots, celery, and garlic. Sprinkle with kosher salt, and mix well. Cover and refrigerate overnight.

2. The next day, line a colander with cheesecloth and pour mixture into the colander. Let drain, and lift up the edges of the cloth over mixture and squeeze to remove all excess liquid.

3. In a large pot over medium-high heat, combine white vinegar, sugar, celery seeds, ground mustard, and turmeric. Bring to a boil, and add vegetables. Simmer for 10 minutes or until vegetables are tender.

4. While vegetables are cooking, sterilize jars by placing them in boiling water for 30 seconds. Remove from water, and let them cool upside down.

5. When both vegetables and the jars have cooled, pour vegetable mixture into the jars. Cover and refrigerate. You can also can this mixture by sealing jars and processing it for 5 minutes. (See Chapter 16 for more information on canning.)

A CLOSER LOOK

Chow-chow is an Amish culinary tradition that dates to their Germanic roots and love of sweet and sour. It's said that at the end of the season, when the ladies finished their canning, they often had odd amounts of vegetables left over from the garden. Rather than throw out these pieces, they combined them and turned them into a relish, calling it chow-chow.

New York State Apple Pie

Sweet, luscious apples wrapped in a tender butter crust—who doesn't love apple pie? For a twist, try eating a slice the English way: with a big wedge of locally made New York cheddar on top.

Yield:	Prep time:	Cook time:	Serving size:
1 (10-inch) pie (8 slices)	1 hour, 30 minutes	40 to 45 minutes	1 slice

1 cup (2 sticks) unsalted butter, cut into ½-in. pieces

3 cups unbleached all-purpose flour

½ tsp. salt

2 tsp. plus 1 cup sugar

8 TB. ice water or more as needed

3 lb. New York state apples (I like 2 York or Cortland, 2 or 3 Granny Smith, and 2 Empire or Stayman)

¼ cup light brown sugar, firmly packed

½ tsp. lemon juice

1¼ tsp. ground cinnamon

1 tsp. vanilla extract

¼ tsp. ground nutmeg

1 large egg, beaten

1 TB. turbinado sugar

1. Place butter pieces in freezer for 15 minutes.

2. While butter is freezing, in a large bowl, mix 2½ cups unbleached all-purpose flour, salt, and 2 teaspoons sugar.

3. Remove butter from freezer and add to dry ingredients. Cut in butter by hand or by using a pastry cutter until mixture resembles coarse meal and butter is slightly bigger than pea size.

4. Add ice water a few tablespoons at a time until mixture just sticks together and forms a soft dough. Do not overmix, or dough will become tough.

5. Divide dough in half, shape into round discs, wrap in plastic wrap, and refrigerate for 1 hour. Dough can be made 1 day in advance. Remove dough from the refrigerator 5 to 10 minutes before rolling it out.

6. Preheat the oven to 375°F.

7. Peel, core, and slice apples into ¼-inch pieces.

8. In a large bowl, combine apples, remaining 1 cup sugar, light brown sugar, lemon juice, ground cinnamon, vanilla extract, ground nutmeg, and remaining ½ cup unbleached all-purpose flour. Set aside.

9. Roll out 1 dough disc into a 12-inch circle. You'll need a 10-inch deep-dish pie plate. Fold dough in half and gently lift it and place in pie plate. Unfold and smooth edges and sides. Pour in apple filling.

10. Roll out the second disc the same way. Fold in half, and cut 3 slits in the center of the fold (these are air vents). Place on top of apple pie filling, unfold, and carefully crimp edges.

11. Brush top crust with beaten egg, and sprinkle with turbinado sugar. Bake for 40 to 45 minutes or until golden brown. Cool on a wire rack. Serve warm or at room temperature.

KEEP YOUR DISTANCE

Red Delicious may be a good eating apple, but don't use it for making pies. This type of apple gets mushy when it cooks and loses its shape. It also produces a lot of water, which is why you may have liquid at the bottom of your pie. Instead, use a combination of tart and sweet apples or even all tart (which contrasts nicely with the buttery crust).

Jersey Tomato and Mozzarella Salad

New Jersey is known for growing some of the tastiest tomatoes in the country. Make this salad in August and September when tomatoes are at their peak, and serve it as a main meal with a crusty loaf of bread.

Yield:	Prep time:	Serving size:
6 cups	10 minutes	1 cup

2 lb. New Jersey tomatoes, any kind (about 4 medium), sliced into bite-size pieces

1 cup fresh basil leaves, cut into slivers (about 12 leaves)

¼ cup chopped red onion

8 oz. fresh mozzarella bocini balls or ½-in. cubes

4 TB. extra-virgin olive oil

2 tsp. balsamic vinegar

½ tsp. sea salt

¼ tsp. ground black pepper

1. In large bowl, add tomatoes, basil, red onion, mozzarella, extra-virgin olive oil, balsamic vinegar, salt and pepper, and toss to combine.

2. Let rest for 10 minutes before serving at room temperature.

NATIVE KNOWLEDGE

While at local markets, take advantage of the many heirloom tomatoes sold there. Experiment with different varieties. But remember, never store tomatoes in the refrigerator. The cold temperature causes them to lose their flavor. Bringing them to room temperature before serving can restore some but not all of their goodness.

Vermont Maple Poached Pears

Baking in an orange-maple-rosemary syrup infuses the pears with sweet citrusy notes, which contrast nicely with the tart, fresh slice of goat cheese. Top it with some toasted walnuts for crunch, and this is a perfect dessert.

Yield:	Prep time:	Cook time:	Serving size:
4 servings	10 minutes	30 minutes	2 pieces pear topped with 1 (1-ounce) slice goat cheese

2 D'Anjou pears, peeled, cored, and cut in quarters lengthwise	1 tsp. chopped fresh rosemary
½ cup maple syrup	2 TB. unsalted butter, melted
1 orange zested and juiced	4 oz. fresh goat cheese, sliced into 1-oz. buttons
½ tsp. vanilla extract	¼ cup toasted walnuts, chopped

1. Preheat the oven to 375°F.

2. Place pears in a small roasting pan.

3. In a small bowl, mix maple syrup, orange zest, orange juice, vanilla extract, rosemary, and melted butter. Pour mixture over pears.

4. Bake pears, uncovered, for 15 minutes. Turn over pears and bake for 15 more minutes. Pears are done when tender but still hold their shape.

5. Remove pears from the roasting pan, pour maple syrup mixture over top, cover with slices of goat cheese, and sprinkle with toasted walnuts before serving.

 A CLOSER LOOK

Although there are more than 3,000 varieties of pears, the main ones you're likely to see are D'Anjou, Bartlett, Bosc, Comice, and Sekel. Each has its own distinct flavor, texture, and taste.

South and Southeast

In no place are there more food traditions than the South. Seafood dishes are a mainstay for any state that borders the ocean, and this area has plenty. Here are a few specialties.

Maryland Crab Cakes

Crispy and brown outside and moist and flavorful inside, these crab cakes are chockfull of hefty chunks of crab. Lightly seasoned with only a bit of Old Bay, mustard, and Worcestershire, they're everything crab cakes should be.

Yield:	Prep time:	Cook time:	Serving size:
6 crab cakes	10 minutes	15 minutes	1 crab cake

1 lb. Maryland jumbo or lump crabmeat	1 tsp. Old Bay seasoning
2 slices bread, crusts removed, and cut into ¼-in. dice	1 tsp. Worcestershire sauce
	½ cup cracker crumbs or breadcrumbs
2 tsp. chopped fresh parsley	3 TB. butter
1 large egg	3 TB. vegetable oil
¼ cup mayonnaise	
1 tsp. Dijon mustard	

1. In large bowl, gently mix crabmeat, bread, parsley, egg, mayonnaise, Dijon mustard, Old Bay seasoning, and Worcestershire sauce until well blended.

2. Form mixture into 6 (3-ounce) patties, and coat in cracker crumbs. Set aside.

3. In large sauté pan over medium-low heat, heat butter and vegetable oil. Add crab cakes, and cook for about 6 minutes on each side until golden brown. Serve immediately.

LOCAL LINGO

Maryland blue crab, or *Callinectes sapidus* ("beautiful swimmer that is savory") is native to the Atlantic Ocean and abundant in the Chesapeake Bay. Due to overfishing, much of the blue crab outside Maryland and Virginia is actually the blue swimmer crab *Portunus pelagicus* from Southeast Asia. Luckily, better resource management is bringing Atlantic blue crabs back to life.

Virginia Peanut Soup

Peanut soup was a staple among the colonists in Williamsburg, Virginia. Creamy, mild, and filling, you're sure to love this soup if you love peanuts and peanut butter. A garnish of fresh chopped peanuts gives it some crunch.

Yield:	Prep time:	Cook time:	Serving size:
10 cups	10 minutes	20 minutes	1 cup

¼ cup unsalted butter (½ stick)

1 small onion, finely chopped

2 stalks celery, finely chopped

1 garlic clove, finely chopped

4 TB. unbleached all-purpose flour

6 cups low-sodium chicken stock

2 cups all-natural, unsalted peanut butter

2 cups light cream or half-and-half

1 tsp. lemon juice

2 tsp. chopped fresh parsley

⅛ tsp. ground black pepper

Finely chopped peanuts

1. In large saucepan over medium heat, melt butter. Add onion, celery, and garlic, and cook, stirring, for about 3 to 5 minutes or until soft.

2. Stir in unbleached all-purpose flour, and cook for 2 more minutes.

3. Pour in chicken stock, increase heat to high, and bring to a boil, stirring constantly. Reduce heat to medium, and cook, stirring often, for about 15 minutes or until reduced and slightly thickened.

4. Whisk in peanut butter, light cream, and lemon juice. Warm over low heat for about 5 minutes, whisking often. Do not boil.

5. Mix in parsley and black pepper. Serve warm with chopped peanuts as garnish.

A CLOSER LOOK

Peanuts thrive in the sandy soil of the South and are a major crop in Virginia, Georgia, Texas, Alabama, North Carolina, South Carolina, and Florida. But it's Dothan, Alabama, that lays claim to "Peanut Capital of the World." More than 75 percent of the peanuts grown in the United States are grown within an 100-mile radius of this city.

Low Country Boil

This is a simple dish that takes advantage of fresh local ingredients—shrimp, potatoes, corn, and sausage. Choose these foods when they're at their peak, and you won't be disappointed.

Yield:	Prep time:	Cook time:	Serving size:
12 servings	10 minutes	20 minutes	1 serving (about 2 cups)

4 lb. small red potatoes

6 qt. water

4 TB. Old Bay or crab boil seasoning

3 lb. kielbasa or andouille sausage

8 ears corn, cut in 3-in. pieces

2 medium onions, chopped into 1-in. pieces

2 large lemons, cut into 4 slices

4 lb. shrimp, peeled and deveined

Cocktail sauce (optional)

1. In a large pot over medium-high heat, combine red potatoes, water, and Old Bay seasoning. Cover, bring to a rolling boil, and cook for 5 minutes.

2. Add kielbasa, corn, onion, and lemons. Boil for 10 minutes or until potatoes are tender.

3. Add shrimp. Continue to boil for about 1 or 2 more minutes or until shrimp are done.

4. Quickly remove contents from water, and spread on a newspaper-lined table or counter to drain. Place in large bowl with some juice for dipping and cocktail sauce (if using).

NATIVE KNOWLEDGE

Low country boil is also called Frogmore stew, named after the town its inventor, a soldier aiming to feed a crowd, came from—Frogmore, South Carolina. Low country cuisine features local crab, shrimp, oysters, and fish often paired with rice or grits.

Mississippi Catfish with Roasted Sweet Potatoes

This recipe pairs two classic Southern ingredients: crispy fried catfish and roasted sweet potatoes. Serve it with a side of collard greens for a beautiful and nutritious— not to mention delicious!—meal.

Yield:	Prep time:	Cook time:	Serving size:
4 servings	10 minutes	30 minutes	4 ounces catfish, 1 cup sweet potato

4 cups *sweet potato,* peeled and cut into ½-in. dice

2 garlic cloves, peeled and minced

½ medium onion, chopped

2 TB. olive oil

1¼ tsp. sea salt

¾ tsp. ground black pepper

8 (4-oz.) catfish fillets

1 cup buttermilk

1 cup yellow or white cornmeal

½ cup unbleached all-purpose flour

¼ tsp. cayenne

2 tsp. garlic powder

1 tsp. onion powder

2 cups vegetable oil

1. Preheat the oven to 400°F. Spray a 9×13-inch roasting pan with cooking spray.

2. In the prepared roasting pan, add sweet potato, garlic, onion, and olive oil, and toss to coat. Sprinkle with ¼ teaspoon sea salt and ¼ teaspoon pepper, and bake, uncovered, for 20 to 25 minutes or until tender.

3. Meanwhile, rinse catfish and pat dry. Place in a small bowl along with buttermilk.

4. In large, shallow dish, mix cornmeal, unbleached all-purpose flour, remaining 1 teaspoon sea salt, cayenne, remaining ½ teaspoon pepper, garlic powder, and onion powder. Dredge catfish in cornmeal mixture, coating evenly and patting it down.

5. In large, deep cast-iron skillet over medium heat, add vegetable oil. (Oil should be a depth of about 1 inch and reach 350°F.) Add coated catfish in batches of 3, and cook for 5 or 6 minutes or until fillets are crispy and golden brown. When done, remove with a slotted spoon and drain on paper towels. To serve, place 1 catfish fillet on a plate and top with 1 cup vegetables. Serve immediately.

Variation: Instead of catfish, you can use any mild white fish or shellfish. Try tilapia, shrimp, sole, or hake.

LOCAL LINGO

Popular in the South, **sweet potatoes** are long, elongated tubers that taper at the end and have a moist orange, yellow, or white-colored flesh. What we call *yams* are actually a dry-fleshed sweet potato. True yams (called boniato) are from a tropical plant native to Latin America. Hundreds of varieties of sweet potatoes range in size, color, and taste. Look for hard-to-find-heirlooms like Hayman, Porto Rico, Covington, and O'Henry.

Louisiana Red Beans and Rice

Small red beans cook long and slow until they're melting soft and smooth in this traditional Louisiana Creole dish. If you want a vegetarian version skip the ham hocks and add a few drops of liquid smoke instead.

Yield:	Prep time:	Cook time:	Serving size:
6 servings	10 minutes plus overnight	2 hours, 10 minutes	1½ cups beans and 1 cup rice

1 lb. small red beans	1 tsp. ground thyme
2 TB. vegetable oil	½ tsp. dried oregano
1½ cups finely diced onion	2 bay leaves
¾ cup finely diced green pepper	½ tsp. cayenne
1 cup finely diced celery	2 tsp. sea salt
3 garlic cloves, finely chopped	¼ tsp. ground black pepper
2 TB. unbleached all-purpose flour	1 ham hock/ham bone
8 cups water	6 cups cooked Carolina Gold rice

1. Rinse, pick over, and soak red beans in water overnight.

2. In large saucepan over medium heat, heat vegetable oil. Add onion, green pepper, celery, and garlic, and sauté for 3 or 4 minutes or until soft.

3. Add unbleached all-purpose flour, and cook, stirring, for 3 minutes. Add water, and cook, stirring for 2 or 3 more minutes.

4. Stir in thyme, oregano, bay leaves, cayenne, sea salt, pepper, and ham hock, and bring to boil. Reduce heat to medium-low, and simmer, partially covered, for 2 hours.

5. About ½ hour before beans are done, prepare rice according to the package directions.

6. Remove bay leaves. To serve, ladle 1 cup rice in a bowl, and top with 1½ cups beans. Serve immediately.

A CLOSER LOOK

Louisiana ranks third in the nation for rice production, especially the southwestern corner of the state. The best kind is called Carolina Gold rice, an heirloom variety that stays soft, fluffy, and moist, even after a few days in the refrigerator.

Southern Stewed Okra

Don't knock okra until you try it! The dark green edible pods have a mild taste similar to eggplant and asparagus that perfectly complements this sweet tomato sauce. Crumbled bacon on top adds a bit of crunch as well as flavor. Serve with rice, grits, or cornbread.

Yield:	Prep time:	Cook time:	Serving size:
6 cups	20 minutes	20 minutes	1 cup

4 strips bacon

1 medium onion, cut into ¼-in. dice

1 medium green pepper, cut into ¼-in. dice

2 garlic cloves, crushed

2 lb. tomatoes peeled, seeded, and chopped (about 6 tomatoes)

1 tsp. sugar

½ tsp. ground black pepper

1 tsp. sea salt

1 lb. fresh okra, cleaned and stems cut off, cut into ½-in. pieces

1. In large, deep sauté pan over medium heat, cook bacon for 6 to 8 minutes or until crispy. Remove cooked bacon from the pan and place on paper towels to drain. Set aside. Remove all bacon fat from the pan except for 1 tablespoon.

2. Add onion, green pepper, and garlic, and sauté for about 3 minutes or until soft. Add tomatoes, sugar, pepper, sea salt, and okra, and bring to a boil. Reduce heat to low, and simmer for 15 to 20 minutes.

3. Crumble cooked bacon on top before serving.

Variation: For a vegetarian version, omit the bacon and use 1 tablespoon vegetable oil instead.

A CLOSER LOOK

Although okra likely originated in Ethiopia, it came to the American South from West Africa via the slave trade and is an essential ingredient in Southern cooking. Sometimes called "gumbo," okra was—and still is—used to thicken soups and stews. It's very perishable (fresh okra only lasts a few days after being picked), so grab it when it's fresh.

Florida Key Lime Pie

Florida's tropical climate makes it ideal for growing all types of citrus and especially the Key lime, a small tart fruit that's highly acidic. Key lime pie is a favorite among Floridians for its sweet-tart taste and creamy filling. Although some people use a pastry crust, here I've opted for graham cracker.

Yield:	Prep time:	Cook time:	Serving size:
2 (10-inch) pies (12 slices per pie)	10 minutes	25 to 30 minutes	1 slice

3 cups graham cracker crumbs

½ cup sugar

12 TB. butter, melted

3 (14-oz.) cans sweetened condensed milk

12 large eggs

1 cup plus 2 TB. Key lime juice

1. Preheat the oven to 350°F.

2. In a large bowl, mix graham cracker crumbs, sugar, and melted butter. Divide mixture evenly between 2 (10-inch) pie pans, and press to form crusts. Bake for 8 minutes, and remove to cool on rack.

3. Reduce oven temperature to 300°F.

4. In a large bowl, beat together condensed milk, eggs, and Key lime juice for about 3 minutes or until well incorporated.

5. Pour filling into cooled pie shells, and bake for 25 to 30 minutes or until filling is set. Remove from the oven, cool on a rack, and refrigerate for at least 2 hours before serving with fresh whipped cream.

KEEP YOUR DISTANCE

Despite what you've heard or seen, don't expect your Key lime pie to be green—and don't be tempted to add green food coloring! True Key lime is actually a light yellow color.

Midwest and Middle America

Known as the country's breadbasket, middle America encompasses the Midwest and Northern states, the Great Lakes Region, the Cornbelt, and the Plains states. It's an agriculturally diverse region that boasts a wide range of culinary traditions. Here's just a sampling.

Midwestern Beer Brats

The Midwest is famous for bratwurst—a mild German sausage—made with locally raised beef or pork. Here the sausage is simmered in dark beer (preferably micro-brewed nearby) and onions. Serve with mashed potatoes for a hearty, satisfying meal.

Yield:	Prep time:	Cook time:	Serving size:
4 servings	10 minutes	30 minutes	2 sausages, ½ cup onions

1 TB. vegetable or canola oil

2 lb. bratwurst or other mild German sausage (about 8 4-oz. links)

2 large onions, thinly sliced (about 6 cups)

4 garlic cloves, minced

2 (12-oz.) bottles dark beer like stout

1. In large, deep sauté pan over medium heat, heat vegetable oil. Add bratwurst, and brown on all sides for about 3 or 4 minutes per side. Remove browned brats to a plate and keep warm.

2. To the same pan, add onions and garlic. Cook, stirring occasionally, for 10 to 12 minutes or until caramelized.

3. Return bratwurst to the pan with onions, and pour in beer. Cover, and bring to a boil. Reduce heat to medium, and simmer for 15 to 20 minutes. Serve immediately.

A CLOSER LOOK

Early colonists brought over sausage-making traditions from Europe (primarily Germany). Later, immigrants from Italy, Poland, the Ukraine, and now the Middle East created their own sausage traditions. Today the United States boasts more than 200 varieties of sausage, but this is still just a drop in the bucket compared to the more than 1,200 types made in Germany.

Wisconsin Mac 'n' Cheese

In this traditional macaroni and cheese, a creamy white sauce is blended with extra-sharp cheddar and Colby cheeses, but if you want to change it up a bit, vary the cheeses. Other versions use fontina, Monterey Jack, and Parmesan.

Yield:	Prep time:	Cook time:	Serving size:
8 cups	25 minutes	25 minutes	1 cup

3 qt. water	2 tsp. prepared mustard
12 oz. elbow macaroni (3 cups)	1 tsp. Worcestershire sauce
3 TB. butter	½ tsp. hot sauce (optional)
¼ cup finely chopped onion	3 cups shredded sharp cheddar cheese
2 TB. all-purpose flour	
2½ cups whole or reduced-fat milk	3 cups shredded Colby cheese
½ tsp. sea salt	½ cup heavy cream
½ tsp. ground black pepper	½ cup breadcrumbs

1. Preheat the broiler to low. Butter a 3-quart ovenproof casserole dish.

2. In a large saucepan over high heat, bring water to a boil. Add elbow macaroni, reduce heat to medium, and cook for 10 minutes, stirring occasionally, or until soft. Drain and set aside.

3. In the same large saucepan over medium heat, heat butter. Add onion, and sauté for 2 minutes or until transparent. Stir in all-purpose flour, and cook for about 1 minute.

4. Slowly whisk in milk. Bring to a simmer, reduce heat to medium-low, and cook, stirring occasionally, for about 5 minutes or until sauce thickens.

5. Whisk in sea salt, pepper, prepared mustard, Worcestershire sauce, and hot sauce (if using). Blend in cheddar cheese and Colby cheese 1 cup at a time, and cook for 2 minutes. Stir in heavy cream, and immediately remove from heat.

6. Mix in cooked macaroni, and pour into the prepared casserole dish. Sprinkle breadcrumbs evenly over top, and broil for about 5 minutes or until top is golden brown.

NATIVE KNOWLEDGE

In the kitchen, cheese is best measured by weight. So 4 ounces natural cheese equals 1 cup shredded, 6 ounces soft cheese like blue or feta equals 1 cup crumbled, and 3 ounces hard cheese equals 1 cup grated.

Minnesota Wild Rice Pilaf

This hearty wild rice pilaf is chock-full of carrots, onions, celery, dried cranberries, and pecans. To make it more of a main dish, add cooked cubed chicken or turkey. Enjoy!

Yield:	Prep time:	Cook time:	Serving size:
10 cups	10 minutes	30 minutes	1 cup

3 TB. butter or olive oil

1 small onion, finely diced (about ¾ cup)

1 stalk celery, finely diced (about ¾ cup)

1 medium carrot, peeled and finely diced (about ¾ cup)

5 cups vegetable broth

1 cup wild rice

1 cup long-grain brown rice

¾ cup dried cranberries, coarsely chopped

2 TB. fresh sage, chopped (about 8 leaves)

¼ tsp. salt

¼ tsp. ground black pepper

½ cup chopped pecans

¼ cup fresh parsley, chopped

1. In a large saucepan over medium heat, heat butter. Add onion, celery, and carrot, and sauté for about 3 or 4 minutes or until slightly soft.

2. Pour in vegetable broth, and bring to boil. Add wild rice, and return to boil. Reduce heat to medium, cover, and simmer for 15 minutes.

3. Mix in long-grain brown rice, and increase heat to medium-high. Bring to a boil. Reduce heat to medium, cover, and simmer for 30 more minutes.

4. About 5 to 10 minutes before rice is done, stir in cranberries, sage, salt, and pepper. Simmer for 5 to 10 more minutes, and mix in pecans and parsley. Remove from heat, and serve immediately.

A CLOSER LOOK

Wild rice is technically not really rice at all but rather the seed of a grass that grows in shallow lakes and streams around the Great Lake region and in California. Many Native American cultures, including the Ojiba Indians of Minnesota, consider wild rice sacred. It's the official state grain of Minnesota.

Iowa Pan-Fried Pork Chop with Corn Casserole

Corn casseroles are found throughout the Midwest. In this version, I've added bacon, green bell pepper, and cheddar cheese and paired it with a simple pan-fried pork chop.

Yield:	Prep time:	Cook time:	Serving size:
8 servings	15 minutes	45 minutes	1 pork chop and ½ cup corn casserole

3 TB. bacon fat (reserved from frying bacon) or butter

1 small onion, finely chopped

1 green bell pepper, ribs and seeds removed, and finely chopped

2 garlic cloves, minced

3 TB. unbleached all-purpose flour

2 cups milk

6 ears fresh corn, husks and silks removed and kernels cut from the cob

4 strips bacon, fried and crumbled

2 cups shredded cheddar cheese

2 eggs, beaten

1 tsp. sugar

Salt

Ground black pepper

½ cup fresh breadcrumbs (1 slice bread, crust removed, finely chopped)

3 TB. vegetable or canola oil

8 (6-oz.) center-cut bone-in pork chops, each ½-in. thick

1. Preheat the oven to 350°F. Butter a 2-quart casserole dish or spray with cooking spray.

2. In a large frying pan over medium heat, melt bacon fat. Add onion, bell pepper, and garlic, and sauté for 5 to 8 minutes or until tender. Stir in flour until blended, and heat for about 1 minute. Gradually whisk in milk until mixture thickens and is smooth.

3. Remove from heat, mix in corn, fried bacon, cheddar cheese, eggs, and sugar, and season with salt and pepper. Pour into the prepared casserole dish, and top with fresh breadcrumbs. Bake for 40 to 45 minutes.

4. About 10 minutes before casserole is done, heat vegetable oil in a large sauté pan over medium heat. Season pork chops with salt and pepper and add to the sauté pan. Cook for about 3 or 4 minutes per side, and serve immediately with corn casserole.

NATIVE KNOWLEDGE

Native Americans as well as pioneers preserved corn by drying it. To do this, first cook fresh corn on the cob for 5 to 10 minutes in boiling water, and cool immediately in cold water. Cut kernels off the cob, and spread on a lipped baking sheet. Set in a 150°F oven several hours or overnight. The dried corn will be dry and brittle. Store in glass jars or hemp bags and use in soups, stews, puddings, or casseroles.

American Southwest and Mountain States

Many people think of the Southwest as a dry, hot, desert region where only cactus and tumbleweed grow. Much of it is that, but there are also plenty of pockets of fertile land, characterized by lush green valleys, rolling hills, and vibrant streams and lakes. Here are a few dishes representing this "wild" land.

Southwestern Stuffed Jalapeños

This dish is a study in contrasts. Hot jalapeño peppers are stuffed with cool cream cheese flavored with a hint of smoky chipotle. Then the whole thing is breaded and fried for a crisp, crunchy finish.

Yield:	Prep time:	Cook time:	Serving size:
30 stuffed jalapeño (10 to 15 servings)	60 minutes	15 to 20 minutes	2 stuffed jalapeños

30 large jalapeños

1 (8-oz.) pkg. cream cheese

1 cup finely shredded Monterey Jack cheese

½ tsp. ground chipotle chile powder

2 tsp. chopped fresh cilantro

½ cup unbleached all-purpose flour

2 eggs, beaten

½ cup buttermilk

1 cup plain breadcrumbs

1 cup corn flour

2 cups vegetable oil

Salt

1. Cut off tops of jalapeños, and remove ribs and seeds. Handle carefully—you want to keep the peppers whole and intact.

2. In a medium bowl, mix cream cheese, Monterey Jack cheese, chipotle chile powder, and cilantro. Gently stuff each jalapeño with filling, smoothing off the top with a knife. Refrigerate jalapeños for 30 minutes.

3. While jalapeños are chilling, place unbleached all-purpose flour in a small, shallow bowl.

4. In a second small, shallow bowl, whisk together eggs and buttermilk.

5. In a third small, shallow bowl, toss together breadcrumbs and corn flour.

6. Working with 1 jalapeño at a time, dredge jalapeño in flour, shaking off excess. Dip jalapeño in egg mixture, roll in breadcrumbs, dip in egg again, roll in breadcrumbs a second time, and transfer to a plate.

7. In a 4-quart saucepan over medium-high heat, heat vegetable oil until a deep-fry thermometer reads 325°F. (You can also use a deep-fat fryer.) Working in batches, add jalapeños and cook, turning after about 1½ minutes, for about 3 minutes or until golden brown. Drain jalapeños on paper towels, and season with salt.

Variation: Although it won't come out as crisp, if you prefer not to fry the peppers, you could also spray a cookie sheet with cooking spray and evenly space peppers on top. Spray peppers with cooking spray, and bake in a 450°F oven for 12 minutes, turning over halfway through the cooking time.

KEEP YOUR DISTANCE

Capsaicin is the compound responsible for chile peppers' fire. It's concentrated in the interior ribs and seeds of the pepper, so if you want to lessen the heat, remove this part of the pepper. You might want to wear gloves while handling jalapeños so you don't burn your hands. In any case, do not touch your eyes, mouth, or any other part of your body when working with these peppers.

Texas Chili

Texas chili contains no beans. It's simply beef, tomatoes, and chili powder, among other things. Cooking it long and slow turns it into a rich, meaty chili.

Yield:	Prep time:	Cook time:	Serving size:
6 cups	20 minutes	60 minutes	1 cup

1 TB. canola oil

2½ lb. beef chuck, cut into ½-in. pieces

1 small onion, finely diced

2 garlic cloves, crushed

2 TB. masa harina (cornmeal)

1 (14-oz.) can crushed tomatoes

1 cup low-sodium beef stock

1 cup strong black coffee

½ tsp. ground Mexican oregano

1 jalapeño pepper, finely diced

1 TB. ground cumin

½ tsp. kosher salt

½ tsp. ground black pepper

1 TB. chipotle chili powder

3 TB. chili powder (preferably ancho chili powder)

1. In large, deep skillet over medium-high heat, heat canola oil. Add beef, and cook, stirring occasionally, for about 5 to 8 minutes or until nicely caramelized. Add onions and garlic, and cook for 3 more minutes.

2. Mix in masa harina. When blended, add in tomatoes, beef stock, and coffee. Cook, stirring, for about 4 or 5 minutes or until mixture thickens and comes to a low boil.

3. Blend in Mexican oregano, jalapeño, ground cumin, kosher salt, black pepper, chipotle chili powder, and chili powder. Reduce heat to medium, and cook, partially covered, for 45 minutes.

A CLOSER LOOK

Beginning in the 1860s, young Hispanic women peddled Texas chili (beef, tomatoes, and chili powder) along with tacos and tamales to lonesome cowboys passing through San Antonio's Military Square during the night. As famous for their fiery food as they were for their flirtatious sales style, they became known as the Chili Queens of San Antonio.

Colorado Lamb Chops and Peach Salsa

Colorado is known as the "land of lamb," so lamb chops are a fitting food for the state. Here they are combined with other favorites: sweet peaches, spicy cilantro, and native pine nuts.

Yield:	Prep time:	Cook time:	Serving size:
4 servings	5 minutes	10 minutes	3 lamb chops plus ½ cup salsa

1½ TB. Dijon mustard

2¼ lb. Frenched lamb rib chops

3 cups peeled and pitted fresh peaches (about 3 medium), coarsely chopped

3 cups loose packed fresh flat-leaf parsley, chopped

½ small red onion, finely chopped

3 TB. pine nuts

2 tsp. white or red balsamic vinegar

2 TB. olive oil

Salt

Pepper

1 cup white wine

1. Brush Dijon mustard on both sides of lamb chops. Place chops on a plate, and refrigerate while you make salsa.

2. In a large bowl, toss peaches, parsley, red onion, pine nuts, red balsamic vinegar, and 1 tablespoon olive oil. Season with salt and pepper, and set aside.

3. In a large skillet over medium heat, heat remaining 1 tablespoon olive oil. Add lamb chops to the pan, and cook for 2 or 3 minutes per side. (If you like it well done, go longer.) Remove chops from the pan and season with salt and pepper.

4. *Deglaze* the pan with white wine, scraping up bits from the bottom. Heat over medium heat for 5 or 6 minutes or until mixture thickens and reduces. It should be the consistency of a light syrup.

5. To serve, place 3 lamb chops on a plate, drizzle with 1 tablespoon wine glaze, and top with ½ cup peach salsa.

LOCAL LINGO

Deglazing is to stir a liquid in a sauté pan, dissolving caramelized bits of food from the bottom of the pan into the liquid. It's often done after cooking meat, fish, or poultry. This liquid is highly flavored and usually used as a base for a sauce. A pan can be deglazed with water, wine, or stock.

New Mexican Green Chile Sauce

This green chile sauce pays tribute to the green chiles roasted in large drums that signal fall in New Mexico. It has a mild heat and a slightly chunky texture that goes well on tacos, enchiladas, burritos, burgers, beans, chicken, and fish.

Yield:	Prep time:	Cook time:	Serving size:
1⅔ cups	10 minutes	35 minutes	⅓ cup

4 Anaheim green chile peppers	2 TB. unbleached all-purpose flour
1 TB. unsalted butter	1½ cups low-sodium chicken broth
1 small onion, coarsely chopped	Dash cumin
2 large garlic cloves, minced	⅛ tsp. sea salt

1. Preheat the oven to 400°F. Spray a baking sheet with cooking spray.

2. Place peppers on the prepared baking sheet, and roast for 20 minutes or until dark brown. Remove from the oven, place peppers in a brown paper bag, and seal. After 10 minutes, remove peppers from the bag, peel, and remove the ribs and seeds.

3. In a medium saucepan over medium heat, melt butter. Add onion and garlic, and sauté for about 3 minutes or until soft. Stir in unbleached all-purpose flour and chicken broth until smooth. Add chiles, cumin, and sea salt, and simmer for 10 to 15 minutes.

4. Pour mixture into a food processor, and pulse for 3 or 4 times or until slightly chunky.

5. Serve warm or hot with chicken, beef, pork, tortilla chips, or any type of Mexican food.

Variation: For a thicker sauce, reduce the chicken broth to ½ cup.

A CLOSER LOOK

New Mexico's hot, dry climate makes it ideal for growing chile peppers. Today more than 200 varieties of New Mexican chiles are grown there. Of those, the two most popular are the Hatch, one the hottest of the New Mexican chiles and usually found roasted, and the Anaheim pepper, named after the California city.

Three Sisters Soup

Named after the "three sisters" Native American grew together—corn, beans, and squash—this healthy, fresh-tasting soup comes together quickly. A dash of chipotle chili powder gives it a hint of heat—great on a cold night.

Yield:	Prep time:	Cook time:	Serving size:
9 cups	10 minutes	20 minutes	1 cup

1 TB. olive oil

1 medium zucchini, cut into ½-in. pieces

1 medium onion, cut in ½-in. pieces

2¾ cups cooked pinto beans (cooked from 1 cup dried beans)

3 cups fresh corn kernels cut from 3 or 4 ears of corn

1 TB. chopped fresh thyme

½ tsp. chipotle chili powder

½ tsp. sea salt

¼ tsp. ground black pepper

6 cups chicken stock

1. In large saucepan over medium-high heat, heat olive oil. Add zucchini and onion, and sauté for about 3 or 4 minutes.

2. Add cooked pinto beans, corn, thyme, chipotle chili powder, sea salt, pepper, and chicken stock. Bring to a boil, reduce heat, partially cover, and simmer for 15 minutes.

Variation: You can use just about any bean or squash for this recipe. If using a winter squash like acorn, peel and seed the squash before using.

NATIVE KNOWLEDGE

If you forget to soak beans overnight, don't worry, use this quick method instead: place beans in a pot with water to cover, and bring to a boil over medium-high heat. Boil for 2 minutes, remove from heat, and cover. Let beans sit for 1 or 2 hours, drain, and cook as you would beans soaked overnight.

West Coast, Northwest, Hawaii, and Alaska

The West covers a wide range of areas, and each has its own distinct geography, climate, and ecology. California's warm, balmy climate is similar to the Mediterranean, the Northwest is mild and temperate, Alaska has cool subarctic climate, and Hawaii is a tropical island. Here are some dishes from each of these places.

California Avocado-Almond Salad

In this salad, an orangey yogurt dressing complements strawberries, figs, and almonds. Avocado brings some richness, and the whole thing is served on a crisp bed of romaine lettuce and spinach, increasing volume as well as bumping up fiber.

Yield:	Prep time:	Serving size:
12 cups	10 minutes	3 cups

½ cup plain, nonfat Greek yogurt

4 TB. orange juice

4 tsp. apple cider vinegar

4 tsp. olive oil

2 TB. honey

4 tsp. Dijon mustard

1 tsp. sea salt

¼ tsp. ground black pepper

2 tsp. orange zest

4 cups romaine lettuce

4 cups spinach leaves, rough cut

2 small avocado, peeled, pitted, and cut into ½-in. cubes

16 strawberries

½ cup almonds, roughly chopped or sliced

6 figs, cut into quarters

1. In a medium bowl, whisk together nonfat Greek yogurt, orange juice, apple cider vinegar, and olive oil. Add honey, Dijon mustard, sea salt, pepper, and orange zest, and mix to combine. Set aside.

2. In a large bowl, toss together romaine lettuce and spinach. Divide evenly among 4 plates. Top each lettuce plate with ¼ avocado, 4 strawberries cut in quarters, 2 tablespoons almonds, and 6 fig quarters.

3. Drizzle ¼ cup dressing over top of each fruit and nut salad, and serve.

A CLOSER LOOK

Fresh figs are so fragile they're not often sold in supermarkets, although they are becoming more common. For quality and taste, your best bet is to get them from your local farmers' market when the season hits in late summer and fall. California leads the pack in fig trees, but you can also find fresh figs grown in Missouri, Texas, the Northeast, and New England.

Northwest Cherry Cream Cheese Bars

This sweet cream cheese bar uses two local specialties: fresh cherries and hazelnuts. The cherries are cooked down as a topping for the cream cheese while hazelnuts appear in two places, the butter crust and as a crunchy topping.

Yield:	Prep time:	Cook time:	Serving size:
24 bars	10 minutes chill time	20 minutes	1 bar

1 lb. pitted sweet cherries

4 tsp. cornstarch

½ cup sugar

2 TB. water

¼ cup cherry jam

¾ cup unbleached all-purpose flour

¾ cup whole-wheat flour

½ cup hazelnuts, finely chopped

1 tsp. ground cinnamon

8 TB. unsalted butter, cut into ½-in. pieces

1½ (8-oz.) pkg. cream cheese

¼ cup confectioners' sugar

1 tsp. vanilla extract

½ cup hazelnuts, chopped (for topping)

1. Preheat the oven to 325°F.

2. In a small saucepan over medium heat, combine pitted sweet cherries, cornstarch, ¼ cup sugar, and water. Bring to a boil, and cook for about 1 minute. Remove the pan from heat to cool. When cool, blend in cherry jam.

3. Pour mixture into a food processor, and pulse 4 or 5 times or until coarsely chopped. Refrigerate until ready to use.

4. In a large bowl, combine unbleached all-purpose flour, whole-wheat flour, finely chopped hazelnuts, remaining ¼ cup sugar, and ground cinnamon. Blend in butter pieces until a loose dough forms (just so it gathers together when pressed—*do not overwork*).

5. Press dough into the bottom of a 9×13-inch baking pan. Bake for 15 to 18 minutes or until lightly brown. Remove from the oven, and set aside to cool.

6. In a medium bowl, and with an electric mixer on low speed, blend cream cheese, confectioners' sugar, and vanilla extract for about 2 minutes or until light and fluffy.

7. When all items are cool, assemble. Spread cream cheese evenly on pastry dough. Gently spread a layer of cherry jam on top of cream cheese, and top with chopped hazelnuts. Cut into 24 squares, and serve cold.

> **NATIVE KNOWLEDGE**
>
> The Northwest climate is ideal for growing fruit. Commercially, the majority of our apples, pears, and cherries come from this region. In the city, it's common to see fruit trees, and orchards abound. At local markets, you'll find apricots, peaches, grapes, and a world of berries, including blueberries, strawberries, marionberries, and elderberries.

Alaskan Salmon with Lingonberry Jam

Lingonberries are a sweet-tart cranberry-like berry that grow wild in Alaska, so they're readily available in many forms. Here they're partnered with wild salmon to make a sweet-savory entrée laced with rosemary.

Yield:	Prep time:	Cook time:	Serving size:
4 servings	10 minutes	15 minutes	1 salmon fillet plus 3 tablespoons sauce

½ cup unbleached all-purpose flour

¼ tsp. sea salt

⅛ tsp. ground black pepper

4 (4-oz.) wild salmon fillets, skinless

2 TB. unsalted butter

1 shallot, finely chopped

¼ cup white wine

½ cup lingonberry jam

2 tsp. fresh chopped rosemary

1. In a small shallow bowl, mix together unbleached all-purpose flour, sea salt, and pepper. Coat salmon fillets in flour mixture, and set aside on a plate.

2. In a medium sauté pan over medium-high heat, heat butter. Do not burn. Shake any excess flour off salmon, and place in hot butter. Cook for about 3 or 4 minutes per side or until done. Remove salmon, and set aside on plate, keeping warm.

3. In the same pan, add shallot, and sauté for 2 minutes, stirring quickly (if it starts to burn, lower the heat).

4. Deglaze the pan with white wine, scraping up brown bits. Mix in lingonberry jam and rosemary, and simmer for about 3 minutes. To serve, place 1 salmon fillet on a plate, and top with 3 tablespoons sauce.

 A CLOSER LOOK

Alaska has a vibrant farming community, and what makes it unique is the fact that the sun stays out much longer in the summer than in the lower 48 states—24 hours a day!

Hawaiian Tropical Fruit Salad

Tropical fruit is a year-round mainstay in the Hawaiian diet, and the four used here are always top picks. Top with a dollop of fresh whipped cream flavored with coconut extract and a tad of sugar. Yum!

Yield:	Prep time:	Serving size:
8 cups	10 minutes	1 cup fruit salad plus ½ cup whipped cream

3 cups fresh pineapple, cut into 1-in. cubes

3 cups fresh papaya, cut into 1-in. cubes

1 whole mango, cut into 1-in. dice

2 cups shredded fresh coconut

Coconut water from reserved from coconut

1⅔ cups heavy cream

3 tsp. confectioners' sugar

3 tsp. coconut oil, or 2 tsp. coconut extract

1. About 10 minutes prior to using place a large bowl and beaters in the freezer to chill.

2. In a separate large bowl, combine pineapple, papaya, mango, and coconut. Add coconut water, and mix. Set aside.

3. Remove the beaters and bowl from the freezer. Pour in heavy cream, and begin beating with an electric mixer on medium speed until mixture begins to thicken, about 2 minutes.

4. Mix in confectioners' sugar and coconut oil, and beat for 2 or 3 more minutes or until stiff peaks form. Do not overbeat, or cream will begin to separate. To serve, place ½ cup whipped cream on top of 1 cup fruit salad.

Variation: To make your own coconut extract, simply place 1½ ounces freshly grated coconut (about ½ cup packed coconut) in a glass jar with 4 ounces vodka. Seal and shake. Place in cool, dark place for 5 to 7 days, shaking every day to combine. On the last day, strain out and discard coconut. The remaining liquid is the coconut extract. It will keep for up to a year.

NATIVE KNOWLEDGE

How do you crack a coconut? First you heat the oven to 375°F. Then hammer holes into the coconut's eyes, and drain the coconut water inside. Place the coconut on a baking sheet, and bake for 15 minutes. Remove from the oven. Separate the hard shell from the husk, and peel the brown husk from the coconut meat. Rinse the meat under cool water, and pat dry.

Index

Q-R

Y–Z